"In the quest to define our national identity, the most essential question was asked by the greatest of our literary critics, Northrop Frye: 'Where is "here"?' Finally we have the answer: In the pages of Roy MacGregor's magnificent new book, *Canadians*."
—Peter C. Newman

"Longtime readers of Roy MacGregor, or even fortunate newcomers to his graceful unfolding style, may be excused for thinking the writer is actually trained in medicine. So precise is his diagnosis of Canadian-ness, so clear and crisp are his stories, so full of rich, revealing detail, so apt are his anecdotes and adjectives from a lifetime of storytelling that we come to think of him as a well-trained professional who can see inside the unique creature that is the Canadian.

"Canadians will smile and nod and even wince at times as they travel along with him across this broad body of sprawling bright lands and deep dark waters and [meet] open people who have so much chronic difficulty understanding themselves and, thus, being understood by others. We can only hope that, first, Canadians will grasp the elegant lessons of 'Canada: the line down the middle of the road.' Then, just maybe, if we're lucky, the rest of the world will follow suit. And we'll all have Dr. MacGregor to thank.

"In short, Roy MacGregor's new book is a national treasure."
—Andrew H. Malcolm, author of *The Canadians*

"Writing a book that tries to explain Canada to Canadians is in many ways a gift … MacGregor unfolds a fascinating depiction of Canada … *Canadians* is a sprawling book. But it does capture the essence of our diversity; it does evoke the spirit of this beautiful, undefinable set of contradictions that make up Canada … A couple of the chapters are powerful enough to bring a reader to tears."
—Aritha Van Herk, *Calgary Herald*

"It's hard to think about anyone more qualified than Roy MacGregor to write a book that truly is a portrait of Canada."
—*The Chronicle-Journal* (Thunder Bay)

"MacGregor cuts to the bone of what it is to be Canadian … MacGregor interprets Canada not only as a country and as a nation, but as an idea, an imaginative construct that often defies reason and logic but one that continues to speak to many who call this insistently unknowable place home."
—*The Record* (Kitchener-Waterloo)

"*Canadians* stands as a superior example of reportage and a reckoning of a journalistic career of more than three decades ... MacGregor has a unique ability to balance objective reportage with a keen, emotional core; he has a good eye for the human interest angle, which intensifies his editorial thrust ... *Canadians* is, in the final reckoning, a series of snapshots of our varied and diverse cultures, an insight into worlds and events that may be utterly foreign to some of us, but are, at their heart, fundamentally our own."
—*Ottawa Citizen*

"If passion for our country counts, Roy MacGregor certainly has it. In Canadians he shares that passion with us again, leavened with a generous sprinkling of humour. Perhaps, as he says himself, it is only another exercise in examining our own belly-button lint, but if so, I never imagined lint could be so fascinating."
—*The Hamilton Spectator*

"MacGregor's writing in *Canadians* is clear, crisp, and easy to read—the qualities that have allowed him such a long and successful career..."
—*Quill & Quire*

"MacGregor writes about us while at the same time seamlessly identifying himself as one of us. Canadians is a charming book, and MacGregor is a graceful writer."
—*Winnipeg Free Press*

"He brings a rare—and trust me, admirable—touch to his work ... A worthy and entertaining effort, reminding us of shameful shortcomings and how we can get it so right, even spectacularly so ... In many ways, travelling over time, topics, and geography, often courtesy of MacGregor's first-person, on-site observations, by anecdotes and quotations, Canadians the book reflects that. The overall effect after a read offers quiet, clear-eyed reassurance."
—*Edmonton Journal*

"The book's greatest strength is the sense of the country and its people that emerge—personal, impressionistic, improvisatory, transitory, speculative. This is journalism of a high order ... MacGregor interprets Canada not only as a country and as a nation, but as an idea, an imaginative construct that often defies reason and logic but one that continues to speak to many who call this place home."
—*Guelph Mercury*

PENGUIN CANADA

CANADIANS

ROY MACGREGOR is the acclaimed and bestselling author of *The Home Team: Fathers, Sons, and Hockey* (shortlisted for the Governor General's Award) and *A Life in the Bush* (winner of the U.S. Rutstrum Award for Best Wilderness Book and the CAA Award for Biography), as well as two novels, *Canoe Lake* and *The Last Season,* and the popular Screech Owls mystery series for young readers. He has twice won the Ottawa-Carleton Book Award.

A regular columnist at *The Globe and Mail* since 2002, MacGregor has written for publications including the *National Post,* the *Ottawa Citizen, Maclean's* magazine, and the *Toronto Star.* His journalism has garnered four National Magazine Awards and eight National Newspaper Award nominations.

In 2005, he was made an officer of the Order of Canada. He is described in the citation as one of Canada's "most gifted storytellers."

Roy MacGregor lives in Kanata, Ontario.

Also by Roy MacGregor

The Dog and I: Confessions of a Best Friend

The Weekender: A Cottage Journal

Escape: In Search of the Natural Soul of Canada

A Loonie for Luck

A Life in the Bush

Canoe Lake

The Last Season

The Home Team

Road Games

Chief: The Fearless Vision of Billy Diamond

Home Game *(with Ken Dryden)*

The Screech Owl Mystery Series *(for young readers)*

Forever: The Annual Hockey Classic

ROY
MacGregor
CANADIANS
A Portrait of a Country and Its People

PENGUIN
CANADA

For Helen and Duncan, mother and father,
who passed on their deep love of the land—and
who always had patience for young explorers

PENGUIN CANADA

Published by the Penguin Group

Penguin Group (Canada), 90 Eglinton Avenue East, Suite 700, Toronto, Ontario, Canada
M4P 2Y3 (a division of Pearson Canada Inc.)

Penguin Group (USA) Inc., 375 Hudson Street, New York, New York 10014, U.S.A.
Penguin Books Ltd, 80 Strand, London WC2R 0RL, England
Penguin Ireland, 25 St Stephen's Green, Dublin 2, Ireland (a division of Penguin Books Ltd)
Penguin Group (Australia), 250 Camberwell Road, Camberwell, Victoria 3124, Australia
(a division of Pearson Australia Group Pty Ltd)
Penguin Books India Pvt Ltd, 11 Community Centre, Panchsheel Park, New Delhi – 110 017,
India
Penguin Group (NZ), 67 Apollo Drive, Rosedale, North Shore 0632, New Zealand
(a division of Pearson New Zealand Ltd)
Penguin Books (South Africa) (Pty) Ltd, 24 Sturdee Avenue, Rosebank, Johannesburg 2196,
South Africa

Penguin Books Ltd, Registered Offices: 80 Strand, London WC2R 0RL, England

First published in a Viking Canada hardcover by Penguin Group (Canada),
a division of Pearson Canada Inc., 2007
Published in this edition, 2008

2 3 4 5 6 7 8 9 10 (WEB)

Copyright © Roy MacGregor, 2007

Epigraph on page viii: "Canadians" by Miriam Waddington. Permission to reprint granted by
Jonathan and Marcus Waddington.

Manufactured in Canada.

LIBRARY AND ARCHIVES CANADA CATALOGUING IN PUBLICATION

MacGregor, Roy, 1948–
Canadians : a portrait of a country and its people / Roy MacGregor.

Includes bibliographical references and index.
ISBN 978-0-14-305308-8

1. National characteristics, Canadian. 2. Canada. I. Title.
FC97.M315 2008   971   C2008-901400-6

ISBN-13: 978-0-14-305308-8
ISBN-10: 0-14-305308-6

Visit the Penguin Group (Canada) website at **www.penguin.ca**

Special and corporate bulk purchase rates available; please see **www.penguin.ca/corporatesales**
or call 1-800-810-3104, ext. 2477 or 2474

Contents

... *We look*
like a geography but
just scratch us
and we bleed
history, are full
of modest misery
are sensitive
to double-talk double-take
(and double-cross)
in a country
too wide
to be single in.
Are we real or
did someone invent
us ... ?

—*Canadians*
MIRIAM WADDINGTON, 1968

The Hands of Alexandria

I HAVE NO IDEA who he was.

A Canadian, obviously. And perhaps that's all we need to know about him apart from this:

He stood on the east side of the tracks near Casselman, a small farming community in southeastern Ontario that sits along the rail line between Ottawa and Montreal. He was an older man, wearing rust-coloured coveralls and high green rubber boots, and he stood so dead centre in the field he'd been turning over that it seemed he must have paced it off for effect.

He stood at attention beside his green John Deere tractor. He picked off his cap with his left hand and slowly raised his right over a long weathered face to a forehead white as the day he was born.

And saluted.

One loner to another.

The famous loner—a man who saw himself as a solitary paddler and was seen by others as a stand-alone gunslinger—could not salute back from where he lay on-board VIA Rail train no. 638. He could not toss out one of those easy, sarcastic jibes he periodically threw at farmers— *"Why should I sell your wheat?"*—and he most assuredly could not raise his hand and give the middle finger to those lining the tracks, as he had done years earlier from a train carrying him and his sons through British Columbia. No, Pierre Elliott Trudeau was dead at eighty, the personality who had dominated the first third of this country's second century as surely as Sir John A. Macdonald had dominated the first third of its first century, gone forever and on his way home to Montreal for burial.

Train 638—two locomotives to pull only three cars—could not have chosen a happier route that surprisingly warm second day of October

2000. All along that 187-kilometre stretch the people of eastern Ontario and western Quebec had come out to mark the passing of the unknowable man who had for so very long commanded the attention of their country. In leftover sunshine from summer they gathered at crossings and along the tracks and to the sides of bridges; they carried flowers and Canadian flags and more than a few babies, the infants held up and their tiny heads steered toward no. 638 as if this one simple act might lock its historical significance into a small brain unaware of any past at all, including the last diaper change.

All along the long route lay the unexpected. The surprises began on the outskirts of Ottawa when the funeral train began picking up speed and passed behind the repair shops for the city's public transit system. The mechanics had lain down their tools and made their way to the rear of the buildings where they stood, in dark coveralls, staring through the fence in silence, their big, grease-covered hands folded as if in recital.

Farther down the line, as the train slowed through an Ottawa Valley farm village, it was the volunteer fire brigade, in full uniform, all at attention on one side of the tracks while on the other stood a peewee hockey team, also in uniform, also at attention. None of the hockey players had even been born when the man they were honouring last held office.

At a leaf-littered golf course that ran along the west side of the tracks players stepped back from their putts and removed their golf caps, seeming for once to welcome a distraction. Those playing immediately behind walked away from their carts and also removed their caps, not one of them daring to stand in that wide-stance, arms-across-the-chest sign of impatience that is standard fare for those waiting to hit their approach shots to a green.

At one crossing a woman held up a cherry paddle, a rainbow-coloured voyageur scarf tied carefully around it. At another, a man held up his country's flag with his country's perfect flagpole: a hockey stick. A railway worker at the side of the tracks cradled his hard hat in his left arm while he stood at attention. Construction workers crawled free of the hole they were digging near a culvert to stand in respect, the yellow front-end loader behind them stilled, its scoop raised in its own serendipitous salute.

They came, sometimes alone, sometimes in numbers, to stand and stare into the window of the final link in train no. 638, a special car with draped windows through which the tall among them might make out, barely, the red maple leaf flag that covered the coffin of the man who had been prime minister for nearly sixteen years and prime personality for another sixteen following his retirement.

They came, many dabbing at their eyes, a few holding his signature red rose, some clapping quietly as the train passed. Simple country people, mourning a man from the cities who was born into privilege and lived in privilege; a man they connected to—sometimes off and on—but who could never quite connect to them unless he was on stage; a man who many years earlier had pressed his somewhat Mongolian, somewhat skull-like, somewhat handsome face to the window of the limousine carrying him through a southwestern Ontario night and looked long out at the flickering farm lights before wondering aloud to an aide, *"Whatever do they do?"*

We could debate forever what it was they felt that day—the passing of their own youth? the end of an era where insecure Canada was finally noticed by others? the death of a man who caused so much change, so much controversy?—but we cannot argue whether they felt something that October morning, and felt it powerfully.

Not long into the long, slow ride to Montreal, Jim Munson, then a reporter for CTV, now a senator, and I left the small pack of journalists in the car assigned to the media and stood by a window on the left side, the two of us staring out at the country staring back.

We weren't being rude. We were merely doing what journalists are supposed to do: follow the story. The train had been set up so that, periodically, members of Trudeau's inner circle would be brought from the car carrying the coffin to the car carrying the media, and there a quick formal interview would be offered. Munson and I had listened politely to the reminiscences of Senator Jacques Hébert, Trudeau's great lifelong friend, and of Marc Lalonde, his former finance minister, but it had soon become apparent that what was going on inside the car was insignificant compared with what was going on outside.

It was one thing to talk about the past; quite another thing to witness the present.

WE WERE ON A TRAIN headed for Montreal, the city in which, two decades earlier, I had first realized the great privilege journalism provides those fortunate enough to work in this unpredictable job. *Maclean's* magazine had sent me there to do a profile of Mordecai Richler, then about to publish a new novel. I carried a tape recorder. I did not like transcribing tapes then, and will do anything to avoid it now, but Richler had such a reputation for surliness, not to mention mumbling, that I had taken it along for self-protection.

It turned out to be the luckiest thing I ever did in my journalism career.

We met at the Montreal Press Club for drinks and then headed for his Sherbrooke Street apartment for the formal interview. He insisted on stopping along the way to pick up two large bottles of Remy Martin and several packs of the small cigars he loved.

The interview went much better than I had expected. Richler was almost as eager to talk about his new book as he was to get into the Remy, and he smoked and talked and kept filling up two glasses, the smaller of which he would push in my direction. It was my first encounter with cognac.

The following morning I awoke in my hotel room still wearing the same clothes I had worn to the interview. The bed covers had never even been turned back.

I was certain I was doomed. No memory. No notes lying on the hotel-room desk. Nothing. And then I remembered … *the tape recorder.* Panicking, I rolled off the bed and found it tossed on a chair. Deep in prayer, promising first child, I flipped the tape and pressed the play button. Richler's voice came through loudly and clearly. I flipped the tape again, pressed rewind, and checked again. My voice was now slow and stupid, Richler's still strong and clear as he answered questions without so much as a slur (well, as far as enunciation went, anyway).

We were talking about journalism. I had asked him why he turned so often to magazine work. Wasn't it getting in the way of his novels?

He said, as he had said before so many times, that his sole purpose as a writer was to be an "honest witness" for his times. He needed real material to create that real world in fiction. And journalism provided this.

"It gives me *entrée*," he said, "into worlds I could not otherwise be a part of."

Exactly. This was precisely the sense I felt on VIA Rail no. 638 that morning. We were witnessing the times, history in the making. It was like being a Canadian Zelig, the Woody Allen movie character who keeps showing up everywhere but never actually takes part—just some face in the background of significant events. When you are a Zelig, no one is ever quite sure how you got there or exactly what you're doing. It can be an awkward feeling at times—a sense that you don't belong—but more often it's a quiet delight that you're somehow there and no one has yet thought to kick you out.

I once came across a wonderful short story called "The Leper's Squint" by Vancouver Island writer Jack Hodgins. It was about a fiction writer and the gathering of material for his work. Hodgins's narrator finds himself visiting Ireland's Rock of Cashel, where a guide points out the wall of rock and the tiny opening through which the outcasts were once allowed to watch, but not participate in, the religious services of the day. It was "like looking through the eye of a needle." No journalist could read that passage without relating.

And yet there's a difference in what's done with the gathering. Journalism isn't, or at least shouldn't be, fiction. The journalist can sometimes become a small part of whatever's happening. Once Richler's lovely notion of *entrée* has been gained, there's a responsibility to be that dependable witness to what journalists like to call "history on the run"— but also a chance to determine, even if ever so slightly, even if accidentally, how fast the run and what shifts in direction it might take. A very small part, often insignificant, but still one to be taken seriously.

Looking back on more than three decades of this work, most of it spent running around this impossible and impossibly huge country, usually alone, I've often felt like a bit of an outsider–insider. I've been privy to so much thanks to this strange job where each year tends to begin and end with a blank daybook. Most people fill in their days and weeks in advance, but a journalist has to look back—usually through clippings rather than a pocket calendar—to know where he or she was on a given day. It might be a federal or provincial election. It could be a trip through the Far North. It could be time spent on oil rigs, following Royal tours or the Stanley Cup playoffs, reporting on a Native standoff, analyzing a farm crisis, or simply doing one of those marvellous "people" stories that give this massive body called Canada its face.

Of all those privileged experiences over those years, perhaps the most moving was being allowed on-board VIA Rail no. 638 as it made its way toward Montreal that day. Standing in the rocking train car, periodically greasing the window with my nose, I was acutely aware of the gift *entrée* had given those few of us who decided to look out rather than in during this remarkable journey.

In this part of the country, it was quickly becoming clear, Pierre Trudeau still held an office that had nothing to do with elections or titles.

THE FUNERAL TRAIN picked up speed between the small villages and towns that line the Ontario side of the lower Ottawa River. In a way it was a shame, in that the leaves were late turning that mild fall: poplar just starting to yellow, maple but a hint of the orange splash to come. Only the sumac had already turned dark as dried blood in the sharp light of mid-morning.

The effect, even with the blurring from increasing speed, was of a countryside so soft and warm it seemed winter should be hemispheres away rather than weeks. Not far from the small town of Maxville the train rocked and hurdled through a marsh where a great blue heron lifted off, slowly banked to the north, and was instantly gone from sight. Nearer the Ontario–Quebec line, thousands of gathering Canada geese—suddenly spooked by the train whistle blown for an upcoming crossing—rose as one, all but darkening the eastern sky before they, too, instantly vanished.

It was such magnificent scenery, the October light playing across finished fields, the water along the South Nation and Ottawa rivers military-still on such a windless day. And yet the natural beauty of the countryside lay far more in the people and their faces. Those who had been waiting at crossings in lawn chairs stood and cheered. Youngsters sat in trees and waved small flags. Older couples pulled their cars over on gravel shoulders, got out, and stood silently at attention as the train passed.

To the two of us at the window, these emotions seemed to come from another, less cynical time, as if this train had somehow headed backward into, say, 1967, when everything seemed so possible for this little country then celebrating its hundredth birthday, or 1968, when the curious-looking man from Montreal won his party's leadership and burst on to the Canadian political scene, as CBC broadcaster Gordon Donaldson once so dramatically put it, like "a stone through a stained-glass window."

Near the outskirts of little Alexandria, something else began to happen. The train jerked, lost speed, then shuddered even slower. One of the funeral officials had earlier announced that the train would be moving at "an especially dignified pace," but this seemed but a few turns short of a full stop. The conductor working our car seemed nervous, checking his watch as if playing a part in a French mystery film. Munson and I tried to lean as tight to the glass as we could to look ahead and see what the problem was.

It turned out that, as no. 638 began passing through Alexandria, the crowd, six and eight people deep in places, had pushed forward. Boy scouts and girl guides at attention were squeezed until they were forced to stutter-step closer. Aging members of the local Royal Canadian Legion branch—chests out, service medals flashing—were forced to edge in, the small corps of young cadets lined up beside the Legionnaires following suit as the growing crowd pushed ever nearer to the slowing train.

Through the glass we could hear a single piper playing "The Last Post." The train slowed to a bare crawl. And this was when we heard the hands of Alexandria. Neither Munson nor I knew what it was at first. There was this sound, this rubbery … *squeak* … that we couldn't place. Not the wheels. Not the brakes. But something else.

And suddenly, instantly, we realized what it was.

Skin.

The people of Alexandria were reaching out to touch the train carrying Pierre Trudeau home. They were, literally, feeling his passing, their hands rubbing along the metal of the cars as the train slowly made its way through the small town and on to Montreal.

Munson and I looked down at hundreds of hands—some so young they had to reach up, some so old they shook helplessly—reaching out to touch the funeral train. Their faces, many openly weeping, were the faces of Canada, every age, both sexes, different languages, old Canadians and young Canadians, old Canadians and new Canadians, all reaching out to touch the train that was carrying Pierre Trudeau to his grave.

Jim Munson broke down first. But he was not alone for long.

I do not believe I have heard anything quite so moving as the sound of the skin of Canada on the history of Canada. It sent chills up and down the spines of every person in the funeral car and still, today, sends chills up and down mine to remember that oddly mouselike sound that had baffled us in Alexandria.

But there was more to it than just confusion. It was the surprise—there is no other word for it, the *surprise*—of staring out at a country and seeing a face you had no idea was there, even though your job, day in and day out, is to describe this face and give it voice.

It was also the stark realization that you were staring out at one small corner of a country so large it defies generalities; defies, we sometimes think, even slight understanding.

Staring out at Canada … and yet acutely, startlingly aware that if VIA Rail no. 638—carrying the man who said the state had no business in the bedroom, who brought in bilingualism and biculturalism, who brought home the Constitution, who brought in the Charter, who called in the troops and called out the energy producers—happened this same soft October day to be passing through, say, Salmon Arm, British Columbia, rather than Alexandria, Ontario, the people of Canada would also be reaching out.

But not to touch the train. Rather, to give back the finger.

THAT REMARKABLE EXPERIENCE—the hands of Alexandria contrasted with the fingers of Salmon Arm—accelerated my growing fascination with the contradictions of this bewildering country.

The Europeans believed they had "discovered" a New World that was of course neither new nor without people holding prior claim. They found a vast, rich, fertile country and, initially, actively discouraged settlement. They found a sprawling, seemingly impenetrable land of tree and rock and bog that already had in place the best highway system the country would ever know: the rivers. They arrived thinking themselves the advanced civilization and found that the most ingenious, most necessary engineering marvel had already been invented: the canoe.

What did Giovanni Caboto think of this place that late June day in 1497 when he sailed into Bonavista Bay and discovered the waters so teeming with cod that his men had only to drop weighted baskets to begin hauling in the fish? What, on the other hand, did Jacques Cartier think when the inside walls of his Stadacona shelter coated over with six inches of ice in early 1536 and 25 of his 110 men perished? What was it that Captain George Vancouver, explorer, is supposed to have seen as he sailed up the west coast in search of the Northwest Passage in the early 1790s, something so disturbing to him that he decided to keep it secret? We don't know. We will never know.

Perhaps, like George Vancouver's great secret, such a country is ultimately unknowable.

The political lines run east and west, the economic lines mostly south. We are some thirty million people who line up along the southern border like goldfish against the glass, all the while leaving the North so empty the rest of the world can say, with some legitimacy, that we aren't even in it.

We have a jagged line far up this empty northern stretch with trees on one side and no trees on the other. We begin the real New Year the day after Labour Day Weekend. We celebrate Groundhog Day when winter has just settled in, not when it's supposedly ending. We complain about the cold and yet, in places like White River, Ontario, and Snag, Yukon, we argue over and boast about record lows. We revere our anthem although only professional anthem singers know the words. We mostly like Americans and often dislike America. We drive from flat prairie into mountains. We have three ocean shores—one with high rocks at the Atlantic, one with shrinking ice over the Arctic, one with inviting beaches into the Pacific—and a fourth shore, freshwater, along the Great Lakes, where for long stretches we stare across to the United States at night as if that country were lighted store windows on the far side of a street that's mostly vacant lot on ours. And yet we consider our vacant lot the superior property.

Thanks to journalism's *entrée* I've seen the sun rise at Cape Spear, Newfoundland, knowing there is nothing but water between my sneakers gripping that rock face and Ireland. I've watched that sun set off Long Beach on Vancouver Island and known there is nothing but sea between my bare feet and Japan. I've felt the shine of that sun for days and nights on end in the Far North, and stood on the most northerly spot of Ellesmere Island knowing there is nothing but ice between my rubber boots and Russia. I've touched salt water east, west, and north—and even bathed in salty Little Manitou Lake in the heart of Saskatchewan.

I have travelled the country by train, bus, ferry, camper, car, bicycle, canoe, foot, and thumb. I have flown by helicopter over the harsh coast and breathtaking fiords of Newfoundland; I have flown by bush plane over the wild white rivers of northern Quebec and the ice fields of the Arctic; I have stared down from passenger jets enough to know what early explorer David Thompson meant when he stared up into the Rockies and thought the mountains looked rather like "the waves of the ocean during a wintry storm."

Like any Canadian, I'm familiar with the touchstones: the Canadian Shield, Peggy's Cove, Old Quebec, nuisance grounds, curling, Georgian Bay, Nanaimo bars, maple syrup, the Rockies, muskeg, road hockey, weather talk, late-night newscasts being bumped by *Hockey Night in Canada,* place names like Climax, Saskatchewan, Dildo, Newfoundland, and Medicine Hat, Alberta, soapstone carvings, legends like Mufferaw Joe of the Ottawa Valley and the Windigo of the northern Crees, the Avro Arrow, May two-four weekends, Screech, Céline Dion, the lake, John Deere caps, fiddleheads, *Morningside, Razzle Dazzle, Corner Gas, Trailer*

Park Boys, Don Cherry, Michel Tremblay plays, *Anne of Green Gables,* poutine, "peace, order and good government," with everything held together by Red Green's duct tape.

I have seen flax in bloom, read Sinclair Ross, been to the Quebec Winter Carnival, tried to play Gordon Lightfoot songs on a guitar, skinny-dipped in northern lakes, removed bloodsuckers, figured out the Toronto subway, portaged canoes, trapped beaver, whined about trivial matters, eaten wild as well as flour-and-sugar beaver tails, cheered for fringe theatre, drunk Keith's draft beer to Stan Rogers songs, toured a northern diamond mine, picked Saskatoons, played hockey, swatted mosquitoes, stood at both Mile 0's on the Trans-Canada Highway, made love under the northern lights (just kidding, children), shovelled roofs, jogged the Hotel Macdonald stairs in Edmonton, boiled sap, kissed a cod, slept on an offshore oil rig, complained about banks, used an outhouse, attended the Calgary Stampede, and even rubbed Timothy Eaton's bronze toe in Winnipeg for good luck.

But do I know the country? Sometimes I think so; more often I feel I know nothing.

Canada, I sometimes think, is a country that, like Einstein's theory of relativity, is impossible for virtually any of us to grasp.

Einstein's theory can be worked out on a blackboard. We have a thousand books, dozens of royal commissions, hundreds of learned papers, and millions of panel discussions and late-night bar conversations—yet none has ever satisfactorily worked out the equation that is Canada. All we know for sure is that for every sign that points one way another seems to be pointing back. We are a country of endless contradiction.

Canadians have two languages but rarely speak them both; they have two official national sports but hardly ever play one, lacrosse; they fret over other provinces' separation threats and race to threaten separation themselves; they use Ottawa as both capital city and swear word; they have politicians who are elected to the federal government to work for the elimination of the federal government; they have academics calling for the end of provinces, premiers working for ever-increasing provincial powers, and mayors hoping for the creation of city states at the expense of provincial powers; they argue, still, over whether Louis Riel should have been hanged as a traitor back in 1885 or deserves a statue on Parliament Hill as a Father of Confederation.

It should come as no surprise, then, that this country that saw 42,042 citizens pay the ultimate sacrifice in the Second World War, that takes such enormous pride in its contributions to both wars, would have as a celebrated novel about those times Earle Birney's *Turvey*, the story of an enlisted man who never sees battle.

Not only did different sides of the country hold different views on Trudeau—Salmon Arm, B.C., never forgiving him for giving them the finger—but time, as well as space, also saw him differently. Pierre Trudeau died the ultimate symbol for a strong, central government. He left behind, as his legacy, a Charter of Rights that is based on tolerance and equality. A half-dozen years after his death, however, a book appeared—*Young Trudeau* by Max and Monique Nemni, two Trudeau contemporaries—showing that he began his political life sympathetic to fascism, thought democracy bad for the sort of elite he himself came from, considered himself a revolutionary capable of open insurrection, and once called upon a crowd to "impale alive" those who supported the conscription intended to send more Canadians off to fight for their country. Thirty years later he would himself call out the army, thinking it necessary to save the nation.

No surprise, then, that when John English published his first volume of *Citizen of the World: The Life of Pierre Elliott Trudeau* in the fall of 2006, the official biographer would conclude, after years of studying Trudeau's public and private writings, that the man was "contradictory and conflicted."

Just like the country itself.

IT WOULD BE SIMPLER, perhaps, if Canada were only smaller.

When Luigi Barzini set out to write *The Italians* in the early 1960s he fancied himself a portrait painter whose "sitter happens to be my country." To capture Canada, however, you'd have to be not only a portrait painter but also a cartographer, for the central personality of the

Canadian is landscape. You'd also need to be an analyst, for Canadians often seem far more interested in what they think—or, more accurately, what *others* think—than in how they look. And you'd have to be a seer, to know what lies ahead, if anything at all.

A friend once said, almost as a joke, that "Canada is the painting that Tom Thomson never finished." The final strokes forever out of reach.

How could you ever expect to properly capture such a country? Can you even try to talk about *a*—one, single, specific—Canadian when the personality you're trying to define speaks two official languages, hundreds of other tongues, and is made up of faces in shapes and colours more varied than in any other nation in the world? How can it be that a country so vast and so blessed with natural resources could shift from a place where four of every five lived on the land to a place where four of every five live in the city—and in so short a time that there are Canadians alive who have lived in both realities?

And how, others must wonder, can a people apply such ridicule to government—even to the very notion of Confederation—and yet take such annual pride in being named by the United Nations as one of the very best countries in the world to live?

"Canada is a serious country," candidate Michael Ignatieff grandly told one crowd during the 2006 Liberal leadership race, yet it's also a country where a cross-country driver will come across a giant pickerel, goose, five-cent piece, Easter egg, moose antler, oil can, apple, hockey stick, elephant, tomato, lobster and, in little Beiseker, Alberta, a giant skunk called Squirt.

It is a country where the representative head of state, the current governor general, comes from Haiti and had to renounce citizenship in France to represent the Queen of England in Canada. A country where the government regularly collects far too much in taxes then declares billion-dollar surpluses and acts as if it's somehow managed to turn a profit running the place. A country whose thirteen parts—ten provinces, three territories—are convinced that there's something in this country called "fiscal imbalance" whereby each and every one of them is getting screwed by a plan originally set up to allow for "equalization."

A country where pollsters not long ago discovered that more people believe in the Loch Ness monster than believe their politicians.

It is a country that sells the outdoors and fresh air and nature and wilderness to those outside its borders—yet today is the most urbanized modern nation in the world. A country whose citizens often seem less interested in whether a glass is half full or empty than they are in whether there might be chips in the rim—and yet will still tell pollsters they think of themselves as contented people.

A country whose citizens are suspicious and jealous of their neighbours yet say the Canadian value they treasure above all others is represented by a health system sworn to fairness and universal access. A country so renowned for the tolerance it continually celebrates that writer Margaret Atwood once couldn't help remarking, "In this country you can say what you like because no one will listen to you anyway."

A country with no history of civil war—but only because historians haven't yet come to terms with what the Meech Lake Accord was all about.

IT TAKES CREATIVE MINDS to keep a place like this together—and perhaps the true secret to the little-recognized longevity of Canada belongs to the inventors. After all, as the poet Miriam Waddington asks:

> Are we real or
> did someone invent
> us ...?

Canada, of course, gave the world the telephone, and insulin, and Pablum. It gave the world the CanadArm, kerosene, caulking guns, standard time, the combine harvester, green garbage bags, the electron microscope, instant potatoes, snowblowers, AM radio, the BlackBerry, electric stoves, IMAX, the Robertson screw, Muskol, the snowmobile, the paint roller, five-pin bowling, the Wonderbra, and Trivial Pursuit.

But Canada's greatest gift to the world—and perhaps to itself— might have come from J.D. Millar back in 1930. Millar, an engineer with the Ontario Department of Highways, had an idea so simple that, eventually, his small experiment in northeastern Ontario was adopted around the world.

The line down the middle of the road.

Just maybe it required a Canadian to realize that forces headed in opposing directions might need a little safe space between them, a little order to the traffic.

And perhaps the secret to Canada can be said to lie somewhere between the lines.

One

The Unknown Country

ON A RAINY DAY in the spring of 1991, I headed off to Victoria to pay a visit to Bruce Hutchison.

It was the year following the failure of the Meech Lake constitutional accord. Meech Lake—no matter what one's opinion of the political initiative to turn Confederation into one big, happy, supportive, sharing family—had been a pivotal moment for this country as the century that was supposed to belong to Canada came to a close. Many firmly believed that Meech's death was the end, which it wasn't. What it was, undeniably, was the beginning of a long, perhaps irreparable rift between the governors and the governed.

A civil war without the shooting—but hardly without casualties.

For much of the previous nine months I'd been on the road "taking the pulse of the nation." This, of course, is journalese for moving about the land in airplanes and rented cars, staying in four- and five-star hotels, eating and drinking at company expense, putting in for overtime and generally visiting old friends—but still, it wouldn't be much of a stretch to suggest that Canada was in the midst of the Second Great Depression. Only this one was of the mind, not the pocketbook, and the drought far more one of political imagination than of prairie fields.

I had gone deliberately to Victoria to visit with Hutchison. After all, who better for a wandering journalist holding a stethoscope instead of a pen to call on than the one known as "the conscience of the nation"?

Hutchison had written more than anyone before—or since—on the elusive Canadian identity. In thousands of columns and several books he'd sought to analyze and advise this country, its politicians, and even its people. His writing was vibrant, his optimism renowned. For someone setting out to travel the country in search of answers, Bruce Hutchison was an obvious destination.

Some might even say *he* invented us.

The man called "Hutch" by older journalists had long been a personal hero as well. He was, after all, the author of *The Unknown Country*, surely the most important book published in this nation over the previous half century. Three times he'd been given the Governor General's Award for nonfiction. He'd also been named to the Privy Council and made an officer of the Order of Canada. He had, years earlier, evolved into an icon for just about every working Canadian newspaper columnist, revered as much for his prolific output and common sense as for the fact that he might have been the first to realize that it's possible to avoid the newsroom and send your work in to sit at the desk for you. And this in the days before data transmission.

Bruce Hutchison would turn ninety that year. Born in small-town Ontario in 1901, he was still writing a weekly column for the *Vancouver Sun,* still living on his small acreage just outside Victoria, still obsessively splitting firewood at his rustic cabin retreat farther up Vancouver Island at Shawnigan Lake.

I was coming to visit at a time when many believed that the sometimes blue, sometimes overcast yo-yo that is the sky over Canada might, for once, actually fall all the way. Meech Lake had been intended to bring Quebec into the 1982 Constitution Act that the province had angrily refused to sign when Premier René Lévesque felt the final deal had been struck behind his back without his knowing.

But there was much more to the national angst than the familiar fretting over Quebec and Confederation, no matter how intense it might be at the moment. The economy was sinking. The deficit was drowning the federal government. And even Hutchison's little house in the country was threatening to wash away after a solid week of hard rain.

Jamie Lamb and I had come by rented car and ferry from Vancouver, where Lamb was doing a general column for the *Sun,* and we were joined by Vaughn Palmer, the fine legislative columnist for the same paper. Despite an age difference of half a century, Palmer was Hutchison's closest friend and very much treated as a son by the older man.

We drove up between the tall Lombardy poplars that Hutchison had planted as seedlings sixty-five years earlier. The trees had grown so high they now seemed out of all proportion to the little wooden bungalow perched on a small rise of land. We knocked on the door— the knocker a brass and smiling William Shakespeare—and were greeted by a small, wizened old man with large, black horn-rimmed glasses and a turn-of-the-nineteenth-century British wardrobe that made him seem more a character out of P.G. Wodehouse than of the laid-back Canadian West Coast.

He had a cane in his hand and its presence clearly embarrassed him, but the endless damp of this disappointing spring had turned his sciatica leg pain "excruciating." Up to now the old man's health had always been excellent, but during his annual visit to Ottawa over the past winter—a visit that invariably included a tête-à-tête with whatever prime minister happened to be in office, from Mackenzie King to Brian Mulroney—he'd ended up in an ambulance rushing him to Ottawa General, where doctors had diagnosed a small but cautionary heart attack.

He needed the cane to get about his garden, which he insisted on showing off even though the tulips were bent over as if they'd just run a marathon. "It's not what it used to be," he said, waving the cane over the expansive lot while his spit-and-polished black shoes sank in the long wet grass. "But then, what is any more?"

The very question I'd come to ask.

Bruce Hutchison, after all, had published *The Unknown Country* in the 1940s. A generation later, in the 1980s, seized in an octogenarian fit of energy, he'd penned a follow-up book whose essence could be gleaned from the title: *The Unfinished Country.*

"There won't be a third!" he said in his creaky old man voice.

BRUCE HUTCHISON was only forty-one in 1942 when he wrote what was, for many years, the best-known book in the land. Today, *The Unknown Country* is out of print—its red cover with the gold-embossed maple leaf on the spine sometimes showing up in second-hand bookstores—and has been largely forgotten. The book is undeniably out of date, both socially and historically, yet it remains a mandatory read for anyone trying to gain any grasp at all of this slippery thing called Canada.

It wasn't even a book he'd intended on writing. He said that it came out of a liquid lunch—Hutchison was a very light drinker—with a New York publisher who kept pushing drinks and insisting that Americans needed to know about their northern neighbour—and that Hutchison was the man to do it. Six weeks later he delivered the manuscript.

Right from the well-known opening sentence—"No one knows my country, neither the stranger nor its sons"—there is a sense of the nation's new spirit and of the author's great optimism for what was to come. He saw Canada more as an energetic youth than a mature adult, a youth unaware of its strengths and uncertain of where exactly it might fit in. It had all the trappings of such young ambition: high hopes and deep doubts, delight and despair, but most of all a restlessness about what might become of it.

Hutchison wrote about a then-young country, eleven million strong but spread so thinly in such an impossibly large space that the real story of the eleven million was an uncanny "loneliness"—the people huddled around the lights of little towns and a few cities, the country forever beyond.

The people, he believed, didn't yet know their own country, but it was slowly coming into focus. It was young and filled with great energy, just coming out of the muffling snows of the past and into a promising new season. The very name of the country was to him the shout of a youth, a name filled with sounds of geese returning and melting rivers roaring down mountains, destination uncertain.

It was as if he could hardly wait to see what was coming. *Then.*

In preparing for whatever this book would become, I naturally began my research with *The Unknown Country*. After all, Hutchison had been there first and had certainly stayed longest. I broke open the dark red covers of a second-hand volume, inhaled the must of yellowed pages, and was much heartened to read in Hutchison's introduction that he'd begun with a plan but had instantly abandoned it. The original plan, he hoped, would not matter in the end.

I, too, had a plan and I, too, soon abandoned those detailed architectural designs. It made sense when I mapped it out; it stopped making sense the moment my fingers stepped, uncertainly, onto the opening page. Hutchison's warning on his opening pages might not have been as direct as Mark Twain's in *Huck Finn*—*"Persons attempting to find a motive in this narrative will be prosecuted"*—but he did have a motive, even if he claimed no master plan.

His assignment had been to explain the great empty northern neighbour to the United States. It was released to a country that barely took notice. One year later, however, the book would be published north of the border and would become a remarkable bestseller.

It was *Canadians,* it turned out, who wanted to know about Canada.

Hutchison wrote that he wanted to open up southern eyes to what was happening on the northern half of the continent. In part because of its impressive war effort, he believed that Canada already stood with the significant countries of the world. And he argued that both countries needed to know each other better, for in coming years this North American relationship would prove an essential factor in world politics.

He could not, however, offer Americans any clear-cut description of the northern personality. The Canadian just didn't define as readily as the English or the French or the German, all so firm in people's minds in this time of war; nor as readily as the American, whose personality was increasingly well formed and known to the world. The only truly distinct Canadian was found in Quebec, he said—this was 1942, remember—but the country's overall identity was still far from clear.

The best Hutchison could do was offer up a snapshot of Canada as he saw it at the time. He knew the country was evolving, had to evolve, and that soon enough that snapshot would have to fade. You might capture it for a moment, or even bring into brief focus a sizeable portion of it, but in the end it remained the unknown—perhaps even unknowable—country.

Many years later, historian Pierre Berton, who considered Hutchison a mentor, would say he had it right. *The Unknown Country*'s very title still held up—a wolf howling in the distance, heard but not seen, a personality left largely to the imagination.

Hutchison decided to write his book as a travelogue. He and wife, Dorothy, visit the Maritimes and Quebec, where they are hopeless with the language. They stop off in Ottawa, where Hutchison attends Question Period and describes the House of Commons as "the true heart of Canada." Here, he thought, everything that was felt in the vast nation was spoken of within a matter of hours. He also believed Parliament was floating in a "comfortable vacuum" and disconnected from the reality of the country.

The Hutchisons slip through Ontario—"I do not pretend to understand Toronto"—and then head ever west, stopping in Gimli, Manitoba, to write about Icelandic immigrants and eventually ending up in the lotus land of British Columbia.

At the end of this trip he's so overawed by the magnitude of trying to understand and describe this vast land that the man who would write more than three million words before his death turned to someone else's words to sum up the experience. Hutchison quotes Captain George Vancouver, the eighteenth-century explorer of the west coast: "A lifetime is not enough to explore this country. A man is too small to feel its size. The poet has not been born to sing its song, nor the painter to picture it."

Hutchison had set out to do just that and, judging by *The Unknown Country*'s sales and shelf life, his attempt was successful.

The book is at times lyrical, at times purple, at times terribly out of synch with current reality. French Canadians are pipe-smoking, good-hearted, simple country folk; the Japanese in British Columbia are breeding so quickly he finds no hope of their assimilation over time. The book is also sexist, consistently ignoring the female half of the population. That is, of course, the way men thought and wrote in 1942. Sixty years from now, today's words will carry different weights.

In Winnipeg Hutchison went to see *Free Press* editor John W. Dafoe, a man he considered the greatest Canadian of the times and whom he credited with helping move the country out of its colonial mindset and into full nationhood. Dafoe, he writes, originated Canada's push to find its own role on the world stage as an "honest broker." Sixty years on, that sentiment has fallen badly out of focus, the phrase itself, when it's used at all, invariably tied to Lester Pearson's Nobel Peace Prize work more than fifty years ago. John W. Dafoe, on the other hand, is no longer a name Canadians recognize.

Hutchison knew that the war had revitalized the country's economy following the Great Depression. Canada was now a stronger nation than anyone had imagined possible and, thanks to Dafoe's enlightened thinking, would take its new and rightful place among leading nations once the war was over.

In Hutchison's opinion, Canada in 1942 was on the verge of greatness. "Now our time is come," he wrote, "and, if not grasped, will be forever lost." No wonder that in later years Peter C. Newman would call Hutchison "the eternal optimist."

HE WOULD NOT REMAIN that way.

The four of us—Jamie Lamb, Vaughn Palmer, Hutchison, and I—headed back into Victoria for lunch at his Union Club. He sat in the passenger seat while I drove. To passersby who happened to peer in at this shrunken little hawk-nosed man, his tie perfectly knotted, his black hat fitted so tight it seemed threaded on, he would have looked like a frail senior being taken for a ride by his grandsons. They wouldn't have known that he was the one in charge, barking out directions and condemning a "Road Closed" sign as one more reminder of the new housing developments bearing down on him.

Nor would they have seen his hands, sitting loosely on his lap over the cursed cane. The man who once described Prime Minister William Lyon Mackenzie King as having "the hands of a physician" still had, at nearly ninety, the hands of a woodsman, their size and grip shaped more by axe than by acquaintance.

Hutchison's love of chopping wood was, for me, one more reason to admire him. His friend and neighbour at the lake, Percy Rawlings, often told the story of Hutchison splitting wood and then deliberately hiding it from sight because if Dorothy found it "she'd only burn it."

Hutchison had once said that the simple woodshed "contains not just some fuel but nearly all that mankind has learned, so far, about civilized society." And that "civilized society," he'd come to believe, had taken a distinct turn for the worse in recent months in Canada.

Bruce Hutchison had lost faith. He'd turned his back on the great promise he'd found so readily in 1942 and held on to for decades. At the club he moved into his familiar seat at the very same table former British Columbia premier W.A.C. "Wacky" Bennett had eaten lunch at for twenty years—"a *sacred* table!"—and immediately began railing about the state of the nation, barely pausing to take breath or bite.

"This is a *country* we're talking about here!" Hutchison snapped at one point when the discussion wavered into individual politicians. But he himself swept it off into personality when he began to talk about the death of the Meech Lake constitutional accord and the role played in its death by the likes of Manitoba legislator Elijah Harper Jr. and, of course, the accord's most vocal critic, Newfoundland premier Clyde Wells.

"That *bastard*!" the grand old man barked.

Vaughn Palmer said he'd never seen Hutchison so black and pessimistic. On the ride out he'd warned that the old man had taken "personally" the crushing blows Harper and Wells had dealt the previous year. The accord had been well received in Quebec for its "distinct society" clause and Hutchison was one of many who believed this was the only way to keep Quebec in the fold. But instead, he argued across the lunch table, it "was rejected without serious thought by an English-speaking majority who hadn't bothered to learn its contents."

Not surprisingly, his opinion was not well received by those who had opposed Meech Lake. Some recalled how much he'd always admired Pierre Trudeau—and hadn't the former prime minister declared that the accord, which he opposed, could be rejected without consequence?

"*Balderdash,*" said the old man. Quebec couldn't possibly be stopped now from leaving Confederation; moreover, Canada's very justification lay in the experiment it represents: different languages and different cultures coexisting peacefully and prosperously under one flag. If Quebec were to go, the rest must follow.

"People who think the rest of Canada can survive are mad," he went on. "You can't have a *scarecrow* nation. It would simply fall apart if the Maritimes and Ontario and the West tried to stick it out. The others couldn't deal with such a strong Ontario. The Maritimes would be the first to petition to join the United States and it would be over for everybody else very soon after."

Hutchison was hardly the only Eeyore moaning and groaning about the land in those days, but being the Grand Old Man of Canadian Journalism, his points had an added edge. And it wasn't only the leaders who'd failed Canada, but Canadians themselves. Sitting in the Union Club stabbing air foes with his fork, he suddenly stopped and smiled. "I came across a quote from Emerson the other day in my reading," he said. "'The people are to be taken in short doses.'" He was feeling the same, showing little concern for news of the Citizens' Forum on Canada's Future that was then going about the country listening to "ordinary Canadians" vent over what had happened during the Meech Lake negotiations.

Returning to his plate, he spoke to no one in particular: "Democracy is such a dirty, dirty business, isn't it? *How* does it go on? *How* does it keep working? I honestly don't know.

"It wouldn't matter if Lincoln or Ben Franklin was sitting down to write up a Canadian constitution right now. It wouldn't work. It *can't* work. The country is in too bad a temper. This country has lost its soul— it's like they took you and they ripped out your heart, that's what it feels like."

This wasn't just old age railing at the coming night—despair knew no clear demographic in the months following the collapse of the constitutional talks—but Hutchison was undoubtedly feeling the march of time. He still worked on an old manual typewriter and delivered hard copy to the *Vancouver Sun* at a time when the other three at the table were pressing "send." He was cared for by a loyal housekeeper, Gladys Veitch (Dorothy had been killed in a car accident in 1969 and daughter Joan, who'd kept house for him, had died a few years earlier). He'd had a heart attack. He had trouble walking.

Later, back at the doorway of his little country bungalow, rain forming dimples on his big glasses, he stopped momentarily and shook his cane. "You know," he said, "there is nothing about old age to recommend it. Avoid it. *Avoid* it."

Before that wet day in Victoria was out he'd say that he might have, at best, another year left in him. The country he'd spent a lifetime defining, he said, might have two more years. Bruce Hutchison would prove correct on the one date—he had only one year left.

But he would prove wrong about the country.

BRUCE HUTCHISON'S FAMOUS OPTIMISM did rally slightly in his final months as yet another constitutional initiative, the Charlottetown Agreement, was underway, but he died six weeks before it was voted down in referendum on October 26, 1992.

This rejection would have upset him as much as the death of Meech, perhaps even more so in that the people—the very ones Emerson suggested "be taken in short doses"—were directly involved this time. The journalist who all his life considered himself a man of the people would never have agreed with them on this one.

Bitterness, like arthritis, often seems a common affliction among older Canadians. Hutchison was not the first eminent figure to hit a wall of disappointment near the end of his life. When novelist Hugh MacLennan entered old age—he died in late 1990 at eighty-three—he felt such doom and gloom that he tried to put it all down in one final dark, dystopian novel. *Voices in Time* is a science-fiction account of the hopelessness that prevails decades after a nuclear explosion has destroyed his beloved Montreal. A main character is likened to "a mind trapped in the collapsing vaults of history." He seems to speak for the author himself.

Such a shift seemed improbable for MacLennan, once the great celebrator of his country through his novels, essays, and such nonfiction works as *Seven Rivers of Canada*. He'd ended one of his earlier novels, *The Watch That Ends the Night*, with "It came to me that to be able to love the mystery surrounding us is the final and only sanction of human existence." To think otherwise, it would seem, would be to go against even the MacLennan clan motto: "Where there's life, there's hope."

Yet Hugh MacLennan had clearly lost his. When his last book was about to come out I went to see him at his cottage in North Hatley in Quebec's Eastern Townships, and the old man, sitting under a leafy oak tree on a gorgeous late-summer day, said he didn't know exactly what had happened to his country, but somewhere along the way "the fibre went out of us."

Bruce Hutchison and Hugh MacLennan were hardly alone. Canada can sometimes seem like the land of Grumpy Old Men.

Robertson Davies, at one time Canada's best-known international author, was so put off by the 1980s rush to enter into free trade with the United States that he became convinced "this is the worst this country has ever seen."

And historian Donald G. Creighton, a year before his death in 1979, the year before the first referendum on Quebec sovereignty, had come to regard the country he spent a lifetime writing about as "a good place to live, but that's all Canada is now, just a good place to live."

IF ANYONE WAS GOING TO ENTER his later years in a grumpy mood, I would have expected it to be Walter Stewart.

It stands as one of the good fortunes of my lucky career that I was able to work with, and at one point be hired by, this man. Walter Stewart was the greatest investigative journalist of his generation, a man who muck-raked and took on all comers in the great traditions of William Lyon Mackenzie, the original Canadian revolutionary, and Joseph Howe, the early anti-Confederate.

Stewart, with his mad-professor hair, his bottle-thick horn rims, his cackle, and a squeaky voice that seemed to run on rusty shocks, was at the same time solidly built, muscular, and utterly fearless. He was the very first to take on the instantly iconic Prime Minister Pierre Trudeau, his highly critical *Shrug: Trudeau in Power* coming out only three years into the sixteen that Trudeau would so totally dominate Canadian politics, even when briefly out of power.

Stewart was the ultimate iconoclast in Canadian journalism, the fourth son of committed CCFers in ultra-conservative London, Ontario, and a top student who once described his hobbies as "reading, writing and arguing." He was writing about the perils of globalization before the rest of us could even fit the word in our mouths. He took on the banks, the food industry, the insurance industry, the historians—and even Canadians' very notion of themselves.

As he once wrote in a rant against government cutbacks, "There's just not enough voices out there saying, *'Hey, wait a minute!'*"

Stewart, who died of cancer in 2004 at the age of seventy-three, worked for the *Toronto Star, Maclean's, Today* magazine, and the *Toronto Sun,* wrote some twenty or more books, and served as director of the School of Journalism at the University of King's College in Halifax. "Approach each story as if you just arrived in town that morning," he would advise young reporters, me included, "and write each story as if you're leaving town that night."

He travelled the country extensively, but disliked driving. He had a driver's licence—claiming it had been issued by a local garage even though he ran into a gas pump during the test—but poor vision in one eye made depth perception difficult, so he rarely took the wheel. Instead his wife, Joan, did the driving while Walt sat in the back seat, happily typing away and periodically looking up through his thick glasses to shout *"Are we there yet?"*

One of his books, *But Not in Canada: Smug Canadian Myths Shattered by Harsh Reality,* took a bit of the stuffing out of this gentle, polite, caring country. Stewart had become so put off by Canadians wallowing in their own silly superiority that he believed "smugness has become a national religion, a national disease" and traced its then most recent rise to the American crisis in political trust that had grown out of the Vietnam War, the Watergate break-in, and the impeachment threat that finally forced Richard Nixon from presidential office.

How, Stewart wondered, could Canadians feel so great about their own political process when, only two years before Watergate, a handful of Quebec indépendentistes known as the FLQ (Front de libération du Québec) had kidnapped British diplomat James Cross and murdered Quebec labour minister Pierre Laporte—and, with almost every Canadian politician backing the decision, the government of the day had brought in the old, rarely used War Measures Act? After calling out the army, Trudeau's Liberal government had tossed more than four hundred people in jail without charges or trial and made it illegal to belong to an organization that had been perfectly legal only the day before—never bothering to explain its actions surrounding an "apprehended insurrection" that became known as the October Crisis.

"We view ourselves as a superior people," Stewart wrote, "a sober, peaceable people, a people of extraordinarily decent instincts and firmly entrenched civil liberties, and we reject any contrary evidence."

He'd become convinced that Canada had become "captive" to its own largely self-created myth of the world's most reasonable citizen—patient, neighbourly, sure to stand up against violence and racism and anything that might threaten civil liberties.

"In short," Stewart wrote in his typical take-no-prisoners style, "all the things your average wild-eyed, gun-toting, bigoted, loud-mouthed, venal, aggressive, tyrannical bastard of an American is not."

Walter Stewart did nothing in halves that could be done by the dozen, and he chased after the myth of the perfectly behaved Canadian like a dog suddenly given wings in a forest full of squirrels. He talked about the October Crisis of 1970 and the troops on Parliament Hill and the suspension of civil liberties that had been so widely applauded by the vast majority of Canadians. He cited previous laws passed in Canadian legislatures that required no proof and allowed no defence. He talked about a Native girl who'd been raped and killed by three white youths in Williams Lake, B.C., only to have their convictions amount to two $200 fines and charges dismissed against the third young man. He told the story of how angry whites had once rounded up Chinese "Coolie" workers they believed had taken their railway construction jobs and driven the terrified workers over a cliff to their deaths.

For a country with such a reputation for tolerance, Stewart often found Canada quite lacking in Christian charity. He talked about the Second World War when those Canadians, many of them from Quebec, who refused to volunteer for active service overseas were tagged "Zombies" and openly attacked, spit upon, and sneeringly handed white feathers as a sign of their cowardice. He talked about how sailors from the Canadian navy were often afraid to go ashore in Quebec City, convinced they'd be treated as enemies by those who opposed the war and attacked and kicked in the side streets.

The war and the lead-up to it was indeed a time of widespread intolerance, the most famous being when the *St. Louis,* a ship carrying nine hundred Jewish refugees, was turned away from Canada, the passengers' last hope, and forced to head back for Germany and the Holocaust, where most perished. The prime minister of the day, Mackenzie King, thought there were already too many Jews around Ottawa. According to Irving Abella and Harold Troper's *None Is Too Many,* in Canada in those days "refugee" was code for "Jew." The director of immigration, E.C. Blair, considered Jews inassimilable, a people "who can organize their affairs better than other people" and who therefore were a threat to good Canadians.

To dismiss the myth of the law-abiding, peaceful, nonviolent Canadian, Stewart offered an entire chapter on Canadian riots. Riots to start a rebellion back in 1837–38 and riots over giving reparations to those who'd rebelled in the first place. Riots during Orange parades in "Toronto the Good." A riot in Regina when unemployed men came through on their way to ask Ottawa for help finding jobs—a riot that cost a life and, Stewart argued, was entirely orchestrated by the state to put the labour organizers in a bad light. A riot in Halifax to celebrate V-E Day that saw liquor stores looted and drunken men and women having sex in the streets and even in the local cemetery. A riot in Montreal over a hockey game that became, many believe, the first sound in the Quiet Revolution that would transform Quebec politics.

Many years after writing *But Not in Canada,* Stewart retraced the route he'd taken decades earlier for the *Toronto Star Weekly,* a cross-Canada trip by car. Joan, of course, was in the front seat, driving. And Walt, of course, sat in the back, happily hammering away at accepted wisdom.

THE CROSS-COUNTRY TRIP is as much a tradition in Canadian journalism as talking about the weather is at Tim Hortons. There's something about the 7714-kilometre-long Trans-Canada Highway—in reality, series of highways—that provides not only the natural narrative of a journey but a continuing metaphor for unity. And considering that so many such trips are undertaken in an effort to understand this confusing behemoth called Canada, and often in times of national crisis, the attraction is obvious.

It was the approach Bruce Hutchison chose for *The Unknown Country.* It was what Walter Stewart decided to do, first for the magazine and then for his book. Like Stewart, Thomas Wilby, Edward McCourt, Charles Gordon, and John Nicol travelled the route by car. Kildare Dobbs and John Aitken tackled it by bus, Dobbs saying that the Trans-Canada allowed the nation's scattered communities to be "strung like tiny beads on an infinitely strong thread." David Cobb did it on motorcycle. John Stackhouse hitchhiked. As he wrote in *Timbit Nation: A Hitchhiker's View of Canada,*

> There was no better way to see a country and meet its people than to beg for rides along the way, to have long conversations (sometimes very long) with strangers, to test public generosity, to overcome fears, within oneself and in others, and to see the road, and feel it. Standing on a remote rural road, you could see the vastness of what it was attempting to connect. On a suburban on-ramp, you could feel the pulse of a society as it rushed from office to mall to home. And climbing into the cars of that society—at the invitation of a stranger, who had everything to lose, as did you—you could sense the openness of the nation, along with its fears and prejudices. In short, you could stand on the roadside and put an entire nation on the couch.

Stackhouse ended his journey decidedly more enthusiastic than McCourt was at the end of his trek in the early 1960s. While McCourt agreed with the importance of bringing the various parts of the country closer together, there was a sense of defeat in his overall assessment of the country he had just tried to grasp. "In Canada," he wrote, "there is too much of everything. Too much rock, too much prairie, too much tundra, too much mountain, too much forest."

Vancouver's Daniel Francis took the most recent journalist's journey in *A Road for Canada: The Illustrated Story of the Trans-Canada Highway,* published in late 2006. Francis, who calls the road Canada's "Other National Dream," uses archival material to show where the road began as well as where it ends in both Victoria and St. John's—both marked Mile 0—and includes Prime Minister John Diefenbaker's remarks at the official opening of the highway on September 3, 1962.

Diefenbaker, even then, saw it bringing "a renewed sense of national unity" to the country—though none of us can remember what the crisis was back then. "This highway," he thundered, "may it serve to bring Canadians closer together, may it bring to all Canadians a renewed determination to individually do their part to make this nation greater and greater still."

There is plenty of evidence that this long road—as criticized for its construction work as for its potholes—connects in mysterious ways with Canadians. This is the road travelled by Terry Fox in 1980 when a return of his cancer forced the one-legged runner to stop his valiant run near Thunder Bay, roughly halfway to his destination in Victoria.

Those who would say Canada's most inspirational hero made it only halfway have no sense at all of the country.

This is also the road another one-legged cancer survivor, Steve Fonyo, ran from one end to the other after Fox's attempt. It is the road wheelchair athlete Rick Hansen travelled and then headed the rest of the way around the world. Their triumphs are so much the stuff of legend now that they've inspired an annual summer cottage industry of similar quests, most of which go unnoticed.

There's also evidence that this journey had symbolic value even before the Trans-Canada Highway was a suggestion, let alone officially opened.

Five years after Confederation, in 1872, Sandford Fleming—who would later give the world time zones—decided to lead a grand expedition across the new country to see what had come out of all that big talk in Charlottetown and Quebec City. The Fleming expedition went from Halifax to Victoria, covering an estimated 1687 miles by steamer, 2185 miles by horse, including coaches, wagons, packs, and saddle horses, nearly 1000 miles by train, and 485 miles in canoes or rowboats.

George M. Grant, the man assigned to keep a written record of the journey, described what had already become known as "The Great Lone Land." It is a name that stands up today. Great, and lone, but powerful. The new Dominion, recorded Grant, "rolled out before us like a panorama, varied and magnificent enough to stir the dullest spirit into patriotic emotion."

Even then, it was about unity.

WALTER STEWART was approaching seventy when he wrote *My Cross-Country Checkup,* but he was still up to taking the stuffing out of Canada and Canadians. One of the first stops he made was in the Maritimes so that he might harangue his fellow citizens for an early form of ethnic cleansing.

In 1755 as many as twelve thousand Acadians were driven out simply because these hard-working French-speaking settlers weren't particularly keen on swearing allegiance to an unfamiliar British crown they weren't exactly sure had that much staying power under the circumstances of the day. For dallying, those Acadians who didn't escape into the dense bush were arrested, had their families torn apart and their homes burned, and for the next eight years until England and France finally reached a peace agreement, were sent by the hundreds and thousands to the south, to Europe, and even to the Falkland Islands. Their land, much of it cleared and perfect for planting, was then offered up to thousands of "planters"— the preferred English word for "settlers"—with the only restriction that no Catholics be allowed. Out with six thousand Catholics, in with as many as eight thousand Protestants, most moving up from the southern "Yankee" colonies. Out with the French, in with the English.

Ethnic cleansing seemed like a pretty fair comment.

One of Walter Stewart's most endearing qualities was an ability to embrace outrage and humour at one and the same time. While passing through Nova Scotia's Grand-Pré National Historic Site, he stopped to watch the devout pray before the statue of Evangeline that stands in the little cemetery at Saint-Charles-des-Mines. "Evangeline," of course, is the Henry Wadsworth Longfellow poem about the Acadian couple separated on their wedding day by the expulsion. Evangeline spends her life searching for her lost husband only to find him in Louisiana years later, lying helpless on his deathbed. Gentle Evangeline, unable to save her beloved, dies herself from the shock of seeing him in such a desperate state.

Longfellow, Stewart delighted in pointing out, wrote his poem nearly a hundred years after the expulsion. He'd never visited Grand-Pré. And Gentle Evangeline never existed. The devout Canadians, therefore, were kneeling deep in prayer before a fantasy that existed entirely in the mind of an American poet.

It was the kind of story—the irony, the wonder, the sheer madness of it all—that put the squeak in Walter Stewart's voice and the magnificent tweak in his writings.

JOAN DROVE HER HUSBAND twenty-five thousand kilometres, much of them on the Trans-Canada, much off, over those long months Walt spent doing one final check of his country. He made up a list of "Deep Thoughts"—"Unisex washrooms at gas stations are not an improvement" and "'Country Cookin' means over-cooked in grease"—and entertained himself by jotting down the best and worst of everything they saw. "Best road for scenery—The Dempster Highway." "Worst road for driving— The Dempster Highway."

He poured his love of history and his love of truth into the book. But there is also a love of the landscape, a respect for the natural world that might be expected from a man whose parents, Miller and Margaret Stewart, had once co-authored a long-forgotten book on the natural world they called *Bright World Around Us*.

Walter and Joan Stewart covered every province and then drove north up through the Northwest Territories toward the Beaufort Sea. They visited L'Anse aux Meadows, the ancient Viking site on the Great Northern Peninsula of Newfoundland. They toured historic Lunenburg, Nova Scotia, and drove across the Confederation Bridge to Prince Edward Island. They sat by the statue of Lord Beaverbrook that stands in Fredericton, a statue of a man of astounding wealth built by the nickels and dimes of New Brunswick schoolchildren. They travelled to Quebec City where, three decades earlier, they had driven straight into a language-rights demonstration and Joan, honking the horn and screaming, in English, "KINDLY ... GET ... OUT ... OF ... MY ... WAY!" had pushed through the crowd to get to their hotel while Walt cowered as close to the floorboards as he could get. This time, a much quieter time, they kept running into the same couple from Boston who, at every encounter, extolled the beauties of this glorious city, the middle-aged American woman admonishing Walt to be careful with the way English Canadians treat French Canada because, well, "You wouldn't want to lose this." In Ontario they saw the sights, travelling from the Martyrs' Shrine at Midland to the huge roadside goose at Wawa. They meandered across the prairies talking about everything from rebellion to elevators and asking such pertinent questions as "Why do they paint the barns red?" (Red was the easiest paint to make. Just put iron scraps into a bucketful of buttermilk and wait for the rust to turn the whole mixture the colour of a handsome barn.) They toured over the mountains and down through the Okanagan and talked about everything from ginseng farms to the Nisga'a land claim.

The trip had a profound effect on Stewart. The man who, many years earlier, had written a three-part series he called "My Farewell to Quebec" found now that he'd softened—or perhaps Quebec had softened. He found Canadians warm and open. He found them interesting. And he found the place much changed.

In the final chapter of *My Cross-Country Checkup,* Stewart said his country could still be intolerant, even racist, but that most Canadians now considered these "matters for shame, not pride." Yes, there was still a

vast gap between the wealthy and the poor, but there remained the possibility of that gap narrowing over time. The most promising change of all,
he said, was that Aboriginal issues were now being addressed not by force
but by law.

A modern traveller across this country, he felt, would recognize its vastness and variety but would also gain "a sense that there are no problems
we cannot meet, no challenges we need to fear, no wrongs we cannot
right, given the political will. It's not a bad old place, taken all in all."

Stewart, who dealt in harsh truths and was never shy in sounding the
alarm, did not in the least share the bitterness that marked the later observations of the old newspaperman Hutchison, of the old novelists
MacLennan and Davies, of the old historian Creighton. Iconoclastic to
the end, he would happily contradict their pessimism with his own
surprising optimism.

At the end of what would be his final trip across his country, Walter
Stewart stood on a hill near Inuvik, close by the Arctic Ocean, stared back
through his thick glasses over the vast landscape he and Joan had just
covered, and smiled. "The Canada we have just driven through," he
concluded, "is enormously, immensely better than the nation we first
crossed thirty-five years ago."

He had found it infinitely different from the Canada he and Joan had
first explored in the 1960s. More interesting. More diverse. More hopeful.

I HAVE COME, over time, to see Canada as the Bumblebee of Nations. It
flies, somehow, between all its various contradictions, not least of which
would be Bruce Hutchison, the eternal optimist, losing hope and Walter
Stewart, the grumpy iconoclast, finding hope. It defies logic—but it flies.
Somehow.

I know that scientists have gone to considerable lengths to show how
bumblebees do actually fly despite the fixed-wing aerodynamic calcula-
tions that suggest otherwise. Poor Canada, however, has yet to find a
zoology professor—let alone a *political* scientist—who can explain the
secret of this country. For bees, it might well be, as some researchers
suggest, the extra lift acquired by the air expelled during rapid wing clap-

ping, hence the buzzing sound. But the forces that keep Canada airborne are rather more elusive. Apart from rumours of cabinet shuffles and possible hockey trades, Canadians emit no buzz at all.

In fact, if a visitor from another world were shown a fat bumblebee with its tiny transparent wings and this massive land mass with its sniping regions, historical disputes, constitutional entanglements, and naysaying populace, the betting, surely, would be much higher on the fat insect staying afloat than on the strange, unwieldy creature called Canada.

And yet this country carries on, seemingly without a flight plan, flitting from one distraction to the next.

It's worth pointing out that, in the relative life span of countries, there almost always *has* been a Canada. Yet again we find the contradictions. Canadians talk and write obsessively about the "New Canada" as if Lester Pearson and Rocket Richard and Wayne and Shuster and Hugh MacLennan and Juliette all fell off some turnip truck a few decades back and the country is just now finding its legs. That black-and-white Canada of the newsreels has been replaced, so many would have you believe, by a colourful, vibrant, updated version that may or may not last, depending on everything from disaffected Westerners to disenchanted Newfoundlanders to disavowing Quebeckers. But the rarely acknowledged fact of the matter is that Canada, no matter how it defies logic, is already a greybeard among countries. And it has proven remarkably resilient.

It is the second-oldest federation after the American federation that came together between 1776 and 1792. The rest all came later: Australia in 1901, others after the Second World War. John A. Macdonald and Georges-Étienne Cartier were getting Canada's act together, in fact, around the same time as Bismarck and Garibaldi were working to unite the German and Italian states. And while France may be older, it has struggled through five constitutions compared with Canada's two ... and perhaps counting. The years since Canada became this impossible country have seen fluctuations and convulsions and reorganizations in Russia, in China, in Japan, in Mexico, and in countless other sovereign states.

And yet no one ever talks about Canada's lasting power.

Just how long it can last.

Two

A Canadian Is...

IT IS OCTOBER 17, 2006. A cold rain is falling in a slant along Wellington Street, the lights from cars moving past Parliament Hill washing yellow down toward the parkway along the Ottawa River. It is nasty and miserable and those of us hurrying along the sidewalk are in danger of being splashed from the side as well as having our umbrellas ripped inside out from behind. We are heading this wretched night, heads bowed, collars tight to chin, to the National Library to hear a panel discussion on what, exactly, makes a Canadian.

True story.

Several months earlier, an enterprising young Rhodes scholar named Irvin Studin approached fifty Canadian writers, thinkers, business leaders, politicians, activists, academics, artists, and—obviously running a bit thin on contributors—even a few journalists and asked them to submit two-thousand-word essays beginning with the words *"A Canadian is ... "*

No two answers were the same, as might be expected, and some didn't even answer at all, which I'm tempted to suggest could be as profound an answer as some of those that were actually typed and delivered. It was a strange exercise: two thousand words not nearly enough, two thousand words way too much.

One thing "A Canadian is ...," however, is willing. As Stephen Leacock once wrote about a favourite character, "he flung himself from the room, flung himself upon his horse and rode madly off in all directions."

Leacock, of course, was writing nearly a century ago. The horse ridden today by alarmists is the computer keyboard. And it goes in as many directions as there are fingers on the keys.

I'm not quite sure why Studin included me in his survey, but I do know that the deadline attached to my contribution was outrageously tight, which would suggest the B or even C list, someone who can type fast subbing for a significant name that either dropped out or didn't deliver. And no money was offered, which almost always leads to the journalist's return note beginning "Much as I would love to...."

But the invitation was impossible to turn down. I found my brain riding madly off in all directions, asking the silly question while walking the dog, riding my bike, watching *Hockey Night in Canada,* and even trying to get to sleep at night. For someone who's never had trouble sleeping, this was disturbing indeed. I simply had no idea what the answer was.

In the end, the only way I could think of to complete that suggestive opening phrase was to go to the Statistics Canada website, look up the running census, and start off with "A Canadian is 32,146,547 different things altogether—and counting...." It seemed smart at the time. On reflection, it seemed silly. On rereading, it seemed passable. Unable to make up my mind and, being Canadian, I went with it.

Canadians, I sometimes think, do lead the world in one matter. Not hockey, not pulp production, not snow, not even potholes, but in picking through their own belly-button lint. For a people known for their resourcefulness, this can often seem a dreadful waste of one's most important resource: time.

Compulsive self-introspection, however, seems oddly and uniquely Canadian. Americans don't seem to do much of it, apart from issue-based magazines that occupy but a fraction of the shelf space devoted to celebrity, sports, and even pornography.

British author Jeremy Paxman says that those he studied in his 1998 book, *The English: A Portrait of a People,* "have not devoted a lot of energy to discussing who they are." He finds this most curious, since vanity is also a large part of the English makeup. At one point he quotes Cecil

Rhodes, who ardently believed that the English just "happen to be the best people in the world, with the highest ideals of decency and justice and liberty and peace." Why, then, would they waste time on something already self-evident?

The result is that the British, despite being one of the critical supply sources for the elusive Canadian identity, are a people rather more interested in other parts of the anatomy than the odd little scar where the umbilical cord was once attached.

Not so in Canada.

More than four decades after Hutchison published *The Unknown Country*, Andrew H. Malcolm produced *The Canadians*. Malcolm had been the Canadian correspondent for *The New York Times* from 1978 to 1982 and spent those four years getting out and around this nation far more than any comparable Canadian journalist. An enthusiastic, adventuresome Teddy Roosevelt look-alike, he fell in love with the country of his grandparents, which he took to calling the "Eagle Scout" of nations.

After four years Malcolm began to think that "for many Canadians perhaps their unfortunate identity was to search forever for an identity, a Sisyphean task guaranteed to ensure eternal angst. The search itself had become the identity...."

And yet he, too, found contradiction in those seeking that elusive identity. There was, Malcolm discovered, reserved shyness, self-deprecating humour, a worrying sense of *not mattering* to the world at large, but also—as Walter Stewart had earlier suggested—an occasional but undeniable moral smugness, a condescension toward many things, mostly American. "What is it in Canada's history and character," Malcolm asked, "that explains its superior inferiority complex...?"

I've often thought myself that Canadians ingeniously use this endless "search" for identity as a handy excuse to wallow in their own self-righteousness—particularly at those moments when America has put the stuck-up Canadian nose out of joint. It could be construed as a sort of verbal party trick to turn the conversation around to oneself and all the comforting goodness of being Canadian.

Or it might be, as Malcolm suggested, superiority and inferiority at the same time. That, at least, would be in keeping with the endless contradictions of Canada.

The case for an inferiority complex has been made so often that it's by far the more accepted of the two possibilities. CBC radio ran a contest several years ago challenging listeners to complete the sentence "As Canadian as...." The winner, to wide general approval, was "As Canadian as possible ... under the circumstances."

No wonder we get called the Clark Kent and the Woody Allen of Nations. The metaphors, appropriately, are from American culture; insecure Canadians would never make a national icon out of an awkward weakling. (They might, on the other hand, make him prime minister.)

Several people have suggested that this inferiority mindset has its source in the colonial mentality found throughout the former British Empire, a deep-rooted sense that whatever is Canadian or Indian or Australian or South African is not quite up to standard. The sun never set on the British Empire, but not much light shone down upon it. A sense of unworthiness was just one of the struggles Commonwealth nations had to overcome as they came into their own. "My generation of Canadians," culture critic Robert Fulford told Malcolm, "grew up believing that, if we were very good or very smart, or both, we would someday graduate from Canada."

Canadian heroes seem almost missing from the national canvas. There are some, of course, but hardly in the numbers Americans celebrate. "During my time in Canada," Malcolm told me in an email from California, where he now works for the *Los Angeles Times*, "I was struck by the postage stamps—lacking heroes like Davy Crockett and Babe Ruth who are shared coast to coast generation after generation, the stamps in that era contained pictures of such things as antique furniture.

"Not exactly a stirring call to self-identity."

PICKING THROUGH THE LINT of the national belly button is at once a useful and useless exercise. Useful to authors of thick books and newspaper columnists and talking heads and academics, all of whom have made a cottage industry of it, but rather useless to people getting on with real lives in what has now been a real country for 140 years.

Al Purdy spent a lifetime looking at his country through poetry and prose and would regularly rail against those who dared dismiss the land he so adored. It irritated him that outsiders, usually Americans, acted as if the country were "a kind of vacuum between parentheses." It was not, he said in his essay collection *No Other Country*, some godforsaken place devoid of culture or art or literature, some "4,000-mile wide chunk of Arctic desert."

Purdy believed the country was essential to his own personality, his adult experiences on the road as formative as his parents had been while he was still a child at home. He once drew up a list of all his journeys across Canada and declared, "This is a map of myself, what I was and what I became. It is a cartography of feeling and sensibility: and I think the man who is not affected at all by this map of himself that is his country of origin, that man is emotionally crippled."

A big, hearty man who liked to order his beer two at a time—when I first met him I thought, wrongly, he was ordering for us both—Purdy felt that everyone else should share in his wild enthusiasm for figuring out what, exactly, made Canadians tick. It was his greatest passion during the late 1960s and early 1970s, a time of Centennial Year, Expo 67, and early Pierre Trudeau, a time when Canada seemed particularly anxious to distance itself from the Vietnam War, Watergate and, of course, Richard Nixon.

Purdy set off across the land, writing about the landscape and periodically dropping in to collect the wisdom of some of Canada's most respected minds. At Campbell River on Vancouver Island he called on Roderick Haig-Brown, a renowned nature writer and West Coast judge who considered fly fishing the ultimate court of decision.

The scotch had been poured, the judge's pipe lighted, and Purdy had deftly steered the conversation toward the country. He was certain that the London-born judge would be as puzzled as he was by the parochial nature of most Canadians—a people who, in a direct reversal of Joyce's Stephen Dedalus, might list their address as the universe, the world, North America, Canada, province, city, street, room....

But Haig-Brown would have none of it. "'What does the cockney know of rural England, or the countryman of London?'" he asked Purdy. "'I'm not at all sure that provincialism is such an evil thing at that. No man becomes a great patriot without first learning the closer loyalties and learning them well: loyalty to family, to the place he calls home, to his province or state or country.'"

And as for Purdy's request to have Haig-Brown pontificate on "The Canadian Identity"—this country's equivalent of the number of angels dancing on the head of a pin—the country judge just shook his head. "'That,'" he said, "'is a question manufactured by writers and intellectuals.'"

The judge, it turned out, was far more interested in the coming salmon run.

A CANADIAN COMES to a fork in the road, the old joke goes. The sign pointing in one direction reads "Heaven." The sign pointing in the other direction says "Panel Discussion on Heaven." The Canadian heads straight for the panel discussion.

"The English," Jeremy Paxman says, "at least, have the saving grace of being able to laugh at themselves. Which must be based on a profound self-assurance." That may go some way toward explaining British comedy, but it does nothing to explain the Canadian penchant for self-deprecating humour. It has long been found on Canadian television—*SCTV, Corner Gas, Royal Canadian Air Farce, This Hour Has 22 Minutes*—but increasingly, though not many Americans are aware of this, on U.S. television and in Hollywood movies.

Lorne Michaels, the creator of *Saturday Night Live*, is Canadian, as are, of course, Jim Carrey, Mike Myers, Martin Short, Catherine O'Hara, Dan Aykroyd, Eugene Levy, the late John Candy, and a great many others widely considered *American* comedians by American audiences. If their humour has anything in common, it's in being slightly ... *off* ... neither American slapstick nor British wordplay but a form in which jokester and joke are so often one and the same. A Canadian, Michaels once said, would never have come up with a movie called *It's a Wonderful Life*. That would be bragging. The Canadian version would have to be *It's an All Right Life*.

Scott Feschuk, who's written satirical pieces for the *National Post* and *Maclean's*—and, no laughing allowed, worked as Paul Martin's speechwriter during Martin's brief and disastrous tenure as prime minister—has said that self-deprecation is the cornerstone of Canadian humour. Feschuk also quotes Mark Breslin, the founder of Yuk Yuk's, as saying that "Comedy is the cry of the intelligent and the powerless"—making it, of course, particularly attractive. "Canadians are so funny," Feschuk concluded, "because no one takes comedy more seriously."

Canadians also crave approval. Self-deprecating humour is one way to get people you might have just met onside. Another sits at the very core of the Canadian language, the instantly identifiable "eh?"—a linguistic cap-in-hand begging for a nod, an agreement-in-principle before the speaker moves on from, say, the profoundly dismal weather today to the current dismal state of the government.

When poet Earle Birney described Canada as "a high school land, frozen in its adolescence" more than half a century ago, he was hitting pretty close to the bone on what an abiding insecurity does to a national personality.

I've often thought that, for a Canadian, one of the worst things that can happen is to learn your brother-in-law has won the lottery. Oh sure, most of us would come around eventually, but only after the initial backlash. Unlike Americans, we're not comfortable with easy fortune. Malcolm Lowry once wrote a poem claiming that, for Canadians, "Success is like some horrible disaster." Better, he felt, to have your house burn down.

Encouraging stuff, that.

Australians call this the "tall poppy syndrome," the striking down of any who dare, by intention or accident, stick their heads up above the common measure. Perhaps in Canada we could call it the tall trillium, but then that would only compel those provinces where trilliums don't grow to complain of discrimination. Poet bp Nichol once said that, despite our better instincts, Canadians spend so much time denigrating each other and others that they'd turned their land into "a country of pointless struggles."

Self-denigration, on the other hand, has long been raised to a national art form. "If Canada invented the wheel," Ottawa high-tech guru Denzil Doyle likes to say, "it would drag it on a sled to be marketed in the United States." John Ralston Saul, who's written so much on the psychological makeup of this country, has remarked that in the entire world only Canada and Australia claim to be "so consistently populated by the abandoned and the defeated." He may well be on to something.

Whether it can be blamed on the tall poppy syndrome or not, Canadians have trouble with heroes. George Bowering, the country's former poet laureate, once claimed that "Napoleon would have been a nobody here." When the announcement came in 1957 that Lester Pearson had just been awarded the Nobel Peace Prize, the reaction of one ranking Canadian politician was typical: "Who does he think he is?"

It's not quite true to think Canadians turn their backs on heroes; it's just that they like their heroes quiet. They prefer them to tend toward type—deeply humble, even shy—and nowhere is this more prevalent than in the hockey star prototype: Rocket Richard to Jean Béliveau to Bobby Orr to Wayne Gretzky to Mario Lemieux to today's new star, Sidney Crosby.

My old boss at *Maclean's* magazine, Peter Newman, liked to joke that the classic Canadian hero would have been William Lyon Mackenzie King, the strange prime minister who held power longer than any other, who liked to talk to prostitutes, his dog, and his dead mother, and who once, when invited to visit wealthy American industrialist John D. Rockefeller, took along a half-dozen shoelaces just to make sure he'd have spares if one broke.

So it's a little surprising that it was a Canadian, Joe Shuster, who came up with the Superman character back in 1938. Evidently Shuster knew it would never ... fly ... in his hometown Toronto, so he sent his comic-book hero off to Metropolis, a mythical American city eventually taken as New York, and the rest, of course, is history.

The superhero who stayed home wasn't so lucky.

Captain Canuck, a comic that appeared and disappeared periodically from 1975 on, never took off, despite his amazing superpowers. Wearing a red-and-white body suit, the super-clean-living Captain fought for "peace, order and good government." It was long held that in these watchwords of the Constitution and the "life, liberty and the pursuit of happiness" of its American counterpart lay the essential difference between Canadians and Americans. That, and the "right" to bear arms Americans so treasure.

Captain Canuck, in everyday life, was Mountie Tom Evans, obviously of British descent but perfectly bilingual and with part "Indian blood." The action was set in the 1990s, with Canada—since anything is possible in fantasyland—as the dominant world superpower.

The good Captain, alas, was eventually brought down. Not by kryptonite, but by a force even more powerful and energy-sapping: the economics of publishing in Canada.

George Woodcock, the British-born critic, used to say that Canadians had a deep distrust of heroes and much preferred martyrs—Terry Fox was embraced more easily following his death from cancer than when he hop-skipped along the edge of the highway—because, well, they largely see themselves as victims, particularly when compared with the mighty and often bullying America and Americans.

For John Ralston Saul, hardly a debate goes on in this country that isn't, at core, "a struggle between competing myths of victimization." One side is forever blaming the other. Francophones blame anglophones; the West thinks itself a victim of the East. It can be regional—Newfoundland blaming Quebec for controlling hydro in Labrador, Quebec blaming Newfoundland for laying claim to Labrador—or it can be financial, such as the oil industry blaming consumers and using this as an excuse to do nothing to protect the environment. But the ultimate myth of victimization, he argues in *Reflections of a Siamese Twin: Canada at the End of the Twentieth Century*, the one that unites all regions of Canada and both official languages, is the idea that "Canada exists only because it did not wish to be American."

Not being American is by far the most common definition around, one that's often offered by Canadians themselves. Saul finds it wanting, a negative notion of existence that for him is offensive. But it's out there, and not about to go away on its own. And when it comes to Canada's possible role in the world—the subject of a later chapter—it may actually serve a purpose.

Of the many obvious differences between America and Canada, the first that comes to mind would be weather. Robertson Davies claimed that "cold breeds caution" and thought this suggested a direct link between winter and the reserved, suspicious Canadian personality.

I think it goes much deeper than that. It was winter, and evolution, that created the thick, luxurious furs—beaver, fox, mink, marten, fisher, wolf, ermine, muskrat—that kept the Europeans coming to these shores in the first place, and it might well be argued that the fur trade is what compelled Canadians to be not only well prepared but prepared for the worst.

The fur trade might have brought prosperity for European backers of the trade, but it left behind a strong, almost genetic, sense that nothing will last and bad times are surely coming. The beaver eventually ran thin and European fashion shifted away from felt hats. There were two key lessons here. One was sustainable harvesting. The other was that you're at the whim of outside forces.

That this country should be suspicious of external influence, then, hardly seems surprising. To make sure Canadians *remain* Canadian, we rely on rules. We threaten legislation to keep American football out. We enact laws to promote Canadian music and give Canadian magazine publishing a leg up. We tie film and book publishing funds to Canadian content. We set up a massive bureaucracy to ensure that Canada gets its fair share of the television and cable world. We establish foreign owner- ship controls to keep our communications and arts industries away from outside clutches.

And then, having duly protected ourselves from the rest of the world, we sit back and read British mysteries, rent Hollywood movies, watch American television shows, read New York magazines, listen to rock music from London and country music from Nashville on devices manufactured in Asia—and bet our hard-earned Canadian money on American football.

YOU BEGIN TO SEE, surely, how impossible it might be, in two words, two thousand words, or two million words, to say exactly "What is a Canadian"? The politicians keep talking about a National Portrait Gallery for Ottawa, but perhaps it would be easier if they passed on the paintings and decided, instead, just to nail a little jelly to the wall.

The Irvin Studin book came out in the fall of 2006. It contained a number of worthy opening-sentence attempts, including his own conclusion that a Canadian is "no more and no less than a citizen of the state called Canada."

Mark Kingwell, philosopher: "A Canadian is … an imaginary creature with various mythological traits, some of them charming, some irritating, many of them contradictory."

Christian Dufour, legal expert on federal–provincial relations: "A Canadian is … at the outset a Québécois, a habitant who lives in the St. Lawrence Valley and speaks French. It's worth recalling that the name meant that, and only that, during most of the country's history."

Aritha Van Herk, author: "A Canadian is … part of a jigsaw puzzle, always trying to find that one missing piece that has fallen behind the wainscoting."

Paul Heinbecker, Canada's former ambassador to the United Nations: "A Canadian is … a promissory note, a bearer of hope in troubled times, a bet that diversity will work, that people can get along and that peace is possible."

William Watson, economics professor and author, McGill University: "A Canadian is … as a rule too fond by half of contemplating what a Canadian is."

Sujit Choudhry, University of Toronto law professor: "A Canadian is … a participant in an ongoing constitutional conversation."

Allan Fotheringham, columnist: "A Canadian is … someone who crosses the road to get to the middle."

Perhaps just checking, for all we know, on the invention Canada gave the world.

MY OWN ANSWER arrived well past the point where a contributor could request even a minor spelling change, let alone a complete rewrite. I'd been thinking much more about personality than actual persons and had become trapped in the abstract rather than the actual. I'd seen the question not as disarmingly simple but as overly broad, one that failed to properly consider how wonderfully different people are from one end of this country to the other, and how, in my business, you just never know who you're going to meet next.

In the fall of 2006 I happened to be in the bookstore in my old home-town of Huntsville, Ontario, when the manager, Catherine Wyle, told me there was a very interesting man living just north of town near the village of Sprucedale. He was a hundred years old, she said. And he had taught himself to read in his nineties.

I knew, instantly, there was a good story here—but would never have guessed *how* good.

Clarence Brazier was then living with his daughter Doris and her husband, Jim Villemaire, a retired police officer, on a lovely acreage in the country where they'd put in a pond and built walking trails through the thick bush surrounding their home. I'd been told I would find Clarence in good shape, but had no idea just how vibrant he was at such an improbable age. The previous summer, at ninety-nine, he had finally put his beloved chainsaw away, having nipped his pant leg while cutting a large maple into blocks and frightened himself that the next slip might be more serious. He still liked to head off into the bush on his all-terrain vehicle, though. At ninety-five he'd bought a brand-new one, one that he said should last him "a lifetime." At a hundred, and vigorous enough to walk the trails and spry enough to bound out of his easy chair like a gymnast, that now seemed in some doubt.

I had come to learn about his reading, but Clarence had a much longer story to tell and was determined to tell it all. What had been intended as a short visit turned into a full day of listening.

Clarence had been born not far from this place, on a small, dirt-poor farm near the Magnetawan River. When he was only five his father lost both eyes clearing land when the dynamite he was using to blow out the stumps failed to go off—until the moment he bent over a stump to see if the fuse had gone out.

By the age of seven Clarence was running the entire farm. To pay off the small mortgage on the property, his mother, Fanny Mae, found work as a cook in the nearby bush camps and would be away for weeks at a time. Clarence took care of his father and five siblings, milked the cows, looked after the animals, mucked the stables, and did the plowing, planting, harvesting, and endless repairs. He would lead his blind father by the hand into the nearby woods where he would position him so that they could both work a cross-cut saw through a tree they could then cut into firewood.

"I had his life in my hands," Clarence told me over a third cup of coffee. "I was seven years old, but I had to know exactly how that tree would fall so it wouldn't hit him."

In the winter months the children went to school, but Clarence—sprouting fast to his eventual six-foot-two—was both tallest in his class and furthest behind. He was so humiliated by appearing dull and hearing the other children laugh at him that he never even finished grade one.

Clarence almost died in the Spanish flu pandemic that raced through the country at the end of the First World War, killing some fifty thousand Canadians (almost as many as had died in the war). He was only twelve when it struck. He lay in bed from January through March, chest burning and blistered from mustard plasters and onion poultices, convinced at times that he wouldn't make it to the next day. He did recover, but was so weak it took him until the middle of May to walk again.

Survival became the story of Clarence Brazier. He took odd jobs—haying for other farmers, filing horses' teeth, de-horning cattle, clipping sheep, felling and hauling wood—to keep up the payments on the farm. When he was fourteen a couple of neighbours lied for him so that he could claim to be sixteen and take out a guide's licence and make some extra money leading city hunters out after deer and moose. In winter he took to the logging camps and in spring worked the river runs, where his quickness and strength soon made him a valued employee.

He told a long story about working a log jam with an older man called Earle Molten and how their pointer boat somehow got turned in the current and swept over the rocks, the long boat splitting in two when it crashed on the rocks below. Each man was still in his half of the boat, and when the fractured vessel slipped off the rocks and into the current, Molten jumped into the water and began swimming to safety. It was a tragic decision: another log came over the chute behind them and crushed Molten's head into one of the logs already caught in the swirl. Clarence stayed with his half of the pointer and made land safely nearly a mile downstream. By the time he got back, the other men had already picked Molten's body from the water.

"He had no kin to send him back to," said Clarence. "They took off his boots, wrapped him in a blanket, and put him in a hole underneath a pine tree. Then they took a couple of six-inch spikes and hammered his boots to the tree. That was his tombstone."

All the long afternoon the stories poured out. He worked lumber camps and gold mines, always quitting and moving on the moment his inability to read was about to be discovered. His wife, Angela, knew and covered for him, but they kept the secret from their four daughters. He became president of a local political party and she served as secretary. He headed up the local farmers' union and she kept the notes and handled the correspondence. He pushed his girls to get good educations and they did, all of them eventually moving away from the family home outside Timmins, where Clarence and Angela Brazier retired and began growing old together, Clarence's secret now safe, he figured, for the rest of his life.

But then, one day, he no longer had his crutch. "I learned to read," he told me, "all because I lost my wife."

Clarence Brazier learned out of necessity, and perhaps this is something to consider when trying to fix that nail to the national jelly. Perhaps it's not so much about inferiority or smugness or about whether we're grappling with victimhood or hiding behind self-deprecation or even about not being American, but rather that the real Canadian character seems to have an endless capacity to *make do*.

The radio show may have had it right all along: "As Canadian as ... possible, *under the circumstances*."

Circumstances such as Clarence encountered when his beloved Angela died and he no longer had his reader. Circumstances such as

what so many Canadians before have encountered and somehow overcome simply out of necessity.

I think, for example, of Francis Wharton. When Peter Newman was
researching his brilliant three-book saga of the Hudson's Bay Company
he came across the tale of this British Columbia trapper who lost his
dentures while deep in the bush. According to the story Newman was
told, Wharton simply went out, shot a deer, pulled out the molars, glued
them together, stuck them in his mouth, "and then ate the animal with
its own teeth."

Or, if you find that one a bit of a stretch, think if you will of Cecil
Harris, who was tilling his fields near Saskatchewan's Bad Hills on June 8,
1948, when his tractor flipped on him. Harris was trapped underneath,
one of the wheel lugs piercing his leg. Certain he would bleed to death
before anyone noticed him missing and came looking, Harris pulled out
his penknife and scratched a quick message into the fender of the tractor:
"In case I die in this mess, I leave all to the wife, Cecil Geo. Harris."

The family found him dead under the tractor. The will, however, stood
up in court.

And for those who might think this one a bit of a stretch too, that
fender and Cecil Harris's penknife can still be seen today in the law library
at the University of Saskatchewan. A reminder to us all that resourcefulness may well be the defining Canadian characteristic.

Clarence Brazier was ninety-three years old and on his own when
necessity came into play. He had to eat but didn't even know how to shop.
He took knife and scissors and cut labels off boxes from the pantry and
went down to the store and tried to match colours and symbols, but that
proved only frustrating and embarrassing. "I had used tricks my whole life
to get by," he said.

And now the tricks were failing him. His hearing was also beginning
to fail. He'd always kept up with the news through the radio, and later
television, but increasingly he was finding it harder to hear. The only
solution, he finally concluded, was to learn how to read.

"I started with the junk mail they delivered to my house," he said. The
mail would come and he'd spend hours out on the farmhouse stoop trying

to pronounce words he knew were on the flyers. He knew the Canadian Tire symbol and tried to work through the letters to see how the word formed. He knew "pizza" and "hamburger" and "fries" from the pictures and memorized those letters. Rug cleaning, snow plowing, real estate listings, grocery specials.

Knowing her father was now alone, Doris, a retired schoolteacher, asked if he'd like to move down south. Clarence agreed, even though he was perfectly capable of caring for himself, shopping excepted. He was still working his woodlot, cutting, splitting, and selling a hundred cords of wood each winter.

Doris Villemaire couldn't help noticing how her father was picking through the newspaper for the flyers. She saw him tracing over words, his mouth moving as he worked on their meaning. She asked him if he'd accept some help. She was volunteering for the local literacy council and had access to material. She brought home some primary readers, grade-one level, and together they worked through the alphabet and words so simple he laughed to recall them. "C-A-T, cat! R-A-T, rat! They were not very interesting."

But Doris found him to be an enthusiastic student: "His eyes would actually sparkle when he'd recognize a word. It was just as I'd seen with my students, but it was also kind of funny, too. I was seeing this same thing in my father—and he was acting just like the children I'd taught."

From junk mail he moved to primary readers, and from primary readers to children's books and then into youth novels. From fiction he headed into nonfiction, and now sits surrounded by books on mining, logging, and Canadian history. He reads at least two hours a day. Often, at night, he will wake and read himself back to sleep. "Had I not learned to read," he says, "I believe I would have slowly become isolated from the world beyond my home. I had to learn. I had no choice."

We can all learn, and at any age—even journalists well into their fifties. I was on the road again, heading down Highway 11 from Sprucedale, back to Huntsville and eventually out to the lake where I like to hide away when it came to me that I had it backward.

The question has never been "What is a Canadian?" Nor should the response begin "A Canadian is ..."

The *answer* has always been that Clarence Brazier is a Canadian. With thirty-two million-plus other correct answers to follow.

Three

The Midway Mirror

IT HAS OFTEN STRUCK ME that Canadians are more comfortable in their own skin when they're outside their own country.

I was in Torino, Italy, in February 2006 for the XXth Winter Games. The smaller Olympics, the Cold Olympics, had taken on what has, in recent years, become the usual rhythm for Canadians: high predictions, early panic, pleasant surprises, satisfactory outcome. The defending gold-medal-champion men's hockey team had landed in Torino full of the usual bravado, but had turned out to be a disaster. The team sent over was too old and too slow, naively coached by those who believed the secret to success lay in sticking to the North American game on the larger European ice surface. The strategy had been such a failure that the embarrassed Canadians had been beaten—hell, *shut out*—by unheralded Switzerland while failing even to reach the medal round.

The end of the world lasted about half an hour.

The men's hockey debacle was more than compensated for by the women's gold-medal-winning hockey team, the delightful men curlers, the valiant cross-country skiers, and the irrepressible Cindy Klassen, whose five medals in speed-skating set a new Olympic standard for the country. The Canadian Olympic Committee had brazenly predicted twenty-five medals—and one week into the Games had been soundly slammed for such a prediction—yet the final count was seven gold, ten silver, and seven bronze for a total of twenty-four. Had the men's 2002 gold-medal hockey team flopped only to third instead of seventh, its worst finish ever, the total would have been exactly twenty-five.

In a single Winter Games, the image of Canadian success had switched from the clichéd gap-toothed smile of hockey players to a long line of young and incredibly alive women skiers and skaters, their teeth seemingly as large and white as the snow-capped mountains surrounding Torino.

On that final Sunday of the XXth Winter Games, a number of Canadian journalists found themselves settling down to penne and pizza in a restaurant in the small town of Grugliasco, not far from one of the media villages where many of us had been billeted for the past three weeks. Most of us had been assigned months before—on the presumption of Canada's involvement—to cover the gold-medal hockey game that had been played earlier that afternoon between Sweden and Finland, skilled Sweden triumphing over the valiant but overmatched Finns. We'd attended the game and quickly filed our understandably shortened stories. Because of event overlap and transportation timetables, however, several of us had elected to pass on the Closing Ceremonies, where many of our colleagues were at this moment sitting, shivering, in the open stadium while trying to mesh together an account of the spectacle in front of them with a sober evaluation of Canada's own moving performance now behind them.

The restaurant—a centuries-old building with a large, heated tent built out from the back—was showing those Closing Ceremonies on a big-screen television at one end of the tent. At the other end, an equally large television screen was carrying the soccer match, with local heroes Juventus against dreaded archrivals from nearby Milan.

The place was packed with families: a couple of hundred Italians gathered to spend three or four hours over a meal most Canadians would wolf down in three or four minutes. The men were almost entirely turned in the direction of the soccer match, the women mostly staring straight ahead at the women they were talking to, and the Canadians and assorted others staring in the direction of the televised Olympic ceremonies. The sound was turned up for the Olympic finale, turned down for the soccer.

It made for a fascinating scene. Every once in a while the sombre Closing Ceremonies music would be interrupted by a burst of cheering for a good rush by the home side, a collective groan over a missed opportunity, or periodic jeering and whistling at Milan. Soundtrack and audience could not have been a greater mismatch.

All through the soccer game the Olympic wrap-up was simply ignored by the vast majority of those in the large, heated tent—except for a moment no one saw coming.

It happened during the handing over of the Olympic flag. The familiar banner with the Olympic rings had been given to Torino at the last Winter Games, in Salt Lake City, and was now being passed on to Vancouver–Whistler, site of the next Winter Games, in 2010. The carefully folded cloth was formally passed from Italian hands to Canadian. The camera then switched to big Ben Heppner, who is one of those rare Canadians—as befits a professional anthem singer—who knows all the words to "O Canada."

Heppner's thick chest heaved in, then out, and he began singing in that remarkable voice that, had we all been born with such lungs, might have prevented the invention of the telegraph and telephone.

The Juventus–Milan game was still on, but suddenly the entire restaurant went silent. You could almost hear the male vertebrae crack and squeak as previously locked-in heads turned from one television screen to the other. No more cheering, no more jeering. Just silence from the crowd and the soundtrack of an anthem belonging to a country an ocean and a minimum four-and-a-half time zones away.

As Heppner moved into the second verse—I'd quote here but, being Canadian, am never quite sure of the words—a single man on the far side of the restaurant took to his feet, standing at attention.

Slim, bespectacled, and grey-haired, it was Bertrand Raymond, long-time sports columnist of *Le Journal de Montréal* and an icon in the small world of Canadian sports reporting. Honoured by the Hockey Hall of Fame and revered by his colleagues, both French and English, Raymond is a force in Quebec society unmatched by any Anglo sports reporter in any other part of the country. Sports is far more political in Quebec—

many believe that the Quiet Revolution of the 1960s and even the sovereignty movement itself grew out of a single act of defiance by the
legendary Maurice "Rocket" Richard back in 1955, a story I'll be returning to in a subsequent chapter. Some of the fiercest indépendentistes are
sports personalities, which makes Raymond's standing at attention in that
Italian restaurant in Grugliasco all the more compelling.

Bert Raymond stood, shoulders squared, arms straight, and he stared
hard enough to make the wine boil at a distant table holding Anglo sports
reporters. He stared until we squirmed, and then, awkwardly, somewhat
embarrassedly, I stood and *The Globe and Mail*'s Dave Naylor stood and
finally the whole table got to its collective feet until Ben Heppner wound
down to the final line that, mercifully, every single person in the country
does know by heart:

"... *we stand on guard for theeeeeeeee ...*"

Bert Raymond, distinguished, still at attention, gave the thumbs up to
those standing across the room. We signalled back.

And then, before any of the proud, if slightly self-conscious, visitors
from Canada could sit back down, something swept through the entire
restaurant that took us completely by surprise.

Loud, prolonged applause from the Italians.

THIS RUSH OF *CANADIANISM* by Canadians no longer in Canada never
emerges quite so vividly as during the Olympic Winter Games. It is here
where Canada, which is normally thought of, if at all, as a reserved
country—"almost incoherently polite," travel writer Jan Morris once
said—shows a most distinctive swagger.

The Winter Games provide uniforms for fans as well as athletes, which
makes the bonding easier and the strutting more noticeable. It hardly
matters whether the souvenir gear is supplied by Roots or HBC; the effect
is always the same: red and white, head to toe, invariably with a red maple
leaf tattooed on a cheek, painted on a bare chest or, at times, carved into
a head of dyed electric-blue hair.

The official Canadian gear in Torino—mukluks, thick vests, knitted
toques with ear flaps and chin ties and crown bobs—was semi-trapper,

quasi-voyageur, moderately goofy, and ubiquitous. The over-the-top clothing was purchased, invariably, in a rush of patriotism usually unfamiliar to Canadians, the sort of mad impulse that explains those red-faced Easterners you see walking through the Toronto airport holding, but not daring to wear, the white Stetson they picked up in the Calgary airport. Like the Mexican straw hat and the loud Hawaiian shirt, such items always seem like a good idea at the time. At the time. You realize only in the hours that follow that you'd never be caught dead actually wearing that cowboy hat anywhere but the shop in the Calgary airport, just as you'd be laughed off the street if you ever walked down Yonge or Ste-Catherine or Robson or stood at the corner of Portage and Main in the full red-and-white explosion of the official Canadian Olympic regalia.

In Nagano, eight years before Torino, a Canadian woman turned up at a hockey game wearing a hockey helmet and not much else. She had two tiny, strategically placed Canadian flags on her breasts and a red maple leaf painted on her bare back as she danced wildly about the Big Hat arena, periodically stopping to scream incoherently in the general direction of the ice surface. To the Japanese, whose idea of Canada had been shaped by Lucy Maud Montgomery's *Anne* books, this exuberant young woman—who did not appear to have any freckles at all, anywhere—was as baffling as Japanese toilet seats, heated and capable of taking blood pressure readings, were to the Canadian visitors.

The Strutting Canadian, seen only periodically and usually at sporting events, seems more to delight than offend. The reserved Japanese might have been stunned by the loud and colourful Canadians in Nagano but they were also oddly attracted to them, the Japanese fans increasingly outfitting themselves in Canadian paraphernalia and begging for Canadian pins. When the "*U!-S!-A!*" cheer went up in Big Hat it was solely American; when "*Ca-Na-Da!*" was the cheer it had as much Japanese behind it as Canadian.

Canadians are themselves delighted with these once-every-four-year personality shifts, as if to suggest that only in acting out of character do they reveal their real character. When curler Paul Savage dropped his pants in Nagano to prove to photographers that he did indeed have an Olympic tattoo on his butt, women's curler Joan McCusker was quick to point out that this represented an illegal reproduction of the Olympic rings. He'd better be careful, she warned, or "they'll sue your ass off."

In Torino eight years later I went down to the Medals Plaza at Piazza Castella with *Globe* columnist Christie Blatchford to watch the men's curling team—four Newfoundlanders and a middle-aged ringer from Ontario—receive their gold medals. With a small crowd, we stood at attention while the Canadian flag went up and "O Canada" played. It was a glorious moment, with tears shed and shivers felt throughout the gathering. When the official ceremony was over, Mike Adam, the team's alternative member, bounded off the stage, walked over to us, and lifted his gold medal up so that it almost touched his nose. "Jeez," he said, "if they'd only put a magnet on the back, I could put 'er on me fridge."

And curling, they say, is boring. Boring as Canadians are supposed to be. Boring as Canada—what British journalists like to call "The Great White Waste of Time"—is supposed to be.

At Nagano the Australians, of all people, complained about the Canadian partiers, claiming they were unable to sleep for all the carousing going on in the Canadian section of the village. "How do you know they were the Canadians?" I asked one of the Aussies riding the media bus. The man turned in his seat and sighed as if explaining to a child. "When they're carrying a big Canadian flag and yelling at Americans to get off," he said, "what do you *think* they'd be?"

I would think they'd be Canadians out of their element—which is when Canadians often seem to be most Canadian of all.

Whether it's overcompensation for insecurity abroad or release from some unwritten rule back home that you Do Not Shout Out Who You Are hardly matters; it happens. You find this Canadian boast plastered on backpacks heading through Europe and across Asia. You find it in foreign airports at gates holding passengers for flights back to Canada. You find it on distant streets and in far-off restaurants where a logo on a ball cap, a city name on a sweatshirt, or the tacking on of an "eh?" at the end of the sentence sparks instant recognition. The ensuing conversation is filled with the familiar touchstones of residence and weather, the names that arise—prime minister and premiers, politicians, hockey players, criminals, newscasters, minor and major personalities in arts and business—known only to those who live in what has been called the cold and empty attic over the United States of America.

The Canadian Identity, it seems, is truly elusive only at home. Beyond the borders Canadians know exactly who they are; within them they see themselves as part of a family, a street, a neighbourhood, a community, a province, a region and, on special occasions like Canada Day and Grey Cup weekend and, of course, during the Winter Olympics, a country called Canada.

Beyond the borders, they pine; within the borders, they more often whine.

Again, the contradiction that is Canada.

THIS ABIDING PASSION for the red maple leaf is all the more remarkable given what a difficult time it had getting up the flagpole in the first place. While there remains a smattering of Canadians who rue that day in 1965 when the new flag was first raised—largely those who fought under the Red Ensign, plus the odd curmudgeon who'd still rather crank his telephone—the vast, vast majority of the country embraces the national flag.

Such was not always the case.

It took Canada forty years to adopt its own flag—relatively quick work considering the 115 years it took to get its own Constitution.

And as for its national anthem, the tune took a hundred years from the first performance—at, ironically, a Saint-Jean-Baptiste Day celebration—to formal adoption in 1980 by Parliament. By one count the song has been reworked twenty-one times since its debut—the only words not to be tinkered with being "O" and "Canada"—the result being that the only way most of us can get through it is to mumble.

The flag's history has its own bizarre twists. According to Rick Archbold's delightful *I Stand for Canada: The Story of the Maple Leaf Flag*, a special committee was struck first in 1925 and then again in 1946 to come up with something new. The members picked through thousands of potential designs, but the suggestions either depressed or offended so many of them that both times they decided to just drop the notion altogether.

The wave of nationalism that preceded Centennial Year, 1967, produced yet another push for a flag to call our own. Whether by design or folly, Prime Minister Lester Pearson chose to announce his intentions in front of a Winnipeg convention of the Royal Canadian Legion. He knew it would be a tough crowd, and it was. They applauded when he called for "a patriotism that will put Canada ahead of its parts"—yet booed the idea of a maple leaf and cheered wildly every time the traditional Red Ensign got mention.

It's unlikely, given the times, that the crowd included angry naturalists, but the fact of the matter is that the symbol then being considered, three maple leaves together, involved a species of maple not found west of Ontario. Crabgrass, found in every region and province, would hardly be suitable for a national flag.

Pearson was accused of "selling us out to the pea-soupers" by those who saw the new flag, lacking any British connection, as a sop to Quebec. He was told to "Go home!" But he kept speaking, and by the time he was finished, reports say, the crowd was largely split on the issue, with virtually as many now cheering as booing the national leader. Encouraged by his Winnipeg reception, Pearson soldiered on.

There was such resistance to the idea in Parliament, however, that Opposition Leader John Diefenbaker, the day's most eloquent defender of all connections British, was able to use a filibuster to force Pearson to send the idea off to another parliamentary committee. Diefenbaker likely presumed that if committees could kill the idea twice before, it could happen a third time.

But this committee was different. It opened the design to everyone from schoolkids to Group of Seven icon A.Y. Jackson. Had the committee swayed one way or another, Canadian backpacks might today have small patches showing a beaver surrounded by her ten kits (symbolizing the ten provinces, of course), a leaping salmon, the perennial moose or, my personal favourite, crossed hockey sticks over a single black puck.

The red maple leaf proved a popular motif, though Pearson was accused at the time—and I've seen this claim repeated in print as recently as a few years ago—of a diabolical Liberal scheme to produce a flag that looked like "Liberal electioneering bunting." It's an intriguing point. Each fall I look about the Precambrian Shield forest in which our little cabin sits, but I have yet to come across a Tory blue maple leaf in the cavalcade of colour that is autumn in those parts.

The flag debate, Archbold notes, was one of the nastiest in Canadian parliamentary history. Diefenbaker, sensing a groundswell against change, was magnificent, but his efforts came to an abrupt end when his own Quebec lieutenant, Léon Balcer, turned on him by asking the Liberal government to bring closure to debate and call a vote. On December 15, 1964, the House of Commons passed the bill 163–78, with many Conservatives, including Balcer, voting with the government.

Diefenbaker had his own small last laugh, though, in his instructions for his funeral, which took place in the summer of 1979. As stipulated, the Canadian flag draped his coffin but, in a sly symbol of dominance, the Red Ensign draped over a small portion of the red maple leaf.

Diefenbaker, much to his disappointment, was on the wrong side of this one. The effect of the new flag on the rest of the country was powerful and practically instantaneous. By 1967 Canada's pre-eminent historian Arthur Lower could say:

> Since the adoption of the new flag, something very interesting has happened to the Canadian psyche, something that probably cannot yet be put into words.... There is nothing in this of turning backs on a hated past, nothing suggesting that old ties were irksome. The point is simply that the country is growing up, coming to see itself as an entity, taking the interest in itself that any organism, to be healthy, must. Each time that the average citizen looks at the new flag, he unconsciously says to himself, "That's me!"

WELL, NOT QUITE, SIR. If it were that simple, there would be no Great Canadian Identity Crisis, which would also mean no cottage industry for academics, no need for national and provincial royal commissions, no panel discussions, no CBC town hall meetings—and this book would be about hockey-playing dogs.

Canadian patriotism is as fickle as Canadian weather. It was on display the day Pierre Trudeau took his final train journey; it flares periodically at sporting events, on certain holidays and, most assuredly, whenever tragedy strikes the Canadian armed forces.

There is some thought, though, that it has been on the rise in recent years, owing not so much to Canadian success at the Winter Games as to … beer ads.

The best example began in 2000 when Molson televised the first of its Great Canadian Rants, starring an actor who came to be known as "Joe Canadian." Casually dressed and standing in front of a simple, squealing microphone, Joe railed against a string of American false assumptions about his country before closing off with the defiant shout "MY NAME IS JOE—AND I AM CANADIAN!"

The Joe Canadian ad became a national sensation, shown for months on arena scoreboards and as loudly cheered at hockey games as the three stars. A couple of years later Molson's sold out to Coors, the American beer company. Joe's Great Canadian Rant was, suddenly, just another American product.

EVEN SO, this notion of defining oneself in terms of what one isn't—the Joe Canadian rant readily boiling down to "I am *not* American"—remains the quickest and simplest reflection in the national mirror.

Author Pierre Berton is often credited with the most novel definition— "A Canadian is somebody who knows how to make love in a canoe"—and often argued that being not American does matter and shouldn't be dismissed, as others would have it, as some backward, negative notion that does more harm than good.

Not long before his death in late 2004, Berton talked to his old friend Peter Newman about the outrage he felt about the takeover of Canada's iconic CPR hotel chain—including Quebec's Château Frontenac, Ottawa's Château Laurier, and the world-famous Banff Springs Hotel— by the American-based Fairmont chain. It was important to preserve those things that separate Canadians from Americans, he believed, whether it be public policy or culture. Canadians, he argued, are different in background and geography and even dreams, and it is important to protect these dreams "or we won't have a country at all."

Canadians spend so much time spinning this Rubik's Cube of national identity that it has, from time to time, captured the attention of outsiders, usually Americans. At a Pittsburgh gathering of the Association of Canadian Studies a few years ago, Tom Barnes of the University of California suggested to a *Toronto Star* reporter that Canada needs to quit fretting so much. "Why all the angst, for God's sake? *Why? Why? Why?*"

At the time, Canadian bookstore shelves were featuring such titles as *Canada in Question, Nationalism Without Walls: The Unbearable Lightness of Being Canadian, The Anxious Years,* and former prime minister Joe Clark's *A Nation Too Good to Lose.*

"How can you *lose* a nation?" Barnes asked.

Perhaps the question isn't so much losing it as finding it in the first place. No one seems to know exactly where to look. Or, for that matter, what to look for....

Yann Martel, whose *Life of Pi* won the 2002 Booker prize, described his country as the world's greatest "hotel" while stressing that, to him, it's one of the more admirable qualities of the nation. "You bring your own cultural baggage with you," Martel said, "and the government provides room service, heat, water and, on television, those quaint Heritage Minutes."

Even if he means no harm, I think Martel sells both the country and its citizens short, but much worse has been said. Richard Rodriguez, an American commentator, once told the Canadian Library Association that "Canada is the largest country in the world that doesn't exist." Even some Canadians would say the equivalent. When Lucien Bouchard was premier of Quebec he once argued that "Canada is divisible because Canada is not a real country."

Matt Jackson would beg to disagree.

Jackson is neither an academic nor a politician, but a hitchhiker. Not long ago he completed a four-year trek through this country, travelling by thumb, car, truck, van, canoe, horseback, Twin Otter, and sail. When he returned to his Calgary home he published a small book of his photographs and notes, freely admitting that he'd been unable to find any simple and convenient definition.

"I think I had this grand notion when I set off," Jackson told the *Calgary Herald*, "that I would cover the country and discover the Canadian identity. And really … I found that we're very different all over, so I don't know that there's one thing that ties everybody together completely…. I think that Canada is a lot more exotic than we give it credit for."

My sentiments exactly.

Four

The Wind That Wants a Flag

"WHY ALL THE ANGST?" the academic from California asked. *"Why? Why? Why?"*

Here's why—or at least part of the reason why. In the autumn following the demise of the Meech Lake Accord, Prime Minister Brian Mulroney announced the establishment of a Citizens' Forum on Canada's Future. The commission was struck in response to continued criticism over the manner in which constitutional reform had been handled. It would travel the country, hearing out what were called "ordinary Canadians."

It became the catchphrase of the times and inadvertently underlined the very problem the political and media elite had stumbled up against in trying to push the accord through without the slightest thought of public input. To far too many supposedly intelligent observers, the term meant "stupid, dull citizens"—people with little education, no power and, for that matter, no personality. Ordinary. Unimportant. The masses. The very phrase, to the establishment, called up images of farmers with flat, uninteresting faces, suburban dwellers with insignificant jobs and dead imaginations, seniors with nothing to do but gripe, office workers more worried about their lawns than their jobs, truck drivers thinking about their next stop, taxi drivers who never shut up and never say anything, airport security workers bitching about who's late coming back from break....

It was a telling misread of their own country.

THAT THE PEOPLE were outraged by the Meech Lake process, and remained so, was undeniable in the fall and winter of 1990–91. There was a fury in "the peaceable kingdom."

Looking back after so many years, the vitriol surprises me—even my own. "Angry" is not a word normally used to describe the daily column I have written now for four different newspapers. Stupid at times, insightful once in a while ... sentimental, silly, sensible on a good day. But not "angry." And yet, there it is right in the headline over the column I filed for the *Ottawa Citizen* on June 5, 1990: "The People Will Repay Our Devious Politicians."

It was the week Mulroney and the Canadian premiers had come to Ottawa for one last-ditch push on the accord that was scheduled to become law on June 23, 1990, now less than three weeks away. Three years earlier the deal had begun as a worthy attempt to bring Quebec into the Constitution Act it had refused to sign in 1982. But in execution it had evolved into a firestorm of controversy as critics, including Pierre Trudeau, argued that "distinct society" status for Quebec would unravel the very idea of ten equal provinces joined together in Confederation.

By June 1990 the accord had come to symbolize an arrogance and an elitism that clearly rubbed the people the wrong way. It had become eleven men in suits deciding, behind closed doors, for an entire country that was denied any say at all. Those who were fronting the accord were saying it had no "egregious error" and couldn't possibly be opened to discussion. The lone premier who was balking, Newfoundland's Clyde Wells, was being beat up by the others to the point where the rumours around the Congress Centre had him in tears and on the verge of a mental collapse—merely because he dared challenge some of the premises behind the deal his predecessor had signed three years earlier.

Before the week was out, the prime minister—using everything from heartfelt persuasion to, some said, control over bathroom breaks—managed to get the premiers to push on to the final date for confirmation, though Wells had insisted on an asterisk to his signed agreement. Two days later, Mulroney, already accused of gambling with the future of the country, would hold his famous interview in which he likened the constitutional gambit to knowing when to "roll the dice"—even further infuriating the people.

Canada seemed very much in the midst of one of those "cataclysmic events" that Andrew Malcolm suggested the country had somehow missed in its history.

The prime minister was saying Canada itself was at stake. And there was something about the arrogance of the closed meetings and the irrational sky-will-fall threats, something about that pretentious word "egregious," that had seriously teed me off.

In that column I contended that the media was missing the story by concentrating on the prime minister, the premiers, their spin doctors, and the various scrums that took place in and around the Congress Centre. "The big story is out among the people," I wrote, "and it is a tale of such fury and anger that God be with the first of these secretive and devious politicians that dares call an election and ask the people what they think about the way things have been going. Somewhere, sometime, the people will have their revenge."

It did not take long to begin. The failure of Meech led directly to the emergence of the Bloc Québécois, when a handful of disenchanted members of Parliament, both Conservative and Liberal, decided to give up on Canada, combine forces, and work toward sovereignty for Quebec. Meanwhile, the anger "ordinary" Westerners felt was pivotal in the now-soaring fortunes of the Reform Party that had been founded in 1987. Parliament itself was about to change dramatically.

Before that first summer was out Ontario premier David Peterson, barely three years into his mandate, called a snap election—and was flattened by the New Democratic Party under Bob Rae. Some survived their next elections and some went down to crushing defeat, none quite so dramatically as the Conservative government itself. In the 1993 federal election the two great majorities of Brian Mulroney evaporated into a mere two seats; among the defeated was Kim Campbell, the leader who for a few short breaths had replaced Mulroney upon his retirement. None of the English-Canadian originals survived their support for the accord: within a little more than three years all were gone from office. It became known as "The Curse of Meech."

Ordinary Canadians, it turned out, were in an extraordinary and lasting snit.

MULRONEY NAMED KEITH SPICER to chair the Citizens' Forum on Canada's Future. Spicer had once been Commissioner of Official Languages and had gained more ink in that job—thanks, in no small part, to an equally brilliant young assistant named Michael Enright—than any commissioner since. It had been Spicer, with Enright's help, who had coined the phrase "Westmount Rhodesians" to make the point that for bilingualism to work, everyone had to buy into it.

Spicer was a genuine eccentric, equally capable of telling an off-colour joke as quoting Shakespeare at length. He could be charmingly and impossibly absent-minded. He'd hired me at the *Ottawa Citizen* four years earlier and, two weeks after the lunch that sealed the deal, did not know who I was when I showed up for work. He could play, by ear, dozens of national anthems on the piano. He was so devoted to an old floppy-eared mutt that, when it lost the ability to climb, he carried the dog in his arms up and down the stairs to his Sandy Hill apartment so that it could relieve itself several times a day. Spicer showed up at the *Citizen* office wearing a safari suit; he insisted on spending time in every possible facet of the paper; he once asked for a Greek headline over his own weekly column; and he basically gave everyone at the paper his or her own head to the point where it was openly questioned whether he himself even read the publication.

No matter; for some of us he could not have been a better boss— endlessly enthusiastic, open to any suggestion at all, no matter how expensive or how ludicrous. In many ways the newspaper thrived as never before, particularly after Spicer brought in the impossible-to-put-up-with, impossible-to-put-down Marjorie Nichols as his main political columnist. He gave the paper a presence that stretched far beyond the bright yellow rural paper boxes of the Ottawa Valley.

Spicer had then moved on from the *Citizen* to chair the Canadian Radio-television and Telecommunications Commission, the government's arm's-length broadcast regulator. He was a surprise choice to head up the new Citizens' Forum. Some said it was inspired—if Spicer was anything, he was unpredictable—and some said it was a ploy, Spicer having been largely predisposed toward the Mulroney government while editor and having left for a government appointment at the CRTC.

Spicer himself would later write in *Life Sentences*, his 2004 memoir, that he was chosen for being the only high-profile Ottawa type "crazy enough" to take on such a "bizarre adventure."

"Bizarre" would be a fair, if somewhat inadequate, description of what was to come.

Twelve commissioners were named to the Forum, with Spicer serving as chair and the other eleven representing the various regional concerns and special interests. The general notion, deliberately loose right from the opening announcement, was that the Forum would travel across the nation to listen to Canadians talk about their country and then take that message back to the federal government.

It would be a psychological report on the general state of a depressed nation.

It wasn't the first time such an analysis had been attempted. Following the shocking election of a sovereigntist government in Quebec on November 15, 1976, Ottawa had established a task force on unity headed by former cabinet minister Jean-Luc Pépin and former Ontario premier John Robarts. The report, which took months to prepare and cost millions, argued in favour of a classic federation, with constitutional recognition of Quebec's francophone reality and the extension of increased powers to all provincial governments. Critics tagged it a "dog's breakfast." Robarts himself had all but admitted defeat, claiming "It was the best we could get." The government of the day ignored it.

The announcement of the Forum was met with ridicule by those in the media who, by dint of time and station, had themselves become part of the very elite that had misread the country over the Meech Lake Accord. The Citizens' Forum was cast as just another foolish government venture to make it *appear* to be in touch; Spicer was ridiculed as too goofy to be taken seriously and too beholden to be feared. He would, if anything, produce a highly literate report that would become the parliamentary equivalent of *War and Peace*—unread even by those who meant to read it.

I have my own admission here. I chose the sneering route at the start and laughed continually at the commission that began with Spicer heading north in search of "poetry." I started calling myself "Commissioner 13" and wrote columns that were intended to look like inter-office memos, Commissioner 13 sending briefing notes to the Chairman.

Knowing Spicer's freely admitted interest in women, particularly busty women, I early on supplied him with a list of strippers on their way to Ottawa—Busty Brittany and her 52EEs heading for Gypsy Rose's, L.A. Bust (65-22-32) coming to Barbarella's—and then compared those breasts with the far-less-endowed strippers working the capital in the weeks leading up to June 23, 1990, the day the Meech Lake Accord died. I think I made some ridiculous point about insecurity or something, but looking back at the column today I cringe to imagine what I was thinking, if anything at all. Sometimes columnists get desperate—perhaps that explains it as well as anything.

The Forum did not begin well, either. A Quebec commissioner resigned. A prospective British Columbia commissioner, well-known television broadcaster Jack Webster, bailed, claiming he was too busy with "other commitments." Spicer convened an early closed-door session with a government pollster that seemed to go against the very spirit of the Forum and then unadvisedly told the media that "I don't think Canadians give a damn about how we organize our meetings." Perhaps not, but the media sure did. There were instant rumours of disorganization and ballooning costs, which Spicer himself had joked would fall "somewhere between a shoestring and an orgy."

Spicer's hope that volunteers would take over the Forum fizzled as federal "facilitators" and commissioners jockeyed for power. He set off, alone, for Tuktoyaktuk in the Northwest Territories and happened to tell Robert Matas, the *Globe* reporter along for the ride, that he'd prepared for this trip into the Far North by reading Inuit poetry, which led to a frenzy of satirical editorial cartoons and an inept attempt by Spicer to fight back by spouting doggerel that no one seemed to find very funny in such a serious time.

None of the media slagging came as any great surprise to those of us who'd worked with Spicer, but this talk had none of the delight in it that our banter had had at the *Citizen*. It was malicious. I myself wrote, two weeks into the commission, that already "the wheels have all but fallen off."

The Forum seemed to have crashed before takeoff. Spicer was fortunate that Canada had no late-night talk show equivalent or Canadians would have not only chuckled at the latest Forum fiasco story in their morning papers but gone to bed laughing at him too.

"I thought I was singing 'This Land Is My Land,'" Spicer would later remark, but "media and public heard the theme from *Looney Tunes*." Things got so bad that he came within a whisker of quitting and starting up his own, non-government-connected volunteer Forum.

But then, slowly, matters began to change. David Broadbent, a senior public servant with impeccable organizational skills, came in as executive director. Laurier LaPierre, an excellent communicator, took on the task of training moderators. Patrick Gossage, once Trudeau's press secretary, came in to talk publicity and planning. And Spicer himself hired on some gifted advisers and writers, among them Martin O'Malley, one of the country's best magazine writers; Nicole Bourget, who'd worked with Spicer at the CRTC; and Nancy Gall, a woman with sharp mind, tongue, and sense of humour who'd worked for Spicer at the *Citizen*.

There was such a good reaction to the "Commissioner 13" columns that they began to appear throughout the wide Southam chain stretching from Montreal to Vancouver (though not, significantly, in Toronto, the national media centre, where Southam had no paper). The papers decided to send me on the road and essentially cover the commission full time until Spicer would table his final report the following June.

It was an education the likes of which I couldn't possibly have imagined. We began in Charlottetown, Prince Edward Island, the oft-called "Cradle of Confederation"—even though the island would initially have nothing to do with Canada's creation in 1867. When the future Fathers of Confederation held their first conference there in 1864, Charlottetown was, in the words of one historian, "a small, isolated, violent little bailiwick" too caught up in its own infighting and petty politics to care about the larger picture.

When they met again in London two years later, P.E.I. was in such a sulk about the way negotiations had gone it didn't even bother to attend. And when it finally did join in 1873—striking an astounding deal that guaranteed this tiny enclave would forever enjoy four members of Parliament and four senate seats—it was only out of economic necessity. Without federal help the island was headed for bankruptcy thanks to overspending on railways. Still, there was no sense of going cap-in-hand to Ottawa. When the governor general of the moment, Lord Dufferin, came to check out the latest addition to the growing confederacy, he wrote to Prime Minister Sir John A. Macdonald that "I found the island in a high state of jubilation and quite under the impression that it is the Dominion that has been annexed to Prince Edward."

Those who came to Charlottetown early in 1991 to sit in the cradle and talk about the current state of this aging confederation were, like the original gatherers, mostly older and completely white. They did include an equal number of women, however, whereas none had been present in 1864. That first Charlottetown Conference had its twenty-two partici-pants sit around a mahogany table in a room that remains largely unchanged since those times and has long been a major P.E.I. tourist attraction. Sharon Larter, the provincial guide working that day, told Spicer that, since the Meech fiasco she'd seen Canadians stand and weep in that room, some even getting down on their knees to pray.

It had been a tough few years for Canadians. The bumblebee was on its back. The economy was sour, the deficit soaring. The Mulroney govern-ment had brought in free trade and the GST, much to the outrage of many. Wayne Gretzky had been sold to a hockey team operating out of Hollywood, the Canadian dollar was slipping and, of course, the Meech Lake Accord had upset ordinary Canadians more than all the above combined. No wonder they were falling to their knees in Charlottetown.

The Canadians who came this cold evening listened politely as Spicer made some opening remarks about the aim of the Forum and then let them know he hadn't come to talk but to listen, and that they should feel free to express themselves. After all, it was their country. One participant practically spit, telling Spicer that Canada had become "a disgusting example of a nation" that couldn't be bothered talking or listening to its own people. Another participant, an elderly man, stood up to tell Spicer he personally could not see what the fuss was all about if Quebec left— "sure as heck shorten up the drive to Toronto."

It is difficult now, looking back sixteen years, to accept the near utter despondency of those who came out to this first formal session of Spicer's Forum. One bespectacled, grey-haired seventy-six-year-old blueberry farmer, who had served as premier of this, the smallest province, from 1979 to 1981, wanted it known that, in his considered opinion, "We've been hoodwinked into thinking the Fathers of Confederation did a very good job."

He pointed off toward a far wall: "I know there's a plaque over there saying that, but I think they did a very poor job. I'd have to say, in hindsight, the Fathers of Confederation botched it."

Angus MacLean, of course, could not be numbered among the "ordinary Canadians" Spicer was seeking out. But Bonnie Howatt could be, and she'd let her sentiments be known even as she worked her way past the former premier to take a seat nearer the front.

"Evening, Angus."

"Evening, Bonnie."

"Oh my God but things are in a terrible state, Angus, are they not?"

"Yes, they are."

The quiet, polite people of Prince Edward Island could not possibly represent all the other citizens in Canada, but this first sense of a "terrible state" held for the entire length of the Forum and the breadth of the country. Canada, in the minds of most of those who turned out, was either going to hell in a handbasket or was already there, the handbasket nothing but smouldering ash.

During the nine months of the Spicer Commission it seemed that everywhere people looked they saw signs indicating the very end of the country. The Hudson's Bay Company decided to get out of the fur business. Renowned Canadians who passed on included literary scholar Northrop Frye, the great mind that once asked "Where is here?"; Eugene Forsey, the constitutional expert and inveterate letter-to-the-editor writer who served as conscience to the nation; former Newfoundland premier Joey Smallwood, the last living Father of Confederation; Roland Michener, the governor general who had once so inspired Canadians; and Hugh MacLennan, the novelist who made "Two Solitudes" part of the Canadian lexicon and left this world as bleak as, perhaps even bleaker than, Bruce Hutchison would be about the country's future prospects that wet day in Victoria.

The real Meech Lake, high in the Gatineau Hills overlooking the capital, might be filled with clear, cold water, but the paper Meech Lake held nothing but poison. Quebec was leaving, institutions were falling, faith was evaporating, and the end was nigh—a half hour later in Newfoundland.

"Like a dying person clinging desperately to the life he knows," the *Charlottetown Guardian* ("Covers Prince Edward Island Like the Dew") had editorialized the snowy day Spicer rolled into town, "Canadians have sunk their claws into a nation of the past, and perhaps even of the imagination...." A letter to the editor wanted Mulroney charged for what he'd brought about. A wire story carried a survey claiming that Canadians were so anxiety ridden over the state of their frail nation that they'd stopped having sex.

This sense of apocalypse—almost comical looking back—could be found everywhere during 1991, even on the bestseller lists, where the summer's top-selling book was on suicide and was bumped off in the fall by a book titled *The Betrayal of Canada.*

Canada, it appeared, was ending the second millennium not far removed from those Europeans who'd approached the end of the first with such a sense of Doomsday panic that families took to caves to hide and inventors desperately rushed to create a flying machine that could somehow lift people free of a world about to blow up on them.

Such is progress.

FOR TWO HOURS in Charlottetown, with Spicer and the other commissioners listening carefully and periodically scribbling notes to themselves, ordinary Canadians railed against the GST, Quebec language laws, sovereigntists, the handling of the Oka standoff between Natives and the army, the prime minister, the bungled accord, and even the media.

The media was out in force for this first meeting, CBC's *The Journal* running satellite interviews, all the major papers and all the main columnists poised to comment on what happened when the Spicer Circus came to town—just as another circus, albeit a real one, had been in town 127 years earlier during the original Charlottetown gathering.

None of the cameras picked up the small bust along one wall of Joseph Howe, an original invitee to the 1864 conference and a journalist who later worked to keep Nova Scotia out of Confederation. Howe eventually became so disenchanted with the idea of this thing called "Canada" that he stopped using the word "Confederation" in his columns and editorials and took to calling it "Botheration." A year after Confederation actually took place, however—without Prince Edward Island, incidentally— Howe was ready to concede that he'd lost the fight and that harping on against Confederation was as meaningless as "the screams of seagulls around the grave of a dead Indian on the coast of Labrador."

There was little doubt that most of the media considered this exercise in Charlottetown just as meaningless. They stifled yawns, whispered among themselves, made plans for a late dinner, and sighed, gratefully, when one of Spicer's commissioners, Susan Van de Velde, began to close matters down by saying that they'd listened and what they'd heard would not be lost.

It was at this point that an old man with soaring black-grey eyebrows suddenly took to his feet near the back of the room. He hadn't said a word all evening but was now determined to be heard. He said he was a farmer from Pownal and a father of twelve. He said he'd been born dirt poor and was still dirt poor. He spoke with an incredible calm and certainty of voice. The entire room stilled as he stood, carefully unfolded his scarf, and placed it around his neck. He was leaving. He put on his coat and held his gloves in his hand, a man dressed for the cold as he spoke under the hot lights.

Leo Cannon had a story to tell about his garden. He talked about the magic he feels when he takes a small carrot seed in his huge hands and pokes it down into the soil and how, a few months later, thanks to a lot of care and a little faith, the next time he moves the earth aside it reveals a beautiful, full-grown carrot. That is how you grow a carrot; that is how you should grow a country.

"The problem with this country," Leo Cannon wanted the Citizens' Forum on Canada's Future to know, "is that we have lost our faith. This country is morally bankrupt. It's about money and profit and greed. We are morally bankrupt, and unless we are willing to change, there's not a hope in hell."

And with that he pulled on his gloves and walked away, off into the night where the snow was just beginning to swirl again along Charlottetown's University Avenue.

FROM THE OPENING SESSION at Charlottetown to the moment Spicer reported at the end of June 1991, Commissioner 13 trailed after the Citizens' Forum on Canada's Future. After Charlottetown, nothing about the Spicer Commission seemed quite so funny any more. Ordinary Canadians, most so angry they visibly seethed and shook, were being listened to by Spicer and his eleven real commissioners. And these people—most often older, most often white, far more often in one official language than the other—had a great deal to say.

The ones not usually listening were the media, and it wasn't entirely the media's fault. I had noticed before, but it struck me particularly during the Spicer hearings, that Canadians do not speak as themselves when television cameras are around. Perhaps it's our innate politeness, perhaps our desire to please, perhaps even some genetic connection back to the days when we automatically deferred to authority. Whereas Americans seem eager to reveal, to star in their own fifteen-second movie, Canadians seem keen to conceal, to let stardom remain where, in their minds, it should be—with the television interviewer.

Spicer was highly attuned to media and wanted television to be a part of his travelling circus. He himself was superb on television, a master ad-libber, capable of saying things like "I'd like to make four points" and then actually making four. He could quote from Shakespeare, Euripides, and Dizzy Dean. He was equally comfortable in French as in English. He liked the camera. He was hardly an ordinary Canadian himself, yet he assumed that televised town hall meetings would draw out the thoughts of everyday people and that a little community centre or church basement could somehow, magically, be electronically transformed into a huge meetin' tent that would cover the entire country.

Spicer did not, at least not at this point, understand the ordinary Canadian. One bright light, one camera, one earplug connecting these people by satellite to some distant interviewer and they instantly changed. Rather than say what they thought, they'd say what they thought they *should* be saying, what the interviewer wanted to hear. Instead of the anger pouring through, reason seemed the order of the day. On television they sounded tolerant, reasonable, hopeful, resigned; off camera, and in the sessions where no cameras showed up, they seethed, they accused, they threatened, they swore to avenge and punish those politicians who'd been involved in the whole sorry process leading up to the Meech Lake debacle. Ontario premier David Peterson had already paid the price; others would follow. Even the prime minister would have the sense to bail before daring to face such wrath.

Commissioner 13 argued that the televised town hall meetings were a disaster and not at all reflective of what people were feeling. What television—particularly the then-powerful CBC news program *The Journal*—had done, even if inadvertently, was create a *third* official language that Commissioner 13 took to calling "BarbaraSpeak" after Barbara Frum, then the most recognizable news media personality in the nation. People spoke as if they were on stage.

The commissioners swept across the country. Hardly a night went by when there wasn't a meeting somewhere. They met to talk about the meaning of Canada, the current state of Confederation, the Constitution. They discussed how they might fix things through everything from senate reform to a full Constitutional Assembly that would start from scratch to redesign this bumbling bumblebee called Canada.

There were official meetings and unofficial meetings, meetings in people's houses over wine and cheese, meetings in community centres over tea and those little multicoloured crustless sandwiches that seem as much a part of church life as Sunday prayer. And it worked.

In Brandon, 472 people showed up to talk to Spicer. The crowd was so large that organizers came up with a rather novel, made-in-Canada scheme to deal with the situation.

They brought in uniformed Canadian Tire cashiers to act as ushers.

BETWEEN MEETINGS and panel discussions, Commissioner 13 stopped in across the country to visit with various touchstones of its history.

In Quebec City I visited the Ursuline convent to check what was going on in the head of the Marquis of Montcalm, the last man to declare this North American turf French rather than English property. Only a short walk away, on an early September day in 1759, the English under the command of James Wolfe scaled the cliffs overlooking the St. Lawrence River and moved on to the Plains of Abraham. There they encountered the French defenders and, following a volley that lasted all of fifteen minutes, Wolfe lay dying in the grass, the wounded Montcalm was being carried off to be hidden in the fort, and that great can of worms that would become Canada's "two founding nations" was opened.

Montcalm died the following morning despite the Ursuline sisters' best efforts. For reasons that baffle, the sisters held on to his skull, and to this day they display it, yellowed and toothless, in a glass case beside the chapel. On the stand holding the glass case is a typed note that instead of lamenting Montcalm's shortened life attacks the King of France for abandoning the people of Quebec following his death. Four years after that pivotal battle on the Plains of Abraham, France and England agreed to end their long war. When the King of France was asked what parts of the New World he most valued he immediately listed Santo Domingo, Martinique, and Guadeloupe, three sugar-bearing islands that appealed to his sweet tooth far more than the deep snow of New France.

That's hardly surprising, given that France was well on the way to giving up its stake in the New World anyway. Fur was one thing, but was beginning to wind down as stocks thinned and fashion changed. Champlain had always believed that enormous mineral wealth—gold and diamonds—would one day be found in the rough terrain beyond the riverbanks, but his promises had proved so empty that in Paris "false as a diamond in Canada" had become a popular phrase.

"He let the Canadians down," the Ursuline sister who typed the note had written of the King who loved cane sugar better than maple syrup.

Now, 232 years later, it seemed a remark worth mentioning again—though this time it had nothing whatsoever to do with the King of France.

ON THE BANKS of the South Saskatchewan River on a fine spring day that tortured year, Commissioner 13 went to sit by the grave of John Diefenbaker. Diefenbaker should be the patron saint of all politicians: six straight electoral defeats, then victory, then the leadership of the Progressive Conservative Party of Canada, then prime minister of Canada, then the largest majority victory of the time in the 1958 general election. He would never again rise so high.

Diefenbaker had always been larger than life, with his thundering oratory, the shaking jowls, the searing stare, the scalpel wit, the enormous flaws and, of course, the outrageous ego. Because his wife, Olive, also buried here on the university side of the river that cuts through Saskatoon, had once taught school in the small Ontario town I came from, he was always open to a visit. I would go to his office in Ottawa long after his fall from leadership and listen to him carve, brilliantly, all those who dared succeed him. His death in 1979—only a few weeks after the return of his party to power since his own glory days—had been a national event, his personally planned funeral train easily the rival of the train that carried Pierre Trudeau back to Montreal.

For most of an afternoon I sat by the tomb and watched visitors come and go. They came from all across the country, including his own Prince Albert riding. They were young enough not to remember him at all and old enough to remember, vividly, the way he had once fired the Canadian imagination with his powerful rhetoric.

Those who came to the Diefenbaker Centre said it brought back old memories to visit the gravesite and tour through the small museum with its election posters, photographs, and speeches. To them Diefenbaker was a leader, and today there were no leaders. To them Diefenbaker was a Canada that looked ahead with confidence, not a Canada that looked back with regret.

"It's just not the same any more," Tom McCloy said as his granddaughter ran shrieking about the grounds, oblivious to the gravesite of the former prime minister. "There's just no respect. Changing times, I guess. I don't know...."

McCloy once had a farm in Diefenbaker's riding. He and his wife had once ridden in the local fair parade with the man they still called "The Chief." They were no different from most other Canadians encountered during the months of the Spicer Commission, deploring the state this seemingly fragile country had allowed itself to fall into.

With McCloy as an eager guide, I walked through the museum, staring at photographs of Diefenbaker with the likes of American president John F. Kennedy and French president Charles de Gaulle; Diefenbaker standing on the back platform of a train staring out at a sea of faces that were the "ordinary Canadians" of the time, though never so insultingly called that. Back then, however, it seemed to those faces smiling back that the country was coming together. Now, to those faces frowning down at the photographs, it seemed it was breaking apart.

"This is a time for greatness," Diefenbaker thundered in one speech prominently displayed at the museum. "National unity requires it."

On scratchy black-and-white video, the speech was riveting to a visitor in early 1991. "The object of Confederation," Dief shouted, "was not to produce Siamese twins in this nation.... We are in a national crisis. National goals will never be attained by following uncertain courses designed to secure immediate advantage....

"... We need to instill in every Canadian the spirit of Sir George-Étienne Cartier. 'Before all, let's be Canadians' ...

"... What has the nation done for an ordinary person like me? What can it do for those who are prepared to devote themselves? Your Canada, my Canada. I give you a line from a young Canadian poet, Stephen Smith, who died in Montreal in 1964. He left a memorable line worthy of Rupert Brooke: 'Canada should be a reflection of God's eyes.'"

It was a truly remarkable speech. And it was delivered, history requires me to point out, at the convention that tossed out John Diefenbaker as party leader.

COMMISSIONER 13 also stopped in on the living.

In Edmonton, it was to spend a day with Fil Fraser, the human rights activist and filmmaker who was one of Spicer's eleven commissioners on the Citizens' Forum on Canada's Future—or, as Fraser preferred to call it, the "Yo-Yo Commission." One day up, one day down; one day filled with hope, one day filled with despair.

In his opinion, what the Spicer Commission had done, if nothing else, was show that "a quiet revolution was going on in the country." The immediate anger that flashed across the nation after the accord failed—complete with "Impeach Mulroney" bumper stickers—was merely the opening salvo in a battle still being played out nearly a year later.

"Maybe people aren't marching in the streets," Fraser said as he slipped his black Jaguar through the Edmonton traffic, "but the amount of emotional energy being expended is similar."

Fraser conceded that he'd fallen into a pit of despair over the country. As little as three weeks earlier he'd admitted to himself, and then to those closest to him, that the country was finished, done, over with. But then, he said, came the beginnings of a "sea change." The national venting was having an effect, and a good effect.

"If I had to tell you when I realized how important it was," Fraser told me over lunch, "I'd pick the time I went into northern Saskatchewan. I flew in to Île-à-la-Crosse, the most unbelievably beautiful but poverty-stricken place you ever saw. The village is all Natives and Métis. They used to run traplines but now there's no point, the fur industry is dead. They used to fish, but now the fish are mostly gone. They've got 80 percent unemployment and third world birth rates.

"We sat in a circle and they handed around an eagle feather. Whoever held it got to speak. It took three hours and they just spilled their guts on the floor. One young man said he was going to burn down the whole northern forest because he had nothing to lose. Old people talked about there being nothing for the young but welfare and despair.

"When it was over they came up one by one and some of them shook my hand, but most of them hugged me. Hugged me. And you know what they told me? They said, 'Go and tell them.' ...

"We're going to do that. We're going to tell what people said. Not how many people said this or how many people said that—but *what* they said. We're going to say what we really heard...."

SINCE THE FUTURE of Quebec was a central focus—the theory being that, having been snubbed by the accord's collapse, Quebeckers would now choose to go their own way—Spicer was keen to head straight into the province and find out what "ordinary Quebeckers" were thinking. Wearing his signature trench coat and wide-brimmed black German fedora—looking more as if he was tromping around the set for *Casablanca* than Canada—Spicer took his commission into the Saguenay, straight to the heart of *bluet* country where the sovereigntist movement had long been strongest. On a radio talk show he was asked what he'd gained by bringing the topic of Canadian unity there. Spicer considered a moment, placed a finger over his mouth, then lifted his hand away and held his finger almost tight to his thumb. "About two millimetres," he said.

It might have been a generous estimation. The province was in turmoil and paid scant attention to the Citizens' Forum. It seemed that every day produced a new idea, each new one banging its head against the rising prospects of an independent Quebec.

One man was proposing the "corridor option." It would allow most of the province of Quebec to go its own way while providing for a superhighway running south of the St. Lawrence between the Ontario border and New Brunswick. Surrounding this wide ribbon of highway would be a preserved corridor considered part of Canada.

A political movement calling itself the Equality Party was pushing for the creation of "The Republic of Laurentia." This idea would have Quebec returning to its tiny New France borders as they existed before the 1759 Conquest.

Another group wanted to create "The West Island Nation," a sort of Luxembourg that would hold the West Island of Montreal where most of the Anglos, most of the businesses, and much of the money were to be found.

The grand schemes went both ways, of course, and included a suggestion by a sitting member of Parliament, Pierrette Venne, that Quebec take over Labrador from the huge land mass that is the province of Newfoundland and Labrador. To her it seemed a sensible idea, given that Quebec had already developed the Churchill Falls hydro-electric project in the region. This suggestion, no surprise, outraged the people of Newfoundland and Labrador, who have long railed against the controversial deal that allowed Quebec to dam the Churchill and profit, enormously, from selling the electricity of Newfoundland and Labrador to the New England states.

Then there were the Cree of James Bay, talking about their own separation from Quebec should Quebec try to separate from Canada....

And all this nattering and threatening, of course, didn't even get to the burgeoning topic of Western separation. The farther west Spicer ventured, the greater the fury he encountered over whatever it was Canadians believed had happened when Meech was hammered out behind closed doors.

The sense was growing fast that, under such pounding traffic, the line down the centre of the road could not possibly hold.

I'D CREATED THE COMMISSIONER 13 persona as a lark, thinking that if it got a laugh that was enough. But soon it was getting much, much more. This was a time of faxes and old-fashioned telephones that people actually answered, and Commissioner 13 began receiving inside material and inside calls. Spicer would later say in *Life Sentences* that Commissioner 13 had somehow "become nationally known as the Forum's ultimate, well-informed quasi-insider." I can't say who was passing on the details only because the list was so long it would make "insider information" sound ludicrous. It seemed as though everyone was involved, from the highest level to the lowest. But those working for the commission had noted the same phenomenon as I had: the ordinary Canadian was in an absolute shitfit about the state of the country and that fact wasn't coming across in the media, which had pretty much dismissed the commission and Spicer altogether.

In late winter the commission produced an interim report. It touched on the fuming resentment toward politicians but gave little indication of which way the final report would go. There was obviously a split in the Forum's office. There was also a split among the commissioners, with some wishing to gloss matters over in favour of the government that had appointed them and a very few others determined that the truth get out as to how outraged so many Canadians were about the conduct of the governments they had elected. Spicer himself often seemed to be waffling. Members of his own staff weren't sure which way he was leaning and several were desperately prodding him to go the distance.

These were among the people who wanted Commissioner 13 to keep the coals tight to Spicer's heels. There were rumours, widely believed, that Spicer had been offered the ambassadorship to France if he played along and reported back, mildly, that ordinary Canadians had vented their anger and were now feeling much better for it, thank you very much. Spicer had once lived in France, was a known Francophile, and in fact would later return to live in Paris, so the rumour certainly had legs. In his memoirs, published fourteen years later, Spicer would recount a telephone conversation with the prime minister in which he said Mulroney promised him any embassy he wished—"just name it and we'll work out whatever you like." Spicer says he politely told the prime minister "Thanks, but I don't really want anything. Let's just get on with the job."

By now Commissioner 13 had turned into something never intended and certainly never expected. What had begun as a small joke had become something of a small political force—certainly within the Forum.

But also beyond the Forum, all the way to the Prime Minister's Office. A friend who was tight with Mulroney passed along a memorandum from the PMO in which it was clear that the column was getting to someone. A handwritten note given to the prime minister had suggested that a backward check of *Citizen* archives could produce a number of older

MacGregor columns that would show his political judgment in a bad light. Attached to the memorandum was a November 9, 1988, column in which I'd written that the Mulroney campaign was stumbling over the free trade issue—the suggestion being that the column looked pretty silly when the Conservatives had gone on to win a second majority. The prime minister himself had signed the memo, adding "This is for P&P on Monday"—meaning a three-year-old column was about to be discussed at cabinet's Priorities and Planning Committee, the most powerful decision-making body in the land.

Surely the country had rather more pressing matters requiring attention.

The pressure on Spicer was mounting, and it was beginning to look as if he might buckle. It was undeniable—even if France wasn't in the works—that he could personally benefit by largely clearing the government name on this file. Spicer had always been both iconoclast and survivor, and it seemed now that those two elements were running at cross-purposes. If he chose to gloss over the anger as a sort of temporary venting he'd lose the respect of a great many close to him, but if he went the other way and reported, accurately, the deep disenchantment of ordinary Canadians he might lose his own future prospects—something anyone entering the last decade of a career would surely consider. Spicer was fifty-seven and the stress was telling. He was eating poorly and drinking too much. His assistant, Barbara Ursel, forced him to see a doctor, who wanted to hospitalize him for "burnout" and advised him to stop working for a two-year period. Hardly something Spicer wanted to hear with only two months left before he'd have to report. Instead he promised to cut back quietly, go for a daily walk, and restrict his red wine intake to two glasses—as he put it, "minimum and maximum."

Through May and the first part of June, Commissioner 13 regularly berated Spicer about following through, about telling the truth, about not letting down the 400,000 ordinary Canadians who'd come into some contact with the Forum. Spicer hadn't said a word about what he'd found, but already the case against him was building in the media. There were, of course, exceptions—*The Globe and Mail*'s Michael Valpy, for example— but for the most part the Ottawa media bought into the elite line that

Spicer was a bureaucratic joke worthy only of ridicule. They said the expense, a budget of $27.4 million, required its own commission of inquiry. They laughed at his figures; they said the Forum was unscientific (*of course* it was); they said Spicer was more interested in finding an apartment in Paris than the pulse of a nation he wished to leave behind. They said he'd be offering no solutions, not realizing that solutions had never been part of the mandate. The role of the Forum had been merely to listen—and then to report back.

As Spicer later revealed in his memoir, the government made sure to get certain discreet messages to him that if he played the game right he could be in line for a nice embassy posting or, as he wrote, a $400,000 golden handshake "which nobody would find out about." None of this, of course, was ever put in writing. Nor was it ever denied.

In late June, only days before Spicer was to table this report, Commissioner 13 struck hard, telling Spicer—whom I quite liked and admired—that he had a "sacred pact" with those 400,000 that could not be broken. I advised him to forget the media response because they were only going to laugh anyway. And if there was bound to be widespread knocking because of the Forum's failures in Quebec, go with them rather than deny them and let it be known that this would be the first time ever that the voice of the Rest of Canada had come through so loudly and so clearly. All Canadians—and this included Quebec and the chortling elite—needed to hear this. Commissioner 13 then supplied his own "minority report." I said that Keith Spicer knew better than anyone what Canadians were thinking and saying. No matter where he travelled, they told him about their enormous love of the country and enormous outrage toward those supposedly running it. They were aghast at the political behaviour that had come out of Meech Lake. They were ashamed of their political leaders, the prime minister in particular, and they had lost faith in the political process.

Having been excluded by a process that wanted nothing to do with them, I said, these Canadians wanted *in* on whatever process might follow. They had no interest in abandoning something that, in their minds, had once worked wonderfully and must be made to work again. I mentioned a short note I'd received that said it all. "Let me put it to you this way," the handwritten note said. "If Canada dies, then I die." It was signed "Pete."

Spicer's job, then, was to speak for all the Petes. And Pete lived in every region of the country, was both man and woman, Native and non-Native, new Canadian and old Canadian, young and elderly and everything in between, spoke not only both official languages but several, and when asked by the commission before each session to list the things most treasured about Canada had named medicare first and, to the great surprise of many, but not all, hockey second.

In the days leading up to Spicer's scheduled report, there was panic in his office as the chairman seemed to vacillate. The official report had gone to the printer containing two dissenting opinions—one from Quebec publisher Robert Norman, one from Newfoundland union leader Richard Cashin—that largely questioned the validity of the exercise. The report had also found its way into government hands, though it had never been intended to. Some staff members were convinced Spicer had decided to throw caution, and perhaps his own future, to the wind and tell the truth about what he'd heard. Others were equally sure he was going to downplay the anger and suggest it had passed, much like the tantrum of a small child.

On the day that he was to report, Spicer was said to be carrying two speeches in his jacket pocket, still uncertain which way he'd go in his introductory remarks, though his press secretary, Nicole Bourget, had strongly advised him to ignore the notes he'd been working on and instead just speak "from the heart." Enough of the official document had been leaked to let people like Michael Valpy know that unless Spicer came through it would end up on that infamous Ottawa shelf that holds hundreds of unread and instantly forgotten commission and parliamentary reports.

After 241 days of pulse taking and lint sorting, Spicer finally reported on June 27, 1991. The venue, nicely chosen, was the Grand Hall of the Museum of Civilization, a magnificent structure on the Quebec side of the Ottawa River opposite Parliament Hill.

It could hardly have been a more dramatic setting. Spicer stood nervously on a tall stage in front of the West Coast totem poles, the assembled cameras and media below and, through the vast glass walls opposite, dark clouds gathering over the round Library of Parliament, the sky rumbling and periodically flashing with lightning.

Spicer's personal "Chairman's Foreword," which he verbally summarized with little use of notes, became the story of the nine-month Citizens' Forum on Canada's Future. The *Citizen* would headline it as nothing less than the "Scream of a Nation."

If Spicer did indeed carry two speeches into the building, he elected to go with the one that would take no prisoners. He laid the blame for what had gone so terribly wrong with this country's spirit squarely at the door of Prime Minister Brian Mulroney.

Spicer's contribution was a literary Hail Mary Pass, a play kept from the other commissioners when the official report was sent off to the printer— thirty-five hundred words only, but every one lacking the bureaucratic governor that had been applied to the official report.

Spicer called the current state of the Canadian spirit "a pessimist's nightmare of hell." He said "Our democracy is sick. Citizens do not accept their leaders' legitimacy. This begins with the prime minister, but does not end with him. It includes leaders of the Opposition and provincial leaders...."

He warned that Canada had become a country "dying of ignorance, and of our stubborn refusal to learn." He said Canada faced "twin crises— one of structure, the other more profound and delicate, of the spirit." He said people were losing the symbols and institutions that made a country and made a country's people believe in it.

He even slammed the "consensual editing" of the official report that had muted the degree of fury out there toward the prime minister. Mulroney, Spicer countered, had become a "lightning rod" for all the anger the commission had encountered.

"From most citizens' viewpoint," Spicer went on, "our report lets the PM off too lightly. At least for now, there is a fury in the land against the Prime Minister." Canadians, he said, had become "the wind that wants a flag."

As Spicer finished up the storm broke, thunder and lightning raging over Parliament Hill, rain pelting the high windows of the Grand Hall.

And then the power went out. The sound system that had carried Spicer's hot, surging words had blown the circuits.

IT CAN BE ARGUED that nothing ever came of Spicer's report. It was tabled, reported on for a few days, raised in Parliament a few times, and then carted off to wherever it is politicians put things they never want to see again.

But it would be wrong to say it vanished.

I often think of a stop Commissioner 13 made in Edmonton during those months of the Forum. I took a cab out to a small yellow clapboard house on 85th to sip coffee with seventy-five-year-old Marjorie Bowker, a retired family court judge who for years had been spending her mornings at the University Hospital ministering to the terminally ill and her afternoons in what was once her children's nursery ministering to Canada.

Bowker's tough questioning on free trade in the late 1980s had elevated her to such populist status in this country that *The New York Times* featured her on the front page and Dan Rather interviewed her on the *CBS Evening News*. She had lost the battle against free trade but had warred just as strongly against Meech and was now one for two.

The rubber match was going to be on the very survival of Canada, and at the moment she had no idea which side was winning.

On an old Smith-Corona in the old upstairs nursery Marjorie Bowker had sat, ramrod straight, not a white hair out of place, and hammered out slender treatises on both free trade and the Meech Lake Accord. In a telling tribute to the Canadian penchant for belly-button lint, both had been published and soared to number one on the bestseller lists. She'd even been awarded the Order of Canada for her work—something that surely grated on the political forces of the day.

Bowker's grassroots writing had coincided with the rise of the Reform Party in the West. And it had flourished during the increasingly testy split between the elites and ordinary Canadians that began with the birth of the Meech Lake Accord. She had become, Commissioner 13 wrote, "The Patron Saint of Canadian Crankiness," considered by her followers as the Voice of Common Sense and dismissed by some of her critics as a bigot for her views on the failures of official bilingualism.

"If you do something important," she said, "there will always be critics. If you don't like critics, don't do anything important."

Her interpretation of Meech Lake was widely shared, particularly in the West. Rather than a sop to Quebec, a document intended to bring the one province left out of the 1982 Constitution Act happily back into the Confederation fold, she saw it more as a power grab by the premiers, with the prime minister, desperate to be the one to "solve" the Quebec issue, both witting and unwitting accomplice to the premiers' real designs.

Bowker argued that Canadians wanted, and needed, a strong central government, not one willing to turn over so many powers to the provinces that the balance shift would call into doubt the very need for Ottawa. She endorsed Trudeau's long-ago warning to Joe Clark that giving away too much power had the potential to turn the federal government into little more than a "head waiter to the provinces."

"This debate," the Albertan grandmother said as she straightened the various folders holding her carefully scissored newspaper clippings, "is all about power. The premiers want more power, and not for the people, but for themselves.

"If there's one thing we need in this country, it's a strong central government. We need it because of our geography. And we need it because of our very small population. A strong central government is the ideal structure for Canada."

She did not feel, however, that this ideal structure was going to hold, nor that it would return. If the country survived this crisis at all, she said, it would be at the expense of the core. Meech Lake or no Meech Lake, the provinces were gaining power and the only way to keep this cat's cradle called Confederation together was to continue on at the expense of the old structure.

Over time, under Mulroney, Jean Chrétien, Paul Martin, and Stephen Harper, she would be proved largely right.

"Meech Lake is not dead," she said with a smile. "It will live forever as the turning point for Canadians' distrust of the political system."

SEVERAL WEEKS AFTER the Citizens' Forum on Canada's Future reported, I got a call from Spicer suggesting a lunch with him and David Broadbent, the bureaucrat who put the Forum back on track and carried it through to the end.

We met across the river at Café Henry Burger and, at the end of a lunch in which some astonishing stories were told of government interference and internal fiascos, Spicer reached down beside the table and pulled up a framed certificate. It looked official, complete with the Canadian coat of arms embossed at the top. It read "Commissioner 13—In recognition of your valuable contribution to the work of the Citizens' Forum on Canada's Future" and was signed by both the chairman, Spicer, and the executive director, Broadbent. I will treasure it forever.

A few months later, with the government showing no inclination whatsoever to follow up on any of the Forum's suggestions, Spicer headed back to his post at the CRTC. He was now, he would later say, a "non-person in the style of George Orwell's *1984*," his name gone from official Ottawa as effectively as names were once erased from the *Great Soviet Encyclopedia*.

As for Commissioner 13, he, too, vanished, happily leaving Parliament Hill for a new beat. He'd been assigned to cover the second matter ordinary Canadians said they valued most about their troubled country: a part of Canadian culture that, some would argue—me happily among them—tells as much about this country as anything else.

Hockey.

Five

Hockey, the National Id

THERE ARE FEW MATTERS in Canada that penetrate as deeply into the national soul as hockey. This is hardly surprising. The more dominant of the two national sports, with its heavy equipment and its vigorous effort, is exactly the sport that should have evolved in a land of ice and cold, just as baseball, with all its standing around, its thin uniforms, and its brief, periodic bursts of effort, is the perfect sport for the warmer climes of America.

In some ways, you can know a country better by knowing how it plays. That golf—with its strict rules and orderliness—would develop in Presbyterian Scotland comes as no surprise, any more than the military formations of American football.

"In a land so inescapably and inhospitably cold," Bruce Kidd and John Macfarlane wrote a generation back, "hockey is the dance of life, an affirmation that despite the deathly chill of winter we are alive."

I discovered just how deeply the penetration of hockey into the national psyche goes on two different occasions in the same month in late 2003.

The first was November 5, when I was assigned by *The Globe and Mail* to spend the day with Prime Minister Jean Chrétien in his final week in office. The Liberal leader was retiring after a decade in the top job and having easily won three majority governments in a strange time of little opposition in Ottawa. Only ten weeks away from turning seventy, he should have been taking it easy, but he was up before dawn working on his file folders, in this case signing off on nearly four dozen appointments that would make headlines the next day.

We had breakfast together and then headed in to Parliament Hill, his Royal Canadian Mounted Police security force having chosen one of several different routes they used to break the routine and, theoretically, to foil those who might have nefarious plans. On this day we headed down Sussex Drive and then MacKay Street, just to the side of the Rideau Hall grounds. He was in a good mood, showing me the emergency telephone that was always within reach in the prime ministerial limousine and joking that he didn't think he even knew how to use the thing. There had never been cause. With the exception of the 1995 Quebec referendum, which his side almost blew to the point of losing Quebec altogether, and the growing scandal over the use of sponsorship money following that nail-biting sovereignty vote, there had been fewer bumps along his three terms than there were this fall along Sussex Drive. It had been a relatively easy ride.

But then he settled back and became pensive. And why not? Forty years in Parliament were about to come to an end. He would, very shortly, no longer be prime minister of his country. His lengthy term in office was being compared—with considerable debate—to the records of King, of Laurier, of Macdonald … only I was about to discover he was thinking of none of these names but of a name not even in politics.

"You know," he said, "I am like Rocket Richard. He was maybe not the most elegant player on the ice, but he had the instinct for the net.

"It is a game," he added with a slightly crooked, undeniably sly grin. "And I am the pro."

There was no need to say any more. Any Canadian would understand, immediately, how Jean Chrétien viewed himself as a politician.

Little more than two weeks later, on November 22, the *Globe* sent me to Edmonton for the Heritage Classic, where 57,167 spectators—thousands of them outfitted in snowmobile suits, thousands of them further warmed by hot chocolate and Baileys—showed up in –20°C temperatures. They had come to watch Oilers legends and multimillionaires

Wayne Gretzky and Mark Messier play shinny on an outdoor rink and then, like neighbourhood kids almost anywhere in the country, pitch in to shovel off the ice between periods. Organizers claimed that ticket requests were so wild for the oldtimers' afternoon game and the evening NHL match between the Oilers and Montreal Canadiens that they could have sold 800,000 tickets if only the stands had stretched all the way to the Rocky Mountains.

During the Salt Lake City Games, Gretzky had said that winning gold was not the only goal of the players, but to live up to the expectations of the entire country. I asked Cassie Campbell, the captain of the women's Olympic team, if she felt the weight of the nation, and she agreed. "When you put on the Canadian hockey jersey," she said, "that's what you expect as well, and that's what you want. It's such a great game. The traditions of the game are that this has been passed down from generation to generation."

Campbell knew her history without even having to study it. Back in 1924, when the first Winter Games were held in Chamonix, France, Canada sent the Toronto Granites over to represent the country. The top player on the senior team was a ringer brought in by the Granites, big, handsome Harry "Moose" Watson of St. John's, Newfoundland. Moose made arrangements, presumably financial, to send periodic reports to a Toronto newspaper once the team reached Europe.

"It has been a wonderful and delightful trip," Moose telegraphed from London, "and our only hope now is that we can get to Chamonix at the earliest opportunity, so that we may start heavy training again and justify the confidence that has been placed in us and retain for Canada supremacy in the hockey world."

There was nothing to worry about. Canada, after all, had no competition to speak of in Chamonix. Moose himself set an Olympic scoring record—thirty-six goals, including thirteen in a 33–0 pasting of the Swiss—that will surely stand forever as the Canadian team waltzed through the competition and claimed the first-ever Winter Olympic Games gold medal for hockey.

But that "confidence that has been placed in us" back in 1924 would eventually become an incredible stress on Canadian players, at times all but unbearable. Who among us watching that night in September 1972 will ever forget Phil Esposito's impassioned plea following Canada's 5–3 loss to the Soviets in Vancouver?

"To the people across Canada," Esposito said, near-teary eyes turned not to interviewer Johnny Esaw but full-on to the camera, "we gave it our best. To the people that booed us, geez, all of us guys are really disheartened. We're disillusioned and disappointed. We cannot believe the bad press we've got, the booing we've got in our own building. I'm completely disappointed. I cannot believe it. Every one of us guys—thirty-five guys—we came out because we love our country. Not for any other reason. We came because *we love Canada.*"

Thirty years later, in Salt Lake City in mid-February 2002, the emotional outburst came from Team Canada executive director Wayne Gretzky. "Nobody understands the pressure these guys are under," a livid Gretzky told a post-game press conference following a lacklustre start by the Canadians, a decisive loss to Sweden, an unimpressive victory over weak Germany, and a tie against the Czech Republic. "The whole world wants us to lose," Gretzky said.

Whether Gretzky's rant was calculated, as some—not me, and I was in the room—have argued, or merely an uncontrolled emotional outburst, as many of us believe, the Canadians in 2002 rallied and went on to victory, just as Esposito's Canadians had in 1972. There is, some have said, a "controlled rage" to Canadian hockey that exists but is little understood, even by the players. "It scared the hell out of me that I would have killed to win," Esposito said, looking back on his famous speech a quarter century on. "That really scared me."

It is a passion, fully understood or not, that applies to fans as well as players. Such a grand national *itch* for a game, however, can be difficult to explain to those who don't readily share it, especially those Canadians who disdain the game and who argue, from time to time, that it has no reason to be carried on the Canadian Broadcasting Corporation because, well, it has nothing to do with the culture of the country.

They could not be more wrong.

Bruce Hutchison once wrote in a newspaper column that hockey might be the country's only authentic and indigenous art form. He also said, with uncanny foresight, that few realized the game was even "a political force" in the life of Canadians.

Hutchinson was writing in 1952. Three years later, the most significant *political* act hockey has ever produced in this country would take place in Montreal. And it would involve a man named Maurice "Rocket" Richard—a player who always said he didn't even much follow that other game called "politics."

"MERCI, MAURICE. Merci bien."

Georges Boudreault stood at centre ice, wiping tears from his eyes and speaking to a dead man.

"Merci ... merci ... merci ..."

Boudreault and his grown son, Mario, had driven, hard, more than four hours from their home in the Saguenay, that rough and rolling, rock-and-pine area well north of Quebec City where the wild blueberries grow large and the people, known for their fervent nationalism, are referred to as *bleuets*. The two Boudreault men had taken turns at the wheel, one driving fast, one looking out for cop cars and speed traps, and had pulled off the autoroute, through the exit, and onto rue de la Gauchetière at exactly 10:05 P.M., May 30, 2000.

Five minutes too late.

Georges Boudreault, a man in his sixties with curling grey hair and a face that has known contact sports, had idolized Maurice "Rocket" Richard all his life. He'd grown up on the outdoor rinks of the Saguenay and was no different from young boys all over the province in those years, a time captured so lovingly by Roch Carrier in his children's book *The Hockey Sweater:* "As for church, we found there the tranquility of God: there we forgot school and dreamed about the next hockey game. Through our daydreams it might happen that we would recite a prayer: we would ask God to help us play as well as Maurice Richard."

Carrier's prayers were never answered, nor were those of Georges Boudreault. In that they were, again, the same as all young boys in

Quebec during those years, for no one—not even with the help of God—ever played as well as Maurice Richard, either on the ice of the Montreal Forum or in the imagination.

Now the Rocket was dead. He had succumbed to cancer earlier in the week at age seventy-eight, and the outpouring of grief had caught the rest of the country—but not Quebeckers, and certainly not Quebeckers of Georges Boudreault's era—by surprise. Richard would lie in state at the Molson Centre, the famous Forum having been shut down so it could be converted to a multi-screen movie theatre. When Boudreault saw the television images of the people of Montreal lining up by the thousands to walk by the casket and pay their respects, he knew he had to be there. The Rocket would be lying in state until 10:00 P.M., at which time the doors to the Molson Centre—today known as the Bell Centre—would be closed. The funeral would be the following day.

Georges Boudreault had only one chance to say goodbye to his hero. But the clock was against him. He and Mario had found a place to leave the car and were now running toward the rink.

I was hurrying myself. I had flown to Montreal from Newark, New Jersey, having covered the opening game of the Stanley Cup final the evening before. The New Jersey Devils had beaten the Dallas Stars handily, 7–3, and would go on to win the Cup in six games, but there was far more talk about the death of the Rocket than whatever life might be left in the Stars. Many of the sportswriters covering the playoffs were also heading for Montreal to cover the funeral. I had packed quickly and left immediately for the airport, hoping to get a flight early enough that I might catch the last of the crowds filing into and out of the arena.

The hockey rink lying-in-state fascinated me. Sixty-five years earlier, the great Montreal Canadiens' hero of another generation, Howie Morenz, had entered hospital in late January 1937 after fracturing his leg in a game. He'd been kept in hospital so long that he was reported to have suffered a nervous breakdown. Then, six weeks after being admitted, he suddenly died of a heart attack. He was only thirty-four.

The outpouring of grief had been so great that the hockey club and Morenz family had decided to hold the funeral at the Forum, with fifteen thousand fans/mourners surrounding the casket as it rested at centre ice and thousands who couldn't get in milling about outside in the cold March wind. It is said that his funeral cortège passed by 200,000 more mourners who lined the snowy streets and roads all the way to the cemetery where Morenz was laid to rest.

It gives you a sense of what this game, and its stars, have meant to the people of Montreal and Quebec.

Georges and Mario Boudreault were too late to get in. They were too late even to sign the condolence books that had been set up near the front entrance to the Molson Centre, one of the entries reading: "My first words were Mama, Papa ... and Maurice Richard."

They tried the main entrance but security guards were locking up behind the last few stragglers. Others were there as well, still trying to get in but being turned away. The guards couldn't let Boudreault and his son in without hundreds more demanding the same, so they shooed the two men from the Saguenay away.

Mario suggested he and his father go around the back. Try another door. They took off up the steps along the side of the building and I followed, thinking their desperation might make a few lines in the next day's column. They pounded on the first door they came to. A security guard on the other side of the glass shook his head and walked away. They came to a second door and pounded. No one came. They hurried farther around the building to a third door—quickly running out of opportunities—and both father and son leaned against the glass here, slapping rather than pounding it as if they were running out of air as well as time.

A security guard, an older man with whitening hair and a salt-and-pepper moustache, looked over. He could see Georges Boudreault gesturing as if it was an emergency—and to Georges it certainly was.

The guard came over, opened the glass door a crack, and raised an eyebrow to invite the older man to explain himself—which he did with a passion that the great Richard himself would understand. He had loved the Rocket all his life. He had seen him play. He had talked to Mario all Mario's life about the great Rocket. Mario had never seen him play. They had driven all this way. They had come from the Saguenay to pay their respects.

The guard listened, the eyebrow dropped, and he opened the door wider, with a quick finger lifted to his lips that they should say nothing about this breach of security.

He opened the door for Georges, for Mario, and then kept it open for me. I hadn't said a word. He must have thought that I, too, had come all this way from the Saguenay to pay respects. Had I said I'd come from New Jersey, I wouldn't likely have been allowed in. Had I said I was an Anglo from Ontario, I most assuredly wouldn't have been.

The four of us made our way along a corridor of the Molson Centre and in through a dark pulled curtain to the stands. We were on the second level. The guard led us down the stairs, across a row of seats, and then out through a door in the boards to the rink floor.

We could see the coffin at centre ice, surrounded by flowers and bathed in a quiet, eerie light. The Rocket was all alone.

Georges made Mario take off his cap. They moved toward the casket at what could be described only as a quick funeral pace: hands held in front like mass servers, heads bowed, short steps ... but quick. They were afraid the other guards gathering on the floor might call a halt.

But there were no whistles, no shouts. The guards were milling together and gathering at the far end of the empty rink, leaving the Boudreaults and me to approach the casket and say our farewells.

I hadn't expected this. Trailing them, I was astonished to think that I'd be the last mourner to pass by the Rocket's open casket. I had no right to be there.

I followed the two men closely. Georges crossed himself as he approached the casket. Mario followed suit.

Maurice Rocket Richard was lying in a totally open casket. You could see him from the tops of his shoes to his head. He wore a dark blue suit, a white shirt, dark tie. But that was not what you noticed.

He'd gone much whiter than the last time I'd seen him—far, far greyer than when he used to do those Grecian Formula commercials (*"Hey Richard! Two minutes for looking so good!"*)—and he looked wasted from the cancer. But that still is not what you noticed.

What you could not help noticing as he lay in that strange coffin in that dark blue suit was that the famous eyes were closed.

The black flame had gone out.

SPORTS HEROES become known for many things. Power. Grace. Speed. In hockey it can be for the shot, the stickhandling, a player's skating or his playmaking. In Rocket Richard's case, it was none of these. He was not a great stickhandler. He had a good shot but not the best on his team. He wasn't particularly fast. He wasn't a playmaker. What he did have, in an abundance never seen before and not seen since, was *passion*—a burning passion that shone directly out of those fierce black eyes.

In 1955 *Sports Illustrated* sent William Faulkner to Montreal to write about the Rocket. The Nobel laureate, a southern gentleman, knew nothing about this northern game and could not understand it, but he saw instantly the connection between the crowd and Richard's eyes. Richard's look, Faulkner said, had the "passionate, glittering, fatal alien quality of snakes"—almost as if the goaltender looking up might be hypnotized into helplessness, which so often appeared the case.

It may have been as close as anyone has ever come to putting into words what those eyes said. Yet they were still only words, falling far short of what the photographs held. The photographs themselves falling short of what it was like to be that goaltender looking up and hit harder by the stare than any puck.

"MERCI, MAURICE."

Georges Boudreault was in tears. He was speaking in a whisper, yet in the empty cave that was the Molson Centre at this late hour his whispers seemed as if they were coming from the public address system over the scoreboard.

"Merci bien.

"Merci … merci … merci …"

We stood there a while, a French-only father and son from the Saguenay and an anglophone stranger who'd simply tagged along—and yet it seemed as if, suddenly, we were family. We had lost a favourite uncle, a boyhood hero, a national treasure—the word "national" taking on a somewhat different context in the Saguenay than it had in the rest of the nation. Georges Boudreault stood at the foot of the casket, wringing his big hands and periodically wiping away tears and crossing himself. Mario and I stood to the side, like two sons waiting for a father to finish.

The older guard who'd let us in came over from the far side of the rink floor where other guards had gathered. With a hand signal, he indicated it was time for us to move along. The elder Boudreault bowed a very courtly thank you in his direction and we all moved off, Georges now openly blubbering.

I was at the very end, thinking about the good fortune, as a journalist, to have witnessed Georges Boudreault's great race to say farewell to his hero, thinking, foolishly, that, on a day when it was said 115,000 people had filed by the coffin of Maurice Rocket Richard, I could say now I was the very last person to pay my respects to one of the country's great icons.

But I wasn't.

Just as the three of us were about to go through the Zamboni chute and into the lower corridor and the front doors, I turned for one last glance at the darkened arena with the soft light and the flowers at centre ice. And I saw something I had never anticipated.

The security guards had been organizing themselves into a small military formation. Young men and women with no military training ever, older men who might once have served—likely several had; clearly someone had put this together—were now *marching* across the arena floor in semi-formation. Backs straight, arms swinging, legs mostly in time, they walked across and came to a halt right beside the coffin of Maurice Rocket Richard.

They turned, virtually as one. They faced the casket while still at attention. Several bowed their heads.

The older guard saluted.

ROCKET RICHARD'S FUNERAL was held the following day. They lined the streets by the tens of thousands. I remember standing on a street corner to watch the cortège pass and seeing the look on the faces of two very young girls travelling in the next-to-final black limousine of the long procession. Perhaps they were grandchildren, perhaps great-grandchildren, and they were pressed to the window. The look on their young faces was one of absolute shock, of bewilderment and wonder, perhaps even of a growing realization as they saw, firsthand, with their own dark Richard eyes, what the Rocket had meant to the people.

They were hardly alone in their surprise. Those of us who'd long covered Canada's game knew, of course, that fans of a certain age would turn out, just as the curious would. But we didn't see this coming.

Joseph Henri Maurice Richard had been a difficult man in the precious little time most of us knew him. He'd vanished from the old Forum for years after his retirement in 1960. Periodically, stories would be told of his being bitter and hard up. He sold oil products door to door and for a while had a basement shop where he wound fishing line onto small bails to sell to bait shops. In the rare times he appeared in public, he seemed shy and reclusive. Public appearances amounted to refereeing charity games played by former National Hockey Leaguers, a task he seemed to somewhat enjoy.

Years passed, and eventually the Rocket began to show up at certain Canadiens functions again. He always seemed impenetrable: dark and brooding and desperate to avoid the limelight. He wasn't approachable the way Jean Béliveau or Guy Lafleur, the two great heroes of later *bleu, blanc et rouge* dynasties, were. The last I'd seen him relatively well was the night of March 11, 1996—fifty-nine years to the day since the funeral of Howie Morenz—when the Forum was closed up and the Montreal Canadiens moved down the street to the Molson Centre.

To open the ceremonies, the organizers had the three most famous Canadiens, the Rocket, Jean Béliveau, and Guy Lafleur, bring out the Stanley Cup, held high over their heads as if, magically, the team had just won a twenty-fifth cup. Richard, as the elder statesman, was to be the centre carrier. Béliveau was on one side of the older man—now generally known to be battling cancer—and the much younger Lafleur on the other.

On his first step out onto the ice Rocket Richard slipped and nearly went down with the cup, only to be saved by the quick hands of the other two. Even so, you could see the embarrassment and fury in the old man's eyes.

To Richard, dignity meant everything. Nearly twenty thousand people in the building cringed in sympathy for him, and when he was introduced along with all the other great heroes of the legendary hockey club, the initial burst of cheering was significantly louder than for anyone else. But that wasn't the end of it. The cheering continued, loudly, and then rose once, twice, to higher and louder levels as the entire building stood as one and, it seemed, had no intention of ever stopping the cheering and clapping.

For fifteen long minutes they stood and cheered, an embarrassed and evidently surprised Richard standing at centre ice, sometimes holding his arms up to call an end to the cheering, sometimes raising them to wipe away the tears.

No one wanted to see the Rocket go down; not ever.

BUT NOW, OF COURSE, he was down, and for good. The fire out of the famous coal-black eyes that every goaltender who ever faced the Rocket seemed to remember most about him.

There was no counting the tens of thousands of fans and mourners those two little girls saw as the funeral cortège made its way to Notre Dame Basilica in the heart of Old Montreal. They would have seen old men openly weeping. They would have seen fifteen daycare children lined up in front of Place des Arts, each wearing a special red bib to mark the occasion, all fifteen instinctively waving as if the parade involved a celebration—which, in a way, it did. At one corner, an elderly woman proudly wearing the old red uniform of the Forum ushers stood at attention, tears dropping from her cheeks as she formed a singular honour guard for the Rocket.

Some walked along behind the slow-moving funeral cortège, falling in behind as it passed and finding they could keep up with the limousines, so slowly were the black cars able to move through the gathering throngs. Guy Gagné pulled an old black-and-white photograph of him with the Rocket out of his wallet and showed it to fellow walkers, saying he himself had dropped in on Richard only a few weeks ago to see how he was doing. Not well. He was thinning and very weak. But, Gagné smiled, "I checked the eyes—he was still the Rocket."

Denis Joinville walked along with a Montreal Canadiens flag draped over his shoulders. He counted himself among the luckiest hockey fans of all time in that he'd seen the Rocket play his final game forty years earlier. He'd been only a child and his strict parents had insisted he be in bed by eight o'clock, even on Saturday nights, but on the night of the Rocket's last game he'd snuck out of his room and crawled along the floor to the hallway, where he'd stuck his head around the corner just far enough to see the flickering black-and-white television set and hear the call of René Lecavalier, the voice of *La Soirée du Hockey*.

"I was so afraid my father would catch me," Joinville said as he hurried toward the church steps. "I knew I would get the strap. He finally saw me—and he waved to me to come and crawl into his lap and we watched the Rocket's final game together.

"It is my best memory. I count myself lucky to have lived then."

The hearse pulled up outside the Basilica, pushing its way through what had become a rolling, lolling sea of people pressed into the open plaza in front and along the side streets. The flags that had been flying at half staff fell suddenly limp as the pallbearers pulled out the coffin and lifted it high enough for many to see. The effect was as if all available wind for the flags had suddenly been sucked away by lungs catching their breath.

And then someone began to clap, slowly. Others joined in, clapping faster, louder. Someone whistled. Others cheered.

The Rocket was taking his final shift.

MANY OF THOSE who came to bury Maurice Rocket Richard walked the entire journey from the Molson Centre to the Basilica, a long trek in seasonable weather that took them down the very street that, forty-five years earlier, had burned with rioters who'd gone on a wild rampage simply because the NHL had ruled that their great hero would not be allowed to dress for the next game.

The Rocket always insisted he was "just a hockey player," but on St. Patrick's Day, 1955, he would become far more than that. He would become, despite his refusal to accept this, refusal even to discuss it ever, one of the pivotal figures in Canadian history.

The Richard Riot was, historians now agree, a significant step in Quebec culture toward the Quiet Revolution that would turn Quebeckers from workers to managers, from second-class Canadians to first-class, and that would sow the seeds of "Maîtres chez nous" ("Masters of our own house") and, ultimately, the sovereignty movement that remains, today, at the very heart of both Quebec and Canadian politics.

It was the final week of the 1954–55 hockey season. Richard was at the peak of his abilities then, a decade after hockey's first fifty-goals-in-fifty-games had elevated him to the level of national sports hero. His thirty-eight goals and thirty-six assists by St. Patrick's Day 1955 were leading that year's scoring race. The Art Ross Trophy, awarded to the NHL's leading scorer, was the one honour that had so far eluded Richard in his fabulous career, and the Montreal fans were looking forward to seeing their hero first win the scoring race and then, in the coming playoffs, lead the team to one more Stanley Cup.

But then everything suddenly went wrong.

There had been an incident in a game played the previous Sunday in Boston. Richard, who had a wild temper, had been in a stick-swinging battle with the Bruins' Hal Laycoe, one of the toughest defencemen in the league. Laycoe had started the duel by cuffing Richard in the head with his stick and Richard, following the frontier code of the game, had struck back with his own stick.

The battle had left both men bloodied, the photograph of a seething Richard, black eyes burning and blood rolling down off his face, today one of the game's most familiar, if slightly sickening, memories. Richard, in his fury to get at Laycoe, had tried to go through the officials. When linesman Cliff Thompson grabbed hold of him, enabling Laycoe to continue his attack on the Montreal star, Richard had slugged Thompson in an effort to get free to continue with Laycoe.

There was no doubt Richard was in trouble, but no one in Montreal imagined how much.

On March 17, with the Detroit Red Wings in town to take on the hometown favourites, the NHL office, then situated in downtown Montreal, announced that Richard was being suspended for the remainder of the season, which amounted to only three games—but also the entire playoffs. It threw the city into an instant panic over Richard's scoring title and, of course, the chances of regaining the Stanley Cup from Detroit, which had taken it away from the Canadiens the year before.

Richard's suspension had been handed down by NHL president Clarence Campbell, a famous lawyer and patrician leader of the Quebec establishment. Tall, slim, pale, very anglophone, rich, and connected, the older Campbell was a sharp and unmistakable contrast to the younger, darker, thicker Richard, hero of the francophone working class. It was well known that the two didn't like each other. Earlier in the season, according to *Montreal Gazette* sportswriter Red Fisher, whose first assignment covering the Canadiens took place that very night, Richard had allowed his name to stand on a ghosted column in one of the French newspapers in which he referred to Campbell as a "dictator." It was the considered opinion of most Montrealers, especially at this pivotal moment.

"Clarence Campbell was trying to crush a little French-Canadian with wings," Roch Carrier wrote in *Our Life with the Rocket: The Maurice Richard Story*.

> That's what people are saying. Anger is rumbling in the province of Quebec like the water held captive in the rivers by the winter ice.... From everywhere, insults are flying towards Clarence Campbell. Everyone has his own story of indignity to tell.... They mention a cousin who used to work for somebody like Clarence Campbell....
>
> Maurice Richard has never accepted humiliation. Humiliating the Rocket means humiliating the entire people. This time we won't bow our heads....

The police knew the situation was explosive. Montreal mayor Jean Drapeau pleaded with Campbell not to take his usual seat among the fans at that night's game. Campbell, a stern man who'd served as Canada's prosecution lawyer at the Nuremberg Trials, said he had no fear and fully intended to take his ususal seat. He arrived late, the first period already on, but the crowd was watching for him. Detroit was up 2–0 and the Canadiens seemed lost without their leader.

The crowd erupted as Campbell made his way in and sat down, pretending not to notice. They booed. Men yelled out threats. Someone threw an egg. Then a tomato. Then more eggs and tomatoes. Campbell sat there stoically, not even blinking. At the end of the period, a smiling man walked toward Campbell with his hand outstretched. Campbell instinctively reached for it and the man brought his hand up and slapped Campbell hard across the face. Another man spun the first man around and smashed his fist into his face.

The Richard Riot was on.

A tear gas bomb exploded in the arena, sending yellow smoke into the air and fans screaming and streaming for the exits. Someone yelled *"Fire!"* More panic.

Officials ordered the building cleared and decided the game would have to be forfeited to the Red Wings, but no one else was thinking hockey any more. The crowd flowed like hot lava out into the streets surrounding the Forum, only to be joined by thousands of others who were already outside protesting Campbell's decision. Some carried home-made placards, one reading *"Injustice au Canada français."*

Someone fired a shot through one of the Forum windows.

Several men gathered around a car, rocked it, and then turned it completely upside down. They went on to do the same to a police car. Others began overturning more vehicles as the seething rioters moved down Ste-Catherine Street, breaking windows, looting stores, and setting cars on fire. The rioting continued for most of the night. Vehicles were destroyed, storefronts ruined, windows shattered—but miraculously no one was killed. Police arrested more than forty rioters, four of them mere youngsters, and the following day a badly shaken Richard went before the news microphones and pleaded for calm.

Campbell refused to lift the suspension. Richard's teammate Bernard

"Boom Boom" Geoffrion—Howie Morenz's son-in-law—would use those final three days to slip past Richard in the scoring race by a single point. Geoffrion, not Richard, would be awarded the Art Ross Trophy—a triumph that became a burden Geoffrion would carry the remainder of his life as the man who had denied the Rocket the one championship, scoring, that his name was most often associated with. In the Stanley Cup playoffs that followed, Montreal won its first round against the Bruins, but without Richard in the lineup it lost in the final, once again, to the despised Red Wings.

And yet in other, more significant ways, the province of the Montreal Canadiens didn't lose at all.

The anger continued to simmer after that St. Patrick's Day of 1955 and the province of Quebec would change in the days and weeks and months that followed. Something had happened that night in the Forum that had nothing to do with hockey, nothing to do with suspensions. It was a revolution, at first noisy, then quiet, but a revolution all the same.

Twenty years after that pivotal night, Toronto playwright Rick Salutin was writing a commissioned play on the famous hockey team. A genuine fan of the game and a renowned observer of Canadian culture, Salutin was trying to come to grips with the hold this team and its stars had on a people who, even if they didn't know it then, considered themselves a nation. Salutin spoke to players, to fans, to sportswriters, to academics, to people sitting in bars around the province. In one encounter in Quebec City he watched the game on television and asked the woman having a drink next to him, "How come?" How come the fans were so frenetic, so involved? How come it meant so much?

Her answer said it all: "The Canadiens—they're us. Every winter they go south and in the spring they come home conquerors."

Red Fisher had said much the same thing to Salutin—that when you're up against the seemingly impossible, the too powerful, you may not win the real battles against the perceived rulers, but you can win elsewhere, in another forum. For Quebeckers, it was on the ice.

Four decades after the Richard Riot, the Rocket told Jack Todd of the *Montreal Gazette* that he believed it wasn't only Campbell who wished to see him punished, but other owners as well. That could mean only, Todd presumed, Conn Smythe of the Toronto Maple Leafs. Both Smythe and Campbell were military men, proud soldiers who, like many of their anglophone ilk, harboured a deep resentment toward Quebeckers for failing to embrace conscription in the Second World War.

It had long been said in certain quarters that Richard's legendary fifty-goals-in-fifty-games feat during the 1944–45 season was suspect in that Richard had stayed to play rather than sign up to fight. He was, went the whispers, competing in a watered-down league, given the number of good hockey players who'd temporarily left their teams for their country. Richard had attempted to enlist, apparently, but his numerous early hockey injuries—he was once thought too frail for the professional game—meant he couldn't get past the physical.

No matter; he hadn't enlisted and was French Canadian. For some, that alone was enough to condemn him.

The Richard Riot stands today as a significant benchmark in the evolution of Quebec. Some writers even compared his treatment by the Anglo authorities to that of Louis Riel, who had been hanged seventy years earlier. Richard had taken on authority, authority had tried to break him, and the fans themselves had rebelled against the establishment. No matter that the whole thing had started with a stick-swinging incident. No matter, even, that Richard himself felt that a suspension was his due—though not one that would include the playoffs.

The point was that the people had risen up, and that Rocket Richard had led them, and from this point on the sleepy Quebec world of parish priests and Premier Maurice Duplessis was awakened and on the way to massive social and political change.

Rocket Richard can hardly take credit for all this. He even campaigned for Duplessis, though he didn't consider himself political. It took the death of Duplessis and a few more years for the Quiet Revolution to begin. But Richard had, even if inadvertently, served as a flashpoint for a very different sort of resistance. French-Canadian players were routinely called "frogs" on the ice by other players. Officials deemed tripping and cross-checking worthy of penalties while racial insults went unpunished.

The bigotry was so widespread it was even considered acceptable in certain parts of Canadian society. Toronto Maple Leafs owner Conn Smythe had once opened a Montreal speech with "Ladies and gentlemen—and Frenchmen," as if the vast majority of Quebeckers were a simplistic, insignificant people apart. What Rocket Richard was doing for his fellow Quebeckers, even if metaphorically, was standing up against the schoolyard bully.

"Richard, at least, could retaliate," *Gazette* political analyst Don Macpherson wrote a half century after the riot.

Most French Canadians could only seethe in silence at the indignities to which they were subjected by English bosses and English shop clerks who would not speak their language and English business owners who put up signs in English only along Ste-Catherine St., all the way to the Forum.

When their champion scored against the English, he scored for them. And when he commanded respect from his English adversaries on the ice, with his fists or his stick, he was retaliating for them.

But when he did retaliate, not only to the verbal taunts but also to the physical fouls, it often seemed to them and to him that he was punished more severely than his English tormentors.

The riot certainly wasn't the only impetus—bitter strikes in the asbestos industry and by Radio-Canada producers had also pitted French workers against English bosses—but it stands as the most significant and easily recalled of the many steps toward a modern Quebec. A Liberal provincial government under Jean Lesage arrived in 1960, the Rocket's last year of hockey, and its first act was to nationalize the hydroelectric industry, which meant taking it from the hands of the English—*les maudits anglais*—and making Hydro-Québec the sole provider of power. A key minister in the Lesage government was a young former broadcaster, René Lévesque, who would later leave the Liberals and bring the sovereignty movement its first great victory when his Parti Québécois won the November 15, 1976, provincial election.

"In rather short order," Concordia University history professor Ronald Rudin has written, "the Quebec government was transformed into a powerful agent to advance the interests of its predominantly French-speaking population."

And, many believe, this transformation had its genesis in a hockey rink in another country, when a player with coal-black eyes took the first swing at authority.

"*Merci, Maurice.*

"*Merci bien.*

"*Merci ... merci ... merci ...*"

ON SEPTEMBER 28, 1972, I was on a bus headed for the very first assignment of what was to become my career. Red Fisher's first assignment—the Montreal–Detroit game that became the Richard Riot—had been far more glamorous. I was headed for a marina on Lake Simcoe to do a story for a Maclean-Hunter business magazine—still some months away from being rescued by my first real job offer, from Peter Newman at *Maclean's*. I had no car so took the bus up the milk run along Highway 11 heading north of Toronto. The bus stopped at a tiny store in a village so small it wasn't even on the map. Someone from the marina would drive up from the lake to pick me up. It was a hard day to do any kind of work, as it also marked the final game of the Canada–Soviet series of 1972. Esposito's impassioned speech had rallied his team, and his team's victories in Moscow had rallied the Canadian fans. This was the afternoon of Game 8, the deciding game.

While I waited for my ride I hoped to catch up on the game, and fortunately a small black-and-white television was on in one corner of the little store. I stood with the owners and one other customer and watched, breathless, as Foster Hewitt's familiar voice crackled all the way from Moscow.

"*Here's another shot! Right in front! They score! Henderson has scored for Canada! Henderson right in front of the net and the fans and the team are going wild! Henderson right in front of the Soviet goal with thirty-four seconds left in the game!*"

September 28, 1972. Final game, 19:26 of the third period. The precise moment all Canadians of a certain age know exactly where they were and what they were doing. That moment—Henderson's winning goal in the 1972 Hockey Summit—is to Canadians what the assassination of President Kennedy is to Americans of a certain age, what the end of the war was to Europeans of an earlier age.

It is our defining moment.

That magnificent image—Henderson leaping into the arms of his Team Canada linemates—has been the subject of books and documentaries and has been captured on stamps and commemorative coins, but for most Canadians all that's unnecessary. The goal is now part of our genetic code, just as the game itself has always been in our blood.

Twenty years after Henderson's magical goal, when the Citizens' Forum on Canada's Future was racing around the country, Keith Spicer and the other commissioners were astonished to find that ordinary Canadians placed a priority on two Canadian values—health care and hockey—that outstripped all other national passions. And lest anyone think that passion for a simple child's game has dwindled in recent years, more than ten million Canadians tuned in to watch the men's hockey team win Olympic gold in Salt Lake City in 2002 and more than six million watched the women's gold victory three days earlier.

Even those who cannot bear the game know how deeply hockey permeates the national conversation, from handy metaphors to water cooler chatter to heated discussions over which channel the television will be tuned to Saturday night.

Decades before the Citizens' Forum and the various Olympic victories, Bruce Hutchison was aware of the direct connection between the national game and the national culture. He would even say that the very "soul" of Canada could be found here by those who know how and where to look. A student of Canada would need to know about the laws of the land and the politicians who make those laws. It would be necessary to know about those who write the books and those who paint the pictures, but equally necessary to understanding the culture and strength of a country, he claimed, was to know its game: "… let the student not neglect hockey."

"Music is culture, business is culture, sport is culture," Roch Carrier once told me at, yes, a panel discussion on the importance of hockey to Canadian culture. "And if we neglect a huge element of our national fabric we make a mistake.

"When I was growing up, hockey was our 'politics.' We knew there was somebody in Ottawa and somebody in Quebec—but the people who *really* mattered to us were in hockey.

"Hockey, to me, is about life."

NO ONE REALLY KNOWS exactly how or where the game of hockey began. There are art historians who believe that shinny is being played in a 1565 painting by Pieter Bruegel, *Hunters in the Snow,* that hangs in Vienna's famous Kunsthistorisches Museum. I've seen it there myself— during, appropriately, an afternoon off from covering the 1996 World Hockey Championships—and saw enough to be convinced.

I am less taken by the claim that the game dates back to the third millennium B.C.E. in Mesopotamia. Apparently a tablet of the Epic of Gilgamesh makes mention of men using curved sticks to propel a wooden ring over the dirt. But as no official scoresheet survived, I prefer to reserve judgment.

There is evidence that a game quite like hockey was played as early as 1800 in what is now known as Canada. Writings by Thomas Chandler Haliburton, who taught at King's College School near Windsor, Nova Scotia, refer to the schoolboys of the early 1800s "hollerin' and whoopin' like mad with pleasure" as they skated on a frozen pond with sticks and a hard, round object.

The journals of Sir John Franklin say something about his men playing some sort of "hockey" game on a small lake in what is today the Northwest Territories. Kingston, Halifax, Windsor, and Montreal all claim to be the birthplace of the game.

Whatever. The first actual hockey game with stipulated rules—and, we presume, much bitching and moaning about them—was played on March 3, 1875, by McGill University students in Montreal. And we know, too, that the Stanley Cup was purchased in 1892 for the extraordinary sum of ten guineas by Governor General Lord Stanley and the following year offered up to the best hockey club in the land. Today that fifty-dollar investment is the best-known, most recognizable trophy in North American sports.

Hockey is, many believe, the perfect Canadian game in that its highest values—teamwork, resourcefulness, tenacity, humility, and triumph—are much how Canadians like to think of themselves on the world stage.

The Canadian game also has an amusing element of, well, socialism. The game has no James Naismith, the Canadian-born inventor of basketball, or even an Abner Doubleday, who's often credited, to great debate, as the inventor of baseball. If hockey is a creation of any one thing, it's the work of an entire country. In the 1950s we invented the game every single winter's day up on Dufferin Street on Reservoir Hill in Huntsville, and there are still plenty of eyewitnesses and participants around to verify this claim. And as the NHL proved during the 2005–06 season, the first season after professional hockey's year-long lockout, the game needs reinventing every once in a while.

The lore of early hockey is rich—"One-eyed" Frank McGee scoring fourteen goals one Stanley Cup match; the Dawson City Klondikers coming to Ottawa by dogsled, steamer, and train to challenge, and lose; "Cyclone" Taylor predicting and then scoring a goal by skating the length of the ice *backward*—yet the early game was played entirely differently: an extra forward called the "rover," players on for the entire sixty minutes, goaltenders penalized for going down....

What remains the same is the enthusiasm Canadians have for their game. So alive does it make them feel that, in many instances, hockey takes over their lives. It helps to be Canadian to understand what humorist Eric Nicol was getting at when he wrote, "For any God-fearing young Canadian, the ultimate reward is to be chosen for the NHL All-Star Game. If he later goes to Heaven, that is so much gravy."

The great heroes of this young country have almost invariably been hockey players, Morenz and Richard being only two among them. Richard's torch would be taken up by Gordie Howe, Jean Béliveau, Bobby Orr, Guy Lafleur, Wayne Gretzky, Mario Lemieux, Sidney Crosby—since, of course, the greatest player in the game should be not only Canadian but suitably humble, as the country demands of its heroes. Richard's reserve and Howie's shyness are, in fact, the real torch that is passed down, to Béliveau, to Orr, to Lafleur, to Gretzky, to Lemieux, to Crosby. All exhibit the outward Canadian personality; all burn inside with a flame that all Canadians believe, imagined or not, burns within them.

"Hockey is Canada's game," Ken Dryden and I wrote in *Home Game*. "It may also be Canada's national theatre.... It is a place where the monumental themes of Canadian life are played out—English and French, East and West, Canada and the U.S., Canada and the world, the timeless tensions of commerce and culture, our struggle to survive and civilize winter."

Toronto novelist Morley Callaghan once tried to underline the significance of the winter game to Canadians by calling it "our own national drama." Callaghan's contemporary, Montreal novelist Hugh MacLennan, attempted to explain the game to an American magazine audience by saying that hockey is the counterpart of the Canadian self-restraint. "To spectator and player alike, hockey gives the release that strong liquor gives a repressed man."

I would also dare suggest that hockey has a direct connection to the Canadian sense of humour. Not from anything comical that happens on the ice—though Phil Esposito's trip on a rose during the 1972 Summit Series was pretty fair slapstick—but for the attitude found in the dressing room. There, nothing is sacred and, in truth, nothing seems even praiseworthy. It's all about taking shots and bringing everyone, especially those who stand out, down to size. The star's only defence is self-deprecation or ironic bragging—the essence of so much of Canadian humour.

Only a fool would claim that Canada's national game is all smiles and chuckles, a sport without flaws. Those flaws would fill and have filled another book, and other books beyond that. There are sad tales of greed, as there are in all professional sports. There are horrific tales of abuse—physical, psychological, and sexual—as there are periodically, but still too often, in any structure where positions of power are held over powerless youth eager to please and succeed.

And, in hockey more than in any other team sport, there is the continuing issue of violence.

There's nothing new here. When Lawrence Scanlan was researching his book on hockey violence, *Grace Under Fire: The State of Our Sweet and Savage Game,* he found sportswriters in the 1890s complaining about the tripping and slashing—at a time when players had hardly any protection—as well as the players and fans abusing officials. There were early incidents of players dying after being clubbed by sticks, but despite legal charges and dire warnings nothing ever came of them.

Around the same time equivalent concerns were expressed about American college football. Tactics such as the flying wedge and gang tackles were leading to career-ending injuries and even deaths. Some colleges had already banned the sport, others were talking about it, and there were even those who believed football itself must be outlawed. It took presidential intervention to make things right. In 1905 President Theodore Roosevelt convened two conferences at the White House—at a time, incidentally, when war was threatening in Russia and the Far East—and basically told college presidents to clean up or else. The warning worked. Sweeping new rules were enacted, ensuring the survival of a game that would eventually transform itself into North America's most popular and profitable sport.

None of this weak-kneed backtracking for hockey.

Tex Rickard, who owned the New York Americans of the National Hockey League during the Depression years, used to hire ambulances to park outside Madison Square Garden to attract fans. Conn Smythe, owner of the Toronto Maple Leafs, bragged that "If you can't beat 'em in the alley you can't beat 'em on the ice." Owners believed the fisticuffs actually sold the game for them. As Smythe once responded in reference to yet another outcry against the violence, "If we don't put a stop to it, we'll have to start printing more tickets."

There were periodic attempts to clean up the game, but all failed. There were arrests and charges and dropped charges and even a few hours in jail cells, to no avail. There were royal commissions that recommended, futilely, a cleanup. In 1975, at a Queen's University symposium on the game, Clarence Campbell, still president of the NHL, pronounced that "Hockey is a game of violence. This will never change. What we do in the NHL is control the level of violence at an acceptable level. I'm not saying that we condone violence, but it's there. We set a level and control it at that point."

This will never change, Campbell believed. It can be argued he was right and remains right. Don Cherry, the most powerful public voice the game has, celebrates the fighters on national television, bemoans any new rules brought in to restrict the brawlers and, for years, sold an annual video compilation of the best fights and hits of the season.

"The aspect of violence has caused us grief," Brian O'Neill told a Montreal audience in 1993 when he stepped down as the league disciplinarian. "We can change our image. We can't do it via public relations. We have to do it on the ice." But the ice hasn't seen any change at all, two infamous examples being Boston Bruins defenceman Marty McSorley's clubbing of Vancouver Canucks forward Donald Brashear in February 2000 and Vancouver Canucks forward Todd Bertuzzi's hunting down and sucker-punching Colorado Avalanche forward Steve Moore in March 2004.

Ottawa-area writer Roy MacSkimming, a former editor who's written a biography on Gordie Howe, Rocket Richard's great Anglo rival, says it's naive for Canadians to pretend the game they so love is all about backyard rinks and fuzzy feelings. He cites the contrast between Henderson's famous winning goal during the 1972 series and the pivotal moment during that series when Canada's Bobby Clarke deliberately slashed and broke the ankle of the best of the Russian players, Valery Kharlamov. "Canada won that extraordinary series," says MacSkimming, "not only by one game and one goal ... [but] by another margin as well—one broken ankle."

He adds that "If you make a really concerted attempt to find out who you really are you will find some dark things. There's a shadow side to the collective psyche that comes out. If we're going to treat hockey as a Canadian paradigm, we're going to have to accept the bad with the good."

THE BEST THING that ever happened to professional hockey may have been the owners' lockout in 2004 that led to the loss of the 2004–05

NHL season. It was the first time the Stanley Cup hadn't been contested since the Swine Flu epidemic of 1919, when the death of Montreal Canadiens player "Bad" Joe Hall forced cancellation of the final series.

The lockout also imposed time for reflection. Salaries had increased at such a pace—the average was then US$1.7 million—that the madness had filtered down even into minor hockey circles. So anxious were parents for their hockey-playing children to reach for, and grasp, the golden ring that the absurdities were showing up virtually weekly. A father in Bathurst, New Brunswick, sued the provincial minor hockey association for $300,000, claiming his sixteen-year-old boy had suffered extreme psychological trauma when the league's Most Valuable Player award had been given to a rival. He also wanted the trophy taken from the winner and given to his son. In Mississauga, Ontario, a player's parents sued an opposing coach for $10,000, claiming he'd been heard talking about putting a bounty on their son's head after an on-ice incident. The players involved were all of nine years of age. And the madness wasn't confined to Canada: in Massachusetts a 270-pound trucker beat to death a 156-pound assistant coach in front of his peewee team because, believe it or not, the trucker thought the coach was running too "physical" a practice.

None of this made the slightest sense. Dave King, one of the game's best thinkers and a coach in both NHL and Olympic hockey, once produced research that showed exactly what the odds were for kids "making it," as their parents so fervently hoped. He took thirty thousand kids born in 1975, all of whom had, at ages five to eight, signed up for the Great Canadian Dream.

Of that original thirty thousand, twenty-two thousand were still playing at bantam age fourteen.

Of that twenty-two thousand, only 232 were drafted by junior clubs.

Of the 232, less than half, 105, played a single game or more in junior.

Of the 105 who got onto junior ice, 48 were drafted by NHL clubs and 2 others signed later as free agents, meaning 50 had a shot at the dream.

Of the 50, 38 were offered contracts they signed.

Twenty-two played at least one game in the NHL.

In 1989, when they were twenty-four years old and in their hockey prime, 11 were playing at some level in the NHL.

The odds, then, were approximately one in three thousand for children signing up in what has traditionally been professional hockey's most fertile training ground.

Something for hockey parents to consider.

Where the greatest reflection took place, however, was at the NHL itself. What began as a lockout over "economic certainty" soon evolved into a shutdown where Canadian fans loudly and clearly expressed their displeasure with the owners, with the players, and with the game. And so, once the owners and the players' association began working together to fix the economics of the game, they also began looking at the game itself.

For years critics had decried not only the fisticuffs but the second level of violence—the hooking and holding and slashing. Ken Dryden, a former goaltender and Hockey Hall of Famer, called for hockey to find its next "forward pass," a move that would revolutionize the game much as the introduction of the forward pass had back in December 1929.

An answer was found in, of all places, the rulebook. The powers that be simply decided to start calling the rules as they had long been written down, and in the 2005–06 season it seemed the game had been entirely reinvented, with speed and skill now rewarded instead of hooking and holding. None of this ended the fights, but it did dramatically reduce their number and all but put an end to the brawler role. Toughness was still admired, but toughness alone was happily rendered meaningless. You'd have to be able to play, too.

Instead of the post-lockout lack of interest so many had predicted, Canadian fans were delighted to see the game played on the ice as it had been played for years only in their imaginations. The very ones who'd told pollsters a year earlier that they couldn't care less about the professional game now seemed, at the drop of a puck, to care as much as they had in the glory days of Rocket Richard and Gordie Howe, Orr and Lafleur, Gretzky and Messier. American fans were slow to come back and, in some markets, didn't bother coming back at all.

That Canadians did rush back shows why Calgary poet Richard Harrison calls hockey "the national id."

CURIOUSLY, the game of hockey hasn't attracted nearly as much academic attention as might be expected of something so integral to the Canadian personality. Richard Gruneau, who teaches communications at Simon Fraser University, says that for decades Canadian intellectuals denied that something as basic as hockey could have a "cultural" facet. Gruneau, who co-wrote *Hockey Night in Canada: Sports, Identities, and Cultural Politics* with the University of Alberta's David Whitson, theorizes that perhaps "hockey's physicality has always seemed too far removed from the world of the mind."

Matters began to change slightly in the 1980s when, suddenly, serious—if largely ignored—novels with hockey themes were published. Hockey became substance for movies, for poetry, for songs—even, finally, for a certain dash of academia. "By the late 1980s," says Gruneau, "it was perfectly acceptable to write doctoral dissertations on Madonna, and, in this environment, academic writing on sport—even hockey—became more widely accepted in Canadian intellectual life."

In the years since, the game has sometimes seemed everywhere, and not just on the ice surface. Numerous television series—the most recent being CBC's *Hockey: A People's History*—have covered the game's roots to its economics to its many problems. Hardly a fall goes by without at least one hockey book on the bestseller lists; some, like Ken Dryden's *The Game* and Peter Gzowski's *The Game of Our Lives,* spending months at the very top. It's been the theme for hundreds of children's books. Even toques, of all things, became a must-have item following the Heritage Classic, where the old-timers wore them to ward off the cold and, in the NHL part of the event, Montreal Canadiens netminder Jose Theodore tucked one under his mask–helmet.

"Hockey," says Roch Carrier, former head of the National Library of Canada and himself a renowned hockey author, "is *life* in Canada."

And sometimes more than that, it seems. I am reminded of the great— and mysterious—Freddie "The Fog" Shero, who as coach of the

Philadelphia Flyers in their infamous "Broad Street Bullies" days once sought to fire up his players during playoffs by writing on the dressing room chalkboard: "*Hockey is where we live, where we can best meet and overcome pain and wrong and death. Life is just a place where we spend time between games.*" Canada is, after all, a country where, in any given hockey rink, more fans will know the words to Stompin' Tom Connors's "The Hockey Song" than to the national anthem.

It is a country so attuned to its national game that the Ford Motor Company can run a television spot in which car horns at a traffic jam honk out the theme music to the CBC's *Hockey Night in Canada*—with no explanation required.

It is a country where, for nearly three months each spring, playoff games that mean nothing to the rest of the world regularly bump *The National* news, with the latest score from Iraq and Afghanistan forced to wait until the scores are in from Ottawa and Edmonton.

It is a country where, in the lead-up to the 2002 Winter Olympic Games in Nagano, Japan, the organizers of the Team Canada entry could call a press conference—heavily attended and carried live across ten provinces and three territories—to announce that no decision had yet been made on who would serve as the team's *third* goaltender.

All this for a player who wouldn't even be *dressing* for the games.

Lester Pearson, appearing before a London audience in 1939, many years before he'd win the Nobel Peace Prize or become prime minister, told his baffled audience that hockey is not just a game to Canadians. "It is perhaps fitting," Pearson said, "that this fastest of all games has become almost as much of a national symbol as the maple leaf or the beaver. Most young Canadians, in fact, are born with skates on their feet rather than with silver spoons in their mouths."

Pearson was partly right. Hockey had certainly become a national symbol. The Stanley Cup was the ultimate sports icon. And yet the Grey Cup, the pinnacle of Canadian three-downs football, was always considered fundamental to Canadian unity. After all, except for a few ill-fated years of thoughtless expansion in the 1990s, the Grey Cup has been contested by Canadian teams, for the most part east versus west, with several of the teams community-owned to provide an added dash of passion.

Grey Cup weekend—often referred to as "The National Drunk"—is such a tradition that it attracts millions who haven't paid the slightest attention to the threadbare league the entire rest of the season. In 1962 the Diefenbaker government ordered both national television networks to carry it so that as many Canadians as possible might tune in. As Mordecai Richler once so delightfully wrote in a magazine piece, "Other, more brutalized nations were knit by civil wars or uprisings against tyrants, but Canada, our Canada, was held together by a pigskin."

But even so, football is not hockey. Canadian football, in fact, is more a cousin of American football—slight differences in downs, size of field, and number of players—whereas hockey is absolutely and entirely *Canadian*. And in far more ways than as a game played on frozen water.

The Canadian climate may have given hockey its first ice surfaces, but the makeup of the players and of its burgeoning fans—people of different cultures, different beliefs, more often separated by religion than brought together—was what ensured that the rink and not the church would become where community met, the home team where they kept the faith. That hockey often gets called "the true religion of Canada" is no accident.

The wall plaques that honour the great players of the game in the Hockey Hall of Fame in Toronto ring with the very history of Canadian settlement during the twentieth century: Schmidt, Dumart, Bauer, Delvecchio, Mahovlich, Mosienko, Esposito, Gretzky …

More and more new Canadians are arriving from parts of the world that consider ice a curiosity, if not a luxury, and who know absolutely nothing about this strange winter game until their children insist on signing up with the other kids in the neighbourhood. This new reality was happily realized in recent years when the Calgary Flames' Jarome Iginla— whose father came from Nigeria—became the first black player to win a National Hockey League scoring title.

As Dryden and I wrote in *Home Game,*

Hockey is part sport and recreation, part entertainment, part business, part community-builder, social connector, and fantasy maker. It is played in every province and territory and in every part of every province and territory in this country. Once a game for little boys, now little girls play hockey as well, and so do older men and women; so do the blind and the mentally and physically handicapped. And though its symmetry is far from perfect, hockey does far better than most in cutting across social division—young and old, rich and poor, urban and rural, French and English, able and disabled. It is this breadth, its reach into the past, that makes hockey such a vivid instrument to view Canadian life.

The game also transcends emotion. Love hockey with a passion or hate it with a passion, the game still dominates Canadian small talk at a level comparable only to the weather.

Consider the following: the most-treasured children's story in the land is Roch Carrier's *The Hockey Sweater;* the most-popular modern film in Quebec is *Les Boys* and its sequels, the ongoing tales of a local beer hockey league; and in Mordecai Richler's final novel, *Barney's Version,* the main character descends into Alzheimer's disease, his memory losing all but the crystal-clear recollections of games played by his beloved Montreal Canadiens.

Small wonder, then, that 115,000 in Montreal would wish to file past the coffin of a man who hadn't played a game in forty years, that 57,167 in Edmonton would want to sit in −20°C and watch a bunch of retired players play shinny in a makeshift rink so far away most fans couldn't even see the puck.

Small wonder, then, that when country star Shania Twain—as famous worldwide for her navel as for her songs—appears on stage in Canada with the upper half of her body draped in a bulky, totally non-form-fitting hockey jersey, Canadians will stand and cheer.

If you can understand that one, you're closer to understanding Canadians.

Six

The Canada of the Imagination

THE DARKEST EYES of the national game may have been closed forever that day in Montreal, but the brightest eyes in Canada never shut in Ottawa.

They're the clearest blue eyes in the National Gallery, and though they hang in the European section, they're every blink and tear Canadian. Yet they have nothing whatsoever to do with the likes of Lawren Harris or Emily Carr, Canadian artists whose self-portraits have stared out from the rooms devoted to Canadian art; nothing at all to do with Jean Paul Lemieux's famous portraits or Alex Colville's haunted studies.

They are the eyes of Henry Wentworth Monk—"Wenty" to family and friends—and what he saw, and foresaw, with those eyes should be the stuff of movies and books. But this is Canada, and perhaps he's fortunate to find space in the European section, his portrait more notable by the name of the artist, William Holman Hunt, than by the subject, poor Wenty of Mosquito Cove, not far upstream along the Ottawa River that flows so quietly past the National Gallery of Canada.

And yet, for those very few who know his curious story, Wenty was at one time a force. He was, in fact, the first person ever to use the term "United Nations" as he preached for the creation of an international tribunal that might bring some order to a chaotic world.

A devout Christian, he was first to call for a special land to be set aside for what would eventually become Israel.

He was also the first in this country to suggest that Canada might one day serve the world as a military peacekeeper and peacemaker—a role that has cost some 150 Canadian lives since the United Nations he foresaw began such missions in the 1950s. No other country has paid so large a price.

Monk had the ear of Czar Nicholas II, of Lord Salisbury, and of Horace Greeley of the powerful *New York Tribune*. And yet he couldn't even get in to see Prime Minister Sir John A. Macdonald. They laughed in his face in Canada, dismissed him as a "crank" and, soon after he died, forgot all about him.

"We tend to forget all our interesting characters," says Frederick McEvoy, who has written about Monk in *The Beaver* magazine and hopes one day to produce a full biography.

Monk was most certainly interesting. He was born on April 6, 1827, in a small settlement along the Ottawa River, a pretty cove on the Ontario side now known as Pinhey's Point. He was the sixth of what would eventually number ten children. A wealthy neighbour, apparently so taken with the strikingly intelligent stare of the child, offered to pay for a fine education once he was old enough to head off to boarding school. When the time came the neighbour wasn't nearly so well off, but he did have enough pull left to arrange for seven-year-old Wenty to sail for London. He entered Christ's Hospital School, an institution established by King Edward VI for the promising children of the destitute. Samuel Taylor Coleridge had been a student here, as had Charles Lamb, who later claimed that the school's rigid devotion to religion and starvation was what produced such pronounced oddity in so many of its graduates.

Wenty would prove no exception.

The little boy consumed and was consumed by the Bible. He believed that train travel, the rage of the times, had been prophesied in the Book of Isaiah—the "swift beasts" that were going to bring the believers to Jerusalem. Scholars, on the other hand, have always read that to mean "camels."

But that was only a small part of what Wenty found in his beloved black book. He predicted the telegraph, then only a few years off, but also saw the world connected by a vast and immediate communications network. He saw that one day there would be weapons of mass destruction. He was a modern Nostradamus in that he predicted, accurately as it turned out, Y2K, the bizarre millennium anxiety that was then still more than a century and a half away.

And he didn't even have a computer to back up.

Wenty had an epiphany one Good Friday when, during the collect, he opened his Bible at random and read: "Have mercy upon all Jews, Turks, infidels, and heretics, and so fetch them home, blessed Lord, to this flock, that they may be saved among the remnants of the true Israelites." From that moment on, he believed that world peace was attainable only if, first, a home for the Jews was established in Palestine.

At age fifteen this strange, bookish loner returned to Canada and was struck by culture shock. His father had hoped he'd take over the dismal little farm, but Wenty had no interest. He had a scholarship to divinity school, and was soon off again. But not for long. He quickly became convinced that the clergy were nothing more than "blind leaders of the blind." He decided to take up the farm offer after all.

In his slim 1947 book on Monk, *For the Time Is at Hand,* Richard S. Lambert writes that Wenty couldn't put down his Bible long enough to lift a plow or an axe and that the farm began failing. Wenty decided to give the farm to a brother, renounce materialism, and become a full-time prophet. He headed for Jerusalem to save the world.

It's a long and twisted story, the tale of Henry Wentworth Monk. He travelled by merchant freighter and met up with the soon-to-be-famous religious artist Hunt in Jerusalem. Hunt, who was also a bit strange, believed Monk had somehow modelled by telepathy for a portrait he'd painted of Christ years before the two met. They became fast friends and soon Monk began modelling in the flesh. The portrait that hangs in the National Gallery is but a small study of a much larger Hunt work.

Wenty put all his visions and prophecies into a book, but no Canadian publisher would touch it. He set out for London to prove them wrong but still ran into a lack of interest. When he finally did get a publisher to bite, he had the enormous misfortune of having his book on Bible interpretation published against Charles Darwin's *The Origin of the Species,* and Darwin, as they say in the trade, buried poor Wenty.

He returned to Canada, left for Washington to put a stop to the brewing Civil War—even got in to see Abraham Lincoln—but got nowhere with his grand peace scheme. So, it was off to Jerusalem and, frustrated once more, back by freighter to North America. The ship foundered and sank off Nantucket Island and Wenty, a strong swimmer from his childhood days along the Ottawa River, was the only survivor. He reached shore, was set upon by dogs, and then shot by a farmer who mistook him for a treed bear.

This is a true story.

By March 1865, still weak but recovered from his wounds, Wenty was finally back home. He suffered terrible headaches. He created disturbances in the street—verbally and sometimes physically attacking those who wouldn't listen to him. He was institutionalized at least once.

But he also made it back to London, where Hunt the artist stood by him and proclaimed his friend "a wild genius, a soul of spotless innocence." Others grew tired of him. Doors that were once open now closed. He headed, once again, back to Canada. This time he was home for good.

Wenty ended his days as a Parliament Hill eccentric, wandering the paths under an umbrella and straw hat, his long white beard and hair flowing behind him. He wrote pamphlets and, periodically, for the *Evening Citizen,* at one point informing his bewildered readers, "I am determined that it shall be through no fault, or neglect, on my part, if people shall refuse to take advantage of the 'great light' and understanding that has been imparted to me for their benefit."

He thought Prime Minister Macdonald should arrange for him to take a seat in the House of Commons. He lobbied for a senate appointment. But they were offering nothing. When the idea of a permanent international tribunal began to pick up steam there was some parliamentary debate that poor Monk, the originator of the idea of a United Nations, should be given his credit, but nothing was ever done.

Others, however, did not offer a cold shoulder. Czar Nicholas II of Russia responded to his letters, as did Lord Salisbury, former prime minister of Great Britain.

It seemed, for a brief shining moment, as if Wenty might finally find redemption when, in 1896, a small campaign was mounted to give him his due recognition. The *Montreal Star* even called him "the philosopher of the capital."

Unfortunately, Wenty died of blood poisoning that summer and was buried in an unmarked grave in Ottawa's Beechwood Cemetery.

CANADIANS, UNLIKE AMERICANS, have always had difficulty mythologizing their own past—we are, perhaps in true northern personality, actually quite adept at stripping the past and knocking down the ones who should stand out. As George Woodcock said, Canadians tend to distrust the heroes they could so easily celebrate. Louis Riel, who would surely be considered a democratic renegade and nation builder had he been American, was to a great many Canadians a madman and a traitor. Tom Thomson, the romantic painter whose work has so defined the Canadian landscape and who lost his life so mysteriously in the deep woods in 1917, was a drinker and a philanderer who either committed suicide or fell overboard when he drunkenly stood in his canoe to take a leak. Billy Bishop lied about his war exploits. Sir John A. Macdonald, the first prime minister and the man who, more than anyone else, put this mysterious entity called Canada together, was a drunk.

As Andrew Malcolm pointed out in that email from California, the United States will put Davy Crockett on a stamp while Canada will go with one celebrating antique furniture.

There may be no better example of Canadians turning their collective backs on the great than in whatever became of Will Barker.

Barker, a farm kid from Dauphin, Manitoba, won the Victoria Cross for what many argue was the greatest aerial dogfight of the First World War. On October 27, 1918, Barker was alone in his Sopwith Snipe over La Forêt de Mormal, France, when he was attacked, according to the official account, by sixty enemy aircraft.

So typically Canadian in his self-effacing humility, he always said it was only fifteen. But whether sixty-to-one or fifteen-to-one, what were his chances?

Barker evaded the initial attack, turned, and counterattacked, shooting down three enemy craft while taking fire himself. As the third plane went down, he passed out from devastating wounds to both legs and one arm. His plane plummeted, another enemy aircraft tailing him to make sure he was finished.

Somehow he came to in mid-air, turned on the fighter tailing him, and took that plane down, a fourth kill. But he could hold his plane in the air no longer and crashed within view of astonished British ground troops. The British soldiers had witnessed the battle, seen Barker's heroics, and now ran to where they expected the young RCAF flyer to have surely died. They were stunned to find him still alive, pulled him free of the wreck, and got him to safety.

Those four kills took Barker's list to fifty downed enemy aircraft. He returned to Canada as Lt. Col. William George Barker, VC, DSO, and with enough other medals to lay claim to being Canada's most honoured combatant—if he'd ever cared to do so. He never did.

But as British Air Chief Marshal Sir Philip Joubert wrote, "Of all the flyers of the two World Wars, none was greater than Barker." Billy Bishop, Canada's best-known flying ace, called Barker "the deadliest air fighter that ever lived."

Barker came home and settled in Ottawa, where he went into the aviation business with Bishop, who had also returned with the Victoria Cross. He married Bishop's wealthy cousin Jean Smith and had a miserable dozen years. The business failed; the marriage teetered; he suffered depression and terrible pain from his injuries. The teetotaller became a drinker.

It seemed life was taking a turn for the better early in 1930 when Fairchild hired him to help sell aircraft to the Canadian government. A test pilot had been sent to show off the plane at the Rockcliffe base airport, but the veteran fighter insisted on taking it up himself for a run. He lost it, and crashed near a concrete landing on the banks of the Ottawa River.

Some said Barker committed suicide. Some said he was showing off for the cute teenage daughter of another pilot. Some say he simply made a mistake with an unfamiliar machine.

They held Will Barker's funeral in Toronto, the cortège two miles long, with two thousand uniformed men, honour guards from four countries, and fifty thousand people lining the streets. As the coffin was carried into Mount Pleasant Cemetery, six biplanes swooped down, sprinkling thousands of rose petals over the crowd.

"His name," said Canadian forces commander Sir Arthur Currie, who had led the troops at the battle of Passchendaele, "will live forever in the annals of the country which he served so nobly."

Not quite, sir.

Barker's name didn't live even long enough to be etched on the crypt where he was laid to rest. His wife's snobbish family could never accept, and certainly could not glorify, the rough-hewn outsider from a prairie farm. The only mark on Barker's grave is the most common name imaginable: "Smith."

Many years later, when little Dauphin approached the government to place a small plaque in the town to commemorate his Manitoba birthplace, it was at first rejected.

Today, no one but the military historians remember the name that "will live forever in the annals of the country which he served so nobly." Barker's biographer, Wayne Ralph, thinks that perhaps he was too much the "warrior" for Canadian tastes.

Had Will Barker been born only a little farther south of Dauphin, just over the Minnesota border in, say, Humboldt, he might well have been the Audie Murphy of his day, the much-decorated war hero who became an even bigger hero on the silver screen. But Canadians today don't even know what Barker looked like.

"He was an international superstar," Ralph told me in an interview from White Rock, British Columbia. "Barker had all the traits of the great Hollywood heroes. He was disobedient, gregarious, flamboyant. He was a frontier kid, a classical figure in the American style of hero. Born in a log cabin, went on to fame and fortune, and died tragically at thirty-five.

"Now he's basically buried in anonymity. To me, it's the perfect metaphor for Canada, where we bury our past."

"NATIONS," Aldous Huxley claimed, "are to a large extent invented by their poets and novelists."

Huxley obviously knew nothing about Canada. This country was far more *failed* by its early recognized writers—bad poets, bitter immigrants, and outright frauds.

For the most part, the mirror held up by early writers wasn't for Canadians to stare into to see themselves but for British readers and, to a lesser extent, British theatre audiences to look into and imagine a country that often didn't exist. Such are the realities of the book business. There weren't enough readers in early Canada to bother writing for—so they wrote, instead, for the outside lecture circuit.

Early Canadian literature, then, is the literature of other countries. "The books that are made elsewhere," Father of Confederation Thomas D'Arcy McGee said not long before he was assassinated in 1867, "even in England, are not always best fitted for us, they do not always run on the same mental gauge, nor connect with our train of thought."

In many instances, a connection wasn't even sought. The train of thought—a more delicate phrase than "economic necessity"—that drove many early writers was British first, then American, where the markets lay for magazine serialization, books and, with luck, stage presentations.

The lecture circuit required persona as much as product, and so it's hardly surprising that so many of the early known Canadian writers weren't at all who they said they were. Grey Owl was no "full-blooded Red Indian," as he advertised, but a full-blooded Englishman named Archibald Belaney. Pauline Johnson, though half Mohawk, was not Princess Tekahionwake. Frederick Philip Grove was really Felix Paul Greve, the rich son of a merchant back in Hamburg, Germany. Ernest Thompson Seton, whose eyes were known to cross under the slightest stress, changed his name so many times he ended up telling people to forget all the previous incarnations and just call him "Black Wolf."

Grey Owl, to give Belaney due credit, at least wrote with some accu-racy, unlike Seton, who liked to give his animals names and emotions and reason. Belaney also genuinely loved the wild, of which he had no fear. Seton was almost as terrified of the deep bush as he was of those awful nocturnal emissions that haunted him and could be treated, he believed, only by sleeping on hard boards and splashing his private parts frequently with ice water.

I don't know how much Seton a young Northrop Frye bothered reading—he read everything, it seemed, so would certainly have studied some—but I do know that Frye eventually produced the seminal study on Canadian literature: *The Bush Garden: Essays on the Canadian Imagination.* He looked at a vast array of Canadian poetry and fiction and saw Canadian writing unique in that the question that preoccupies artists in the rest of the world—"Who am I?"—had been replaced in Canada with "Where is here?" and "How do I live here?"

Frye was, and remains, hugely celebrated for his insights on what became known as the "garrison mentality" of Canadian writing. It was a notion he came upon while studying the tragic poetry of his own mentor, E.J. Pratt, author of such epics as "The Titanic" and "Brebeuf and His Brethren." Frye claimed—and the claim was widely accepted—that the story of Canada was one of beleaguered settlers up against the impossible and endless wilderness.

He wrote that, in reading through Canadian literature, he'd been long struck by a tone of "deep terror in regard to nature." It occurred to me, upon first reading Frye, that if I crossed out the word "nature" every time he used it and inserted the word "city," his perception would apply perfectly to my parents. They were completely at home in the bush of Algonquin Park, where they both lived—mother as a child and young woman, father as a lifetime logger—for considerable amounts of their lives. They were terrified driving to Toronto. They worried more about traffic lights than wolves, more about big crowds than heading off into the bush.

And they were hardly alone.

"The line which marks off the frontier from the farmstead, the wilder-ness from the baseland, the hinterland from the metropolis," historian

W.L. Morton said many years back, "runs through every Canadian psyche." And, if I may add, it runs in both directions—as befits this contradictory country.

I began to wonder if it were possible that Frye had it wrong for a vast number of Canadians. For them, nature might be the comfort zone. For them, Frye's "deep regard" and "terror of the soul" would be reserved more for the world, for the different languages and different customs that lie beyond Canada.

Frye, after all, was the direct opposite of my parents and the vast majority of Canadians his age, few of whom would have wasted a moment of their lives worrying about the defining features of early Canadian literature. He was born in the city (Sherbrooke, Quebec), raised in the city (Moncton, New Brunswick), educated in cities (Toronto and Oxford), and taught for decades at the University of Toronto's Victoria College. How much contact, I began to wonder, could he possibly have had with Canada's nature?

According to his own journals, Frye didn't venture much into the countryside. He had terrible hay fever. He also had little inclination. He once wrote in his diary that the work the Lord had chosen for him was to sit happily and think beautiful thoughts, occasionally stopping to write them down.

Find me even a handful of fellow Canadians who could say the same.

In one of Frye's more compelling arguments for his widely accepted theory, he compared the immigrant landing at New York City to the early immigrant reaching Canada. The American-bound immigrant would find New York busy and bustling, the Statue of Liberty welcoming, the harbour safe and filled with promise. Canada, on the other hand,

> has, for all practical purposes, no Atlantic seaboard. The traveller from Europe edges into it like a tiny Jonah entering an inconceivably large whale, slipping past the Straits of Belle Isle into the Gulf of St. Lawrence, where five Canadian provinces surround him, for the most part invisible…. To enter the United States is a matter of

crossing an ocean; to enter Canada is a matter of being silently swallowed by an alien continent.

A brilliant metaphor—the mouth of the St. Lawrence opening up like the mouth of the biblical whale that swallowed Jonah—but, really, get a grip, professor.

The mouth of the St. Lawrence, to the early immigrant, would have felt far more like a safe warm womb than any hungry whale. The poor wretches would have somehow survived the often-terrifying two-month sail across the Atlantic, would have often seen parents, children, spouses die during the passage, and would have lived in filth and vomit and, often, human waste for weeks on end in cramped quarters.

Surely they would *cheer,* would they not, when they saw the green and welcoming banks of the St. Lawrence take them in?

Even that elitist whiner Susanna Moodie—who would later serve as one of Frye's primary examples of this terror—was ecstatic to enter the St. Lawrence when she sailed over on the *Anne* in the late summer of 1832. "Never," Moodie wrote in her day journal, "had I beheld so many striking objects blended into one mighty whole! Nature had lavished all her noblest features in producing that enchanting scene."

Moodie would be swallowed by her whale a bit later. Unable to recreate in Canada the genteel life she pined for back in Britain, she'd become the new country's sharpest early critic and denouncer.

"If," she wrote in *Roughing It in the Bush,* "these sketches should prove the means of deterring one family from sinking their property and shipwrecking all their hopes, by going to reside in the backwoods of Canada, I shall consider myself amply repaid for revealing the secrets of the prison-house and feel that I have not toiled and suffered in the wilderness in vain."

One conclusion to take from Frye's interpretations, even if a tad unfair, is that he spent far too much time sitting in his comfortable office staring at a map of the country and letting an exceptional imagination run away with him. Little did he realize that so many would happily follow.

Frye's enormous reach—and of course there is much to admire in this man and much to agree with—can be found in almost any discussion of Canadian literature. Margaret Atwood's *Survival* largely grows out of her old professor's thinking; Gaile McGregor's *The Wacousta Syndrome: Explorations in the Canadian Landscape* begins with John Richardson's 1832 Canadian novel *Wacousta* and uses its savagery and outside threats to agree with Frye and Atwood that "the Canadian experience is one of the unrelenting harshness of nature, and the characteristic Canadian response to turn inwards, back to the garrison."

Fine, that's part of it, I'll concede. But then she goes on to say that Americans "have generally viewed nature as a source of inspiration, natural wisdom, moral health, and so on. Canadian writers seemingly do not even like to look on the face of the wilderness."

Poppycock.

Perhaps the problem lies in the writers studied. We can safely presume that these academics scrutinized vast amounts of Canadian poetry, from E.J. Pratt to Bliss Carman to Earle Birney, as well as the fiction of Hugh MacLennan, Morley Callaghan, and Sheila Watson, and even those more "literary" nonfiction efforts of the Strickland sisters, Moodie, and Catharine Parr Traill. But many of the early explorers, who surely did not share this Fryean terror of nature, left behind journals. Though there was rarely much introspection, the writings were often wonderfully evocative of a landscape that inspired less fear than awe. The early immigrants to Canada, of course, were often unable to read, let alone write, yet it could be argued—though never proven—that they were quickly very much at ease in the very nature that was supposedly swallowing them up. Even those who were literate would have been so busy with clearing and wood-gathering and planting and harvesting and, yes, simply *surviving* that they might never have found the time to write the celebratory stories of nature they might have felt.

There is, alas, no way to include in the literature of a country the books that never get written.

Wayne Grady, a fine Ontario writer and translator, is another who's become wary of Frye's interpretation of Canada's pre-Centennial printed word. Grady has studied the journals of numerous explorers, and while he rues the fact that so few attempted to be poetic or introspective in their carefully noted observations, he's found ample evidence that appears to contradict Frye. "There is very little in the way of terror in the journals of David Thompson or Samuel Hearne," Grady writes in his introduction to *Treasures of the Place.* "What there is is a continuous sense of wonder at the vastness and the splendour of the Canadian wilderness."

A great deal has changed since 1971 when Frye published *The Bush Garden,* his collection of literary essays written over three decades. Those early explorers' sense of wonder is found increasingly in modern Canadian fiction. Not only that, but the Canadian "landscape" now covers even more ground, from the wilderness of the Far North to the inner city and, for that matter, the inner workings of the northern personality.

In the years since Frye's key pronouncements on Canadian literature, this country found its real literary voice in such writers as Atwood, Richler, Margaret Laurence, and Gabrielle Roy. An entire new generation emerged, including the likes of Jack Hodgins in British Columbia, Sid Marty in the Rocky Mountains, Guy Vanderhaeghe on the Prairies, Jane Urquhart in Ontario, David Adams Richards in New Brunswick, Wayne Johnson in Newfoundland…. And more are just beginning what are sure to be long and creative careers in fiction. Canada has moved from the silly world of Seton into the more rarified literary world of the Giller Prize, international recognition, and summer book festivals that seem as popular as lake regattas and family picnics.

But let Americans debate the greatest character of their literature— Natty Bumppo, Gatsby, Huck Finn, even Moby-Dick. The prime person-ality of Canadian writing has always been, and to a large extent remains, the land itself.

It's telling that, when Bruce Hutchison came to the end of his great book on Canada, he gave the final word to Captain George Vancouver, who was neither a poet nor a novelist.

The Canada of the imagination isn't quite as Aldous Huxley believed it to be for other nations. Here it was invented by its nonfiction writers—

from George Vancouver through Pierre Berton—as much as, if not more than, by its novelists and poets.

THAT SAID, Canada fared far better in its early fiction than it has in American fantasy. When Hollywood does Canada, the results can make Frye's wacky image of the frightening, open-mouthed Gulf of St. Lawrence seem practically scientific. The movie *Saskatchewan* featured extraordinary mountain vistas. The movie *Quebec* turned the 1837 Rebellion into a bunch of horny frontiersmen storming the fortress to get their filthy paws on the sexy heroine....

Long before film tax breaks, and long before Vancouver became a stand-in for virtually any American city you might name, Canada had a special relationship with Hollywood—though reality had nothing to do with it. Many of the great names of Hollywood had Canadian roots: Mack Sennett, Norma Shearer, even Sam Goldwyn, who passed through Nova Scotia as a child. Raymond Massey, brother of Vincent, Canada's first native-born governor general, would play the classic Abe Lincoln. Gladys Smith of Toronto would go on to become "America's Sweetheart" Mary Pickford. Cecilia Parker and Ann Rutherford, both Canadians, would later star with Mickey Rooney in the *Andy Hardy* series—and one day be proud recipients of special achievement awards for so wonderfully representing "the American way of life."

As for the Canadian way of life, Hollywood merely distorted it to suit the needs of whatever movie was being made. In *Hollywood's Canada,* Pierre Berton delights over one B movie scene in which a tycoon snatches his daughter away from his conniving wife and announces he's taking her "Far away in Canada—*safe from the evils of civilization.*" Hollywood films, Berton believed, had "given the world no real image of Canada at all, except that of a geographical absurdity—a vast, empty snow-swept land of mountains and pine trees." It was a country devoid of cities.

It must be said that Canadians themselves are often accessories to the fact here, in that this is an image we not only cling to but actively promote in tourism posters, brochures, and advertisements. And it's very much the image that Canadian Winter Olympians—with their

Hudson's Bay Company toques and mukluks—present to the world every four years.

Berton also charged Hollywood with imposing its idea of the Old West on the Canadian northwest without the slightest thought to reality. The western shot in Arizona with John Wayne riding hard was no different, psychologically, from the western shot in Alberta or Saskatchewan. The American clichés—war-painted Indians, covered wagons, lynchings, posses, standard cowboy and Native dress, and tin-starred sheriffs—"were moved across the border with scarcely a change in the plot except for the presence of the movie Mounties."

This, Berton argued, ran contrary to historical reality. Canada didn't have the same mythological frontier justice. Law in Canada didn't come from the grassroots but from above, and with rare exceptions it arrived ahead of the settlers, not racing behind them to catch up. The truth, Berton argued, was that shootings were extremely rare in the Canadian West. Canadians tended to solve their problems with talk and conciliation, Americans with might and victory. Canadians by and large had no sense of "frontier" that had to be tamed but rather a sense of "prairie" that would accept settlement.

Canada had no Frederick Jackson Turner to voice the quintessential frontier theory as he'd done for America in his famous 1893 address to the American Historical Society. So much of Hollywood's impression of the West comes out of the widespread acceptance of Turner's thesis, a genuinely held belief that the frontier had defined many of the characteristics of the American people, characteristics that would persist for as long as America itself. He found coarseness but also strength, practicality and resourcefulness, great energy, domineering individualism, a rigid sense of good and evil, and an infectious enthusiasm that came from freedom of choice. And the sheer existence of the frontier, Turner said, drew similar qualities out of the more effete East.

The province of Alberta, much of it settled by former Americans, comes closest to Turner's description, particularly in its can-do mentality of which he so greatly approved. Overall, however, the Canadian prairie—I hesitate to use the word "frontier" here—was marked by mutual assistance and as much faith in authority as in technology. If the six-gun was the symbol of the settling of the American West, the building bee would be the symbol for the Canadian West. One co-option, the other cooperation.

And if individualism is the most powerful attribute to arise from the American experience of pushing west, the Canadian equivalent would have to be medicare, in principle and practice its very converse.

The Greatest American might well be John Wayne, Hollywood hero and western movie star, or Ronald Reagan, actor and president. But the Greatest Canadian, according to a 2005 CBC poll, turns out to be a slim little bespectacled prairie preacher named Tommy Douglas, father of universal health care, patron saint of the social safety net.

Douglas stood first after more than 140,000 Canadians had voted, beating out, in order, Terry Fox, Pierre Trudeau, Sir Frederick Banting, David Suzuki, Lester Pearson, Don Cherry, Sir John A. Macdonald, Alexander Graham Bell, and Wayne Gretzky.

Shania Twain, Mr. Dressup, and wrestler Bret Hart all beat Sir Wilfrid Laurier, the prime minister who in 1904 predicted that "Canada will fill the twentieth century." So the poll can hardly be said to be highly scientific. Still, voters passed over hockey heroes like Rocket Richard and military heroes like Billy Bishop to select the little Baptist minister who went on to become premier of Saskatchewan and ultimately spread his medicare gospel to the entire nation.

A man who believed a country's greatness wasn't measured by its heroes, its great leaders, its military victories, or its size, wealth, or literature, but "by what it does for its unfortunates."

Seven

The Shrinking of the World

SIT OUT IN THE SUN on one of the benches that line the main street of Coutts, Alberta, and a Canadian can stare in wonder at the United States of America until the sun goes down.

There is, however, not the slightest sense that anyone living in Sweetgrass, Montana, is sitting on the other side of the fence looking back at Canada. No wonder Margaret Atwood once called this line "the world's longest undefended one-way mirror."

It was the end of October 2004, and *The Globe and Mail* had dispatched me to keep tight to the border while talking to Canadians about America and Americans about Canada. It had been a difficult three years, the September 11, 2001, terrorist attacks followed by a northern wave of sympathy and support for Canada's southern neighbours, the military initiative in Afghanistan a joint effort between the two countries, and then the two going their separate ways over what to do in Iraq.

On such a bright day, the Sweetgrass Hills are spectacular in the late autumn haze that lies just beyond the razor wire and the steel gates and the high-voltage lamps that separate Alberta's Highway 4 from Montana's Interstate 15. On the north side of the razor wire sits the village of Coutts, population 364, and on the south side the Montana village of Sweetgrass, population about 100. Coutts, as the border crossing is best known, is a main trucking corridor for live cattle—during those times when there isn't a mad cow scare—and a regular crossing for everything from lumber trucks to kids in search of a bar that will serve them and to sticker-plastered RVs taking prairie snowbirds south to Arizona and New Mexico and Texas for the winter.

It is said that a truck carrying goods crosses the U.S. border southbound every 2.5 seconds or so, some $1.3 billion in trade a day. A quarter of America's exports head north, but more than three-quarters of Canada's trade heads south, a figure that can only increase now that Canada has become America's main energy supplier. And with Canada holding more oil reserves than any other country in the world but Saudi Arabia—some say time will prove considerably *more* than Saudi Arabia—and with hydrogen, solar, and wind power not likely to replace fossil fuels and carbon any time soon, it won't matter how tight border security ultimately becomes.

The psychology of border towns is fascinating. In Sweetgrass, with its barking stray dog and tumbleweed, the people of Montana sense they've been pushed to extremes, as far north as they can go around here. Sweetgrass is rundown, depressed, marginalized by geography.

To those in sparkling Coutts, on the other hand, with its new lots already measured out and open for bidding, geography is what makes the place. They don't feel pushed to the extremes; they live at the centre. This is where the funnel feeding down into the United States narrows; this place *matters*. The streets are paved and lined with curbs and sidewalks and trim lawns. Coutts has a school, a ballpark, even community tennis courts. The town water tower has a happy face painted on it. There are good jobs here and, given the state of the post-9/11 world, surely more work to come.

The single advantage that goes to ugly little Sweetgrass is the actual border facility itself, two-thirds of which had to be built on the American side so that its border patrol officers wouldn't have to check their weapons on the way to the toilets.

The Canadian border guards have never been armed—a somewhat charming tradition that is quickly coming to an unfortunate end.

HOW THE BORDER CAME ABOUT is largely a story of lack of interest.

Canadians have always felt that Americans give precious little thought to this huge, empty country sitting in the top branches of North America. And many Americans would even agree. "Americans assume Canada to be bestowed as a right," former U.S. secretary of state Dean Acheson told Andrew Malcolm, "and accept this bounty, as they do air, without thought or appreciation."

Yet, except for the fur supply, Canada's two founding nations were never all that interested either. The King of France might have preferred Caribbean sugar islands to the cold, useless tract of land Champlain claimed, but the British weren't much different.

Back in 1960, Canadian historian W.L. Morton gave a series of lectures at the University of Wisconsin on Canada's historical value and importance to its only neighbour. Morton talked about the War of Independence and how, after such a gruelling and unsatisfactory experience, the British were simply looking for peace at whatever cost. Ben Franklin, speaking for the American side, proposed that Britain hand over virtually all its possessions on the continent, including Newfoundland and the territory belonging to the Hudson's Bay Company. Britain didn't even appear to get upset by the proposal, and "Canada" continued on only because George III was keen to give some refuge to the Loyalists and perhaps maintain some sort of what Morton called a "strategic check" on this new republic springing up in the former colonies. In a moment that would have forever changed the makeup of North America, negotiator John Jay of New York proposed that the U.S. border run along the 45th parallel all the way from Maine and the top of his state to the Pacific.

Had Jay won out, this day would have found me sitting somewhere in a field in the heart of Alberta, not on a park bench in a border town that wouldn't otherwise exist. Jay's suggestion would have given Canada a slice of Maine, a portion of Michigan, Wisconsin, Minnesota, Idaho, and Oregon, and most of North Dakota, Montana, and Washington. The United States would have ended up with that area along the north shore of the St. Lawrence and Lake Ontario to which so many Loyalists had fled—as well as what would one day become Toronto and Ontario's Golden Horseshoe all the way up to cottage country.

It's certainly something to think about. Had the 45th line won the day, there might not even *be* a Golden Horseshoe. In *The Canadian Identity*, Morton goes so far as to speculate that if this border had been accepted, "Canada" would have picked up so much fertile western land that, if settled and populated, it could have "spelled continental supremacy."

Had John Jay's proposal taken the day, Canada would now be to the United States what the United States is to Canada. And I might be sitting on this bench wondering why Americans have all this angst about who they are. *Why? Why? Why?*

There but for the stroke of a quill....

Britain, given the choice and eager to give some comfort to the Loyalists, went with the water lines of the upper St. Lawrence and the Great Lakes then out along the 49th parallel—the very line that separates Coutts from Sweetgrass—to the Pacific Ocean. And so, in choosing the higher ground, as it were, Britain destined Canada to be "the country of the northern economy."

In other words, diminished.

John Ralston Saul has called Britain and France Canada's "indifferent mothers." When key treaties were to be signed both had shown more interest in rum-producing islands than the fur-producing colony to the north. In *Reflections of a Siamese Twin* Saul offers a litany of British disinterest throughout history, from failing to back Canada on the inland fisheries in the 1870s to betraying it on the Alaska Panhandle in 1903. A commission had been struck to decide the Alaska/Canada dispute, but the recommendations it was leaning toward so outraged the Canadians on the panel that they pronounced them a "grotesque travesty of justice" and refused to sign.

The lone Brit on the panel, Lord Alverstone, would have the deciding vote. He went with the United States.

From then on, says Saul, Britain's only interest in Canada was to have it pick up a share of the military burden and financial debt brought on by the two World Wars. Once Canada demonstrated its independence during the Suez Crisis thanks to Lester Pearson's negotiations, Britain became rather dismissive of Canada as too soft, too "wet," and a bit of a whiner on the world stage.

As for the North American stage, once those boundaries had been set, proximity and relative size had their predictable impact. The United States of America was so large, so populated, so wealthy, so powerful, and so determined that little Canada, despite an even larger land mass, couldn't help being caught up in the whirlpool that was America in the nineteenth and twentieth centuries.

Early on, Stephen Leacock had noted "a sort of underlying fear that Canada is getting a little too close to the United States. It is the same sort of apprehension as is felt on a respectable family farm when the daughter of the family is going out too much with the hired hand. The idea is that you can't tell what might happen."

SITTING HERE catching a little autumn sun in Coutts, it's impossible not to be struck by the amount of trade heading south. No wonder Hugh MacLennan once suggested that Canada had become "a colony of a sort unknown to the history of Europe or Asia." It is a relationship that can be described only as unique.

Americans, however, seem blissfully unaware of the volume of traffic that passes through dozens of crossings like Coutts and Sweetgrass. Speaking to reporters before an upcoming conference on North American free trade in the spring of 2006, President George W. Bush talked about the impressive "half-billion" dollar annual trade between the two countries. He wasn't even close—the real figure is a half-*trillion* dollars.

The trucks seem to roll endlessly through the border crossing, the traffic heading south on this day several times heavier than the traffic heading north. There aren't many cars, the dollars far closer to par than they have been in years, cross-border shopping no longer the story it was in the 1980s, and the partiers staying home thanks to dropping drinking ages and changing liquor laws.

"It's changed a lot," says Kerv Thiessen, an easygoing, grinning Coutts councillor and businessman. Thiessen can recall a time when "there'd be fifteen hundred over there on a weekend—'cause Alberta had no booze on Sunday."

Thiessen is a great admirer of the American way of life. It appeals to his own cowboy instincts: a respect for the individual, an instinct to stand up for what you think is right and whatever you think is wrong. Canadians, he finds, keep too much to themselves, are too accommodating for their own good. "We have no guts in this country," he tells me as the sun heads for the Rockies. "No courage at all. We put up with all those regulations. It's crazy. A kid falls off his bike and the next thing you know everyone has to wear a helmet. I tell you we have no courage."

Thiessen respects Americans, works with them, sells to them, applauds their all-business attitude, but he doesn't think of himself as one. He is Canadian, even if sitting only a few yards—in his case, metres—from the globe's most powerful nation and dealing with that reality every single day of his life. "Americans are the best neighbours in the world," he says, "but that doesn't make them a relation or a friend."

The exact relationship has always been a puzzle. Robert Thompson, leader of the Social Credit Party, in the 1960s once informed the House of Commons that "The Americans are our best friends—whether we like it or not."

Those "best friends" are separated by a 5061-kilometre line that is still often referred to as the world's longest undefended border. It's only so in places these days, but they're sufficient in number to convince certain Americans that a special fence be erected to reduce the chances of Canadian-located or even Canadian-born terrorists slipping over to do damage.

In the days following 9/11 the CIA's former head of counterintelligence, Vincent Cannistraro, noted that CIA and FBI intelligence "appear to have tracked maybe five of these people to Canada." Senator Hillary Rodham Clinton suggested that Canada might be "a haven" for such terrorists. And much was made of a previous incident where a man at Port Angeles, Washington—a small border crossing not unlike the one at Coutts—tried to enter the United States carrying explosives he intended to use on Los Angeles International Airport. Canada was suddenly extremely suspect.

The popular myth among Americans that the 9/11 hijackers slipped over the border from Canada isn't likely to die any time soon, even though none had ever set foot here.

Ronald Reagan once called the border "a meeting place between great and true friends," and that pretty much describes how it was viewed right from Canada's birth in 1867 up until that unforgettable September morning.

In 1923, shortly before his untimely death, President Warren G. Harding dropped in on Vancouver at the end of a cruise to Alaska. He spoke to a large crowd gathered at Stanley Park—not far from the 49th parallel—and said that Canadians and Americans hardly need a border, for they "think the same thoughts ... live the same lives [and] cherish the same aspirations.

"No grim-faced fortifications mark our frontiers," he told the gathering, "no stealthy spies lurk in our tranquil border hamlets.... Only humble mileposts mark the inviolable boundary line."

Fifty thousand Canadians cheered his every word.

THE BORDER CROSSINGS are no longer "only humble mileposts." They grow tighter every day—the Canadians beginning to arm themselves, the Americans now demanding passports for anyone wishing to travel to the United States. "Good fences make good neighbors," Robert Frost's neighbour keeps telling him in "Mending Wall," but Frost, somewhat like Canada, is never quite convinced. Who says? he wants to know. Why?

... Before I built a wall I'd ask to know
What I was walling in or walling out,
And to whom I was like to give offence ...

And yet there are times when the "good neighbour" theory holds wonderfully true, no matter what the state of the fence that has grown from Harding's humble mileposts to the razor wire that runs between Coutts and Sweetgrass.

No American ally was more involved than Canada when the order came to shut down the airways after the second airliner had gone into the Twin

Towers. More than thirty thousand airline passengers found refuge and welcome in Canada—and yet it seemed to count for nothing. When the president took to the airwaves a few days later to thank those nations that had come to America's aid in its time of need, Canada wasn't even on the list.

Canadians poured out their sympathetic grief on Parliament Hill as they gathered for the first National Day of Mourning since 1967, when Governor General Georges Vanier had died in office. They came to listen to Prime Minister Jean Chrétien say, rather appropriately, "Words fail us." Eighty thousand came to lay floral tributes, release balloons, and sing both national anthems.

"You have a symbol before you," Chrétien told U.S. ambassador Paul Cellucci as a north wind rattled the lowered flag over the Peace Tower. "A people united in outrage, in grief, in compassion and resolve."

He quoted from Martin Luther King Jr., who once said that in difficult times it is not the words of the enemy that one tends to remember, but the silence of your friends. "There will be no silence from Canada," the prime minister said, his words echoing off the office buildings on the south side of Wellington Street. "Our friendship has no limit."

It seemed, at that point, as if it did not. Shortly after the horrific events of September 11, 2001, I travelled across both Canada and the United States to talk to everyday citizens about the effect of these stunning attacks on their lives. It was in some ways a stark reminder of the differences between the two countries—yet in other ways a reminder of the similarities.

When you travel you can't help noticing the endless disparities, even the most basic ones. Better roads in America; better coffee in Canada. No sidewalks in America; people walking everywhere in Canada. When I eat in Canada I think about appetizers and dessert; when I eat in America I stick to the main course—and even that's so large the server will offer to put what can't be finished in a Styrofoam suitcase so that I can work on it later in my hotel room.

In America they turn the homes of past presidents into shrines; in Canada they have to take up public collections to clean up the neglected graves of former prime ministers.

Talk radio in Canada is the CBC, which many in the country find too left for their liking. Talk radio in the United States is from the far right, National Public Radio the exception that proves the rule. What's particularly notable about American talk radio is the constant refrain about how insufferably *liberal* the media is. Evidently they don't listen to themselves—but that, of course, is an affliction on both sides of the border.

All that aside, I found ordinary people much the same. As angry in Arkansas as in Alberta. As terrified in Charlotte, N.C., as in Charlottetown, P.E.I. There were those in Canada insisting that this country should join the war on terrorism, and those who felt that everyone should duck and stay put—"safe from the evils of civilization."

But above all was a deep sense of being in this thing together, and nowhere was this more apparent than in the little Newfoundland town of Lewisporte. It was at this outport community along the rocky edge of Notre Dame Bay that 773 weary travellers ended up after the closing down of North American air space.

The airline passengers were sent here on yellow school buses from Gander, the once-great Newfoundland airport where transatlantic flights used to refuel and where, that unforgettable Tuesday, thirty-eight aircraft holding 6656 passengers and crew were ordered to land and stand by until authorities figured out what had happened in New York and Washington and Pennsylvania and decided when it would be safe again to take to the air.

They arrived in foul moods and often foul odour—the last planeload had been sitting on the ground thirty hours before being processed and sent off in the school buses—and were headed for a place they'd never heard of and where they didn't know if there'd be telephones to call home. Many didn't even speak English.

They stayed the better part of a week, put up in people's homes and whatever other space could be found. Hundreds slept on church pews. "Seven hundred and seventy-three," mayor Bill Hooper boasted, drawing out the number as if he were announcing the next hymn, "and not one complaint."

"Most of them didn't know where they were," Salvation Army major Lloyd George told me when I visited in the weeks following the attacks. "We had to get a map of North America and put it up on the wall and point out where Newfoundland was—and then where we are here.

"They had trouble believing what we were telling them. Someone would ask about a shower and we'd tell them just to head over to the house and take one, here's the directions. Well, they couldn't believe we'd just let them into our houses that way. Then they'd ask about a key and we'd say, 'You won't need a key, the door's always open—most of them don't even have locks.' The one thing they couldn't grasp about us was our trust."

The moment the mayor heard of the air shutdown he contacted the major and they set up a "war room" at the Sally Ann. They contacted the other churches and the various service groups and the major himself okayed every imaginable expense without the slightest thought of where the money, some $15,000 eventually, might come from in a town that has seen lumbering vanish and the fishery dwindle.

The little community put on skits and entertainment each night for the stranded passengers. They fed them partridgeberry jam on toast in the mornings. They held banquets in the evening. The local fishermen, with nothing better to do, took them out on the sea and showed them the harbour and the near islands. They organized hikes through the country-side. They held elaborate cod-kissing ceremonies to make the visitors "Honorary Newfies."

Some of the stories coming out of Lewisporte made it difficult to think there could be such gaps widening between Canadians and Americans. When one seventeen-year-old American girl broke down when she realized she couldn't possibly make it home now in time to attend her grandfather's funeral, the Lewisporte women running the community-centre kitchen came out, took the girl in their arms, and simply took turns holding her as she sobbed.

When the passengers were finally allowed to leave there were many more tears. Steve Kimberling, an American Airlines captain whose best friend was piloting the plane that had been hijacked into the Pentagon, bought Newfoundland T-shirts for the entire crew to wear home.

On Delta Flight 15 they partied all the way back to Atlanta. "It was like they had been on a cruise," one of the crew members emailed back to a new friend in Lewisporte. "Everybody knew everybody else by their name. They were swapping stories of their stay, impressing each other with who had the better time. It was mind-boggling. Our flight back to Atlanta looked like a party flight. We simply stayed out of their way...."

The email went on to tell the story of a business-class passenger asking, and receiving the quite unusual permission, to speak over the PA system. The passenger reminded all aboard what they'd just been through at the hands of complete strangers and suggested they work together to give something back to Lewisporte. The passenger, a medical doctor, suggested a trust fund be set up in the name of Delta 15. Nine months later, four-teen scholarships were given out to Lewisporte students.

"Why all of this?" the email continued. "Just because some people in faraway places were kind to some strangers, who happened to literally drop in on them."

"It just shows you," Major Lloyd George said after he'd shown me this remarkable email, "how much the world has shrunk. Fifty years ago, if something like this had happened, it would have seemed so far away—'That's in New York, that's not here'—but look at what email and cell phones and cable television have done to us.

"It happened in New York and it happened here almost instantly right after."

"LAST CALL for Canada."

The announcement came over the public address system at Disney's Epcot Center. I was hurrying—carefully side-stepping puddles from an overnight downpour—but wasn't exactly sure where I was going.

Much like Canada itself at this moment.

It happened to be the same February morning in early 2003 that Secretary of State Colin Powell's treasured reputation went up in smoke. It wasn't immediate, of course; in fact, his reputation might never have been brighter than at that very moment. Powell was in New York City, standing in front of photographs and maps as he methodically walked the United Nations Security Council through the necessity of moving quickly and decisively against Iraq and the weapons of mass destruction that President Saddam Hussein had undeniably assembled.

I'd been in Florida covering the tragedy of the Columbia space shuttle, which had blown up over Texas upon re-entry. It marked the second time in seventeen months that a massive wave of sympathy for Americans had swept through Canada. First September 11; now this. Twice in less than a year and a half. It all seemed too much, too unfair.

I'd driven to the Orlando area from Cape Canaveral, where the Kennedy Space Center was still in a state of shock in the days following the disaster. The telling story in Cape Canaveral had been the silence. So attuned had the population become to space missions that they'd learned to look up at the familiar sound of re-entry, the twin sonic booms that meant the big silver ship would come into view within moments. The locals of Cocoa Beach and Titusville and Cape Canaveral call this double explosion the "welcome home." Re-entry had been announced for 9:17 A.M., and seventy-five-year-old Charles Lee, whose astronaut son had been on four such missions, had been walking the beach when he realized his watch had passed 9:17 and there had been no sound. And silence, Charles Lee said matter-of-factly, meant "something had gone wrong."

Columbia had blown up over Texas as it came back into Earth's atmosphere. It was an American story first and foremost, but also an international one. Israel had lost an astronaut on the mission and one of the American astronauts was of Indian heritage. There were Canadian workers at the Space Center and Canadian astronauts training for future flights. Canada, of course, immediately offered condolences for the Columbia tragedy. But as for Iraq and weapons of mass destruction and whether or not Canada, so often an ally, would join in any action against Saddam Hussein, so far there had been only the same thing Charles Lee picked up on the beach that awful morning: a telling silence.

"Last call for Canada!"

It was an unusual moment to be a Canadian in America. Powell's multimedia presentation—designed to show how Iraq had deceived the naive United Nations arms inspectors—was a tour de force. *USA Today* had compared his use of photographs and maps and pointers and argument—"... *photos that I am about to show you are sometimes hard for the average person to interpret ...*"—to that of Adlai Stevenson back in 1962, when the United Nations ambassador had convinced the council that the Soviets were behind a massive buildup of nuclear missiles in Cuba.

Even perennial American dove Senator Edward Kennedy had been swayed. The Doubting Thomases, at that moment, had been seemingly routed by Powell's calm voice and convincing evidence—"*The truck you also see is a signature item. It's a decontamination vehicle in case something goes wrong.*" British prime minister Tony Blair, who was already onside, was suddenly an American darling. The French and German doubters were being pilloried. If anyone happened to think of Canada, unlikely as that might be, it was only to puzzle over where it stood.

"*Final call for Canada!*"

THERE HAD BEEN a disengagement in Canada over much of the previous decade, in terms of both world politics and national affairs. There had been flare-ups—the most dramatic being a second failed referendum on Quebec sovereignty in 1995—but for the most part people seemed rather disengaged. The endless constitutional debate had taken its toll. Ordinary Canadians were burned out.

History has already recorded that the sky did not fall the day after Meech Lake died, nor did it fall—again as widely predicted by much of the establishment—the day after Meech's replacement, the Charlottetown Accord, was turned down by referendum on October 26, 1992. The report of the Citizens' Forum on Canada's Future was quickly shelved and forgotten. The people simply turned their backs on constitutional talk, most of them hoping never again would they have to squirm while the politicians played with the strings of this Confederation cat's cradle.

There was the usual doom and gloom. Constitutional expert Eugene Forsey had earlier warned that if Ottawa continued to hand off powers at such a pace it would eventually turn itself into a Cheshire cat—"with nothing left but the smile." Yet the Bumblebee Nation carried on, defying almost everyone with any manner of opinion on its survival. The economy, so dismal at the time of Meech, rebounded magnificently. The deficit, if not the national debt, was wiped out and soon government "surpluses" became a virtual tradition. The oil industry boomed in the West and manufacturing was healthy in the East. People were too busy watching their house values rise to waste energy worrying about where they lived.

Perhaps it's only fitting for a country with water on three sides that things tend to come in waves in Canada. Meech and Charlottetown had pounded the shore and the 1995 Quebec referendum had threatened to turn into a tidal wave, but then relative calm, albeit with the usual ripples, had followed. That Meech had led to the rise of the Bloc in Quebec and reinforced the rise of Reform in the West only underlined the old theory, first voiced by Trudeau cabinet minister Jean Marchand, that Canada is more like five countries than one. Its face automatically includes at least one nose out of joint.

And yet, in surprising ways this increased regionalization turned to an advantage. Jean Chrétien came to office in 1993 with a clear majority and an opposition so regionalized and marginalized that he was able to return to a style of prime ministership not seen since the days of Mackenzie King, running the country more as a part-time hobby than anything else. As F.R. Scott wrote of King in his marvellous poem "W.L.M.K.," the secret of Canada's longest-sitting prime minister had been to "Do nothing by halves / Which can be done by quarters."

Chrétien wasn't Mackenzie King, but he did vow not to resurrect the issue of the Constitution. His government concentrated on jobs and the economy, as promised during the election campaign. And despite that one chilling scare in the fall of 1995, when Premier Jacques Parizeau and Lucien Bouchard came within a whisker of winning the Quebec sovereignty referendum, the country largely went back to sleep on those matters that turn the bumblebee on its back.

Canada, however, woke up that bright Tuesday morning in September 2001 to a world that had changed. The country quickly joined the NATO-led deployment against the Taliban forces in Afghanistan, but when talk of invading Saddam Hussein's Iraq followed, Canada balked. It became popular for politicians and Canadians to take the moral high ground, but closer to the truth was that Canada couldn't afford it. The military, once so proud, had been allowed to decline over the years of constitutional warring to a point where barely enough "might" was on hand to get to Afghanistan.

The Chrétien government had its UN ambassador, Paul Heinbecker, work hard behind the scenes to bring about a Security Council resolution that would have given UN weapons inspectors more time to determine whether Iraq really did possess the weapons of mass destruction that Powell had so convincingly argued it had. Five years later Heinbecker would tell me he was being quietly encouraged by both American and British UN officials who saw the planned invasion as "a catastrophe unfolding." As he so wistfully put it, "what we might have avoided."

Powell might not have won the day with the Security Council, but he certainly did with the American people and, backed up by Tony Blair, a U.S.-led coalition invaded Iraq. No weapons were found, of course, and the quick, definitive victory began turning into what, by the winter of 2006–07, was being regularly compared to the American fiasco in Vietnam a generation earlier. But early on in the military action no American sympathy was to be had for doubters either inside or outside its borders.

When Canada, like Germany, like France, raised initial questions about the advisability of the military action, what little glow was left on its friendship in the hours and days following the 9/11 attacks quickly dissipated. First there was the prime minister's communications adviser calling Bush a "moron" for his decision to take his "War on Terrorism" into Iraq when no clear link had been established between Saddam Hussein and Osama bin Laden and no firm evidence of Powell's feared weapons of mass destruction. A member of the Liberal caucus, Toronto MP Carolyn Parrish, was caught saying "Damn Americans—I hate those bastards!" and months later exacerbated the situation by gleefully stomping a George W. Bush doll on CBC's satirical show *This Hour Has 22 Minutes*.

Then it got nasty.

By the time President Bush came to Canada on an official state visit eleven days after the Parrish stomp, the media on both sides of the border were in full sniper mode. When Parrish—who'd been immediately booted out of the Liberal caucus and forced to sit as an Independent—appeared on CNN's *Wolf Blitzer Reports*, *Crossfire*'s rather precious bow tie, Tucker Carlson, suggested that "without the U.S., Canada is essentially Honduras—colder and a lot less interesting." Not particularly witty, but more than enough to get well under Canadians' thin skin.

The American media piled on. The country was ridiculed by Pat Buchanan as "Canuckistan." It was mocked as "limpid, flaccid" and as "third-rate," "a made-in-Taiwan version of the United States." The Fox Network's acerbic Bill O'Reilly was particularly vituperative, with a ridiculous disregard of reality—at one point characterizing *The Globe and Mail* as "a far-left newspaper." It had become the bilateral equivalent of "Your mother wears army boots."

The Canadian government even hired a polling firm, Millward Brown Goldfarb, to conduct a quick survey on what Americans were thinking of Canadians in the early months of the conflict. Not much, it turned out. They dismissed Canada's offer of $220 million toward the rebuilding of Iraq once victory was assured as "unimpressive."

There was also a growing American apprehension about Canada's stance on social issues. "Directions to Canada," said the headline over one *New York Times* feature, "Head North and Turn Left." The paper even quoted Canadian comedian Rick Mercer connecting the U.S. concern over Canada to the American attempt to find Saddam and his henchmen: "Between the pot smoking and the gay marriage, quite frankly it's a wonder there's not a giant deck of cards out there with all our faces on it."

No politician was as dramatically anti-American policy as Carolyn Parrish, but the Liberal government under both Chrétien and his brief successor, Paul Martin, grew increasingly testy. At one point Canada's ambassador to Washington, Frank McKenna, a former Liberal premier of New Brunswick, called the American government "dysfunctional."

On January 23, 2006, Canadians elected Stephen Harper prime minister with a minority government. Harper, a deeply conservative Westerner,

immediately launched a strategic effort to repair diplomatic relations—
including McKenna's swift replacement by former Conservative finance
minister Michael Wilson. Harper and Bush got along so famously that
Bush took to calling the rather stiff and formal Harper "Steve," much to
the delight of the Canadian media. U.S. secretary of state Condoleeza
Rice and new Canadian secretary of state for foreign affairs Peter MacKay
struck up such a quick friendship that the media filled with gossip about
possible romance.

What mattered much more was that the new Harper government set
out to rebuild the armed forces that had fallen into such sorry disrepair,
committing an additional $11 billion to new equipment and recruitment.
It also significantly increased Canada's Afghanistan commitment by estab-
lishing a base in Kandahar and taking over leadership of the International
Security Assistance Force. With casualties rising rapidly—more than forty
Canadian soldiers had been killed by the beginning of the year—the
notion that "flaccid" "Canuckistan" wasn't pulling its weight was a sad one
to embrace.

And yet it still held water in whatever parts of America were paying
attention.

"CANADA FILM starting now."

Beside the Epcot Center's Future World is Disney's World Showplace,
constructed back in 1982. Nine nations were involved in the original
launch—the United States, Canada, Mexico, France, Germany, Italy,
China, Japan, and the United Kingdom—with Morocco and Norway
added later. Some, like Mexico, had since updated their pavilions, but, for
reasons unknown, Canada had remained frozen in 1982.

The 1982 film *O Canada* still being shown at the Canadian pavilion
was technologically impressive—shot in 360-degree "Circle Vision" and
spread out over nine screens—but was sadly out of date with reality. The
faces no longer represented the near-cosmic shift in demographics that
had occurred since the year the Constitution was repatriated. The Royal
Canadian Mounted Police musical ride was featured, as were Niagara Falls
and the Rockies—both timeless—but the one brief shot of the country's

largest city, Toronto, didn't even include the SkyDome. Given that the World Series champions would be playing in the Dome a decade after the film was shot, even American viewers must have been struck by the omission.

O Canada depicts a country of the postcards, not of the history books. Geese take off, deer leap, caribou race, salmon run, skiers ski, hockey players knock pucks around until one scores. It seems a country where hardly anyone lives, where the vistas go on forever and the seasons come and go. The voiceover uses "eh?" more than once too often.

Had any Americans been searching the film for support in the upcoming invasion of Iraq, they would have found only military bands both smaller and less well outfitted than most American high school marching bands and a circle of period-costumed soldiers firing … muskets.

If this was Canada as Americans see their neighbour, heaven help Canadians. The pavilion itself has as its centrepiece a miniature CN hotel that looks to be a combined Château Frontenac, Château Laurier, and Banff Springs Hotel—all since 1982 bought out by the American-based Fairmont Hotels chain. Alongside the hotel are a miniature "Victoria Gardens" and a pile of false rocks intended to be the Rockies though they look rather more like Arizona or New Mexico. The young workers at the pavilion wear black-and-red lumberjack shirts reminiscent of the Canadian yokel parodies of Bob and Doug McKenzie familiar to American fans of *Second City TV*. The souvenir booth sells, as expected, hockey pucks, but also Davy Crockett coonskin caps—perhaps to remind Americans that Canada is still a place where we trap our own clothes.

You wouldn't expect American ignorance of all things Canada to surprise the young people who work there, but even they sometimes get caught off guard. "I know this is going to sound stupid to you," one American man asked in the days before I happened to drop in, "but *where's* Canada?" They thought at first he was joking. He wasn't.

"You know where the continental United States sits?" one of the lumberjack-shirted workers asked him.

"Yes."

"You know where Alaska is?"

"Yes."

"Well, all that green in between—that's Canada."

Green ... pink on the old school maps in the days of the British Empire, white on the weather maps, the country no more considered than a hallway whose occasional new paint job goes unnoticed. No wonder that when Toronto won that 1992 World Series—played in the SkyDome that doesn't exist at the Epcot Center—U.S. Marines headed out into Fulton County Stadium in Atlanta in a dignified procession featuring the Stars and Stripes held high on one pole, Canada's red maple leaf on the other—upside down.

Canadians, of course, were outraged.

And yet, characteristically, they were also delighted—as if knowing "right side up" on one's own flag translates into some greater worldliness, some undeniable superiority. Ridicule of America is a northern necessity of life, as Canadian as blueberry pie.

The modern master of the art is Newfoundland comedian Rick Mercer. Beginning with *This Hour Has 22 Minutes* and moving on to his own *Rick Mercer Report*, Mercer applied to America a variation of the old Newfie joke he himself would have been acutely familiar with. He would head down to the States posing as a journalist, complete with microphone and camera crew, and ask famous and not-at-all-famous Americans about matters Canadian.

The Canadian audience howled at the always-friendly, eager-to-please Americans earnestly responding to queries about Prime Minister Jean "Poutine," the hockey puck on the Canadian flag, Saskatchewan seal hunts, dogs finally being allowed as house pets, rhinoceros roaming the northern hinterland, and Canada finally catching up to the rest of the world by dumping its traditional twenty-hour clock in favour of the more universal twenty-four-hour version.

The show's producer told *The Christian Science Monitor* that the brilliance of the scheme lay in the fact that it "taps into an age-old inferiority complex." But surely it draws equally upon the superiority complex to which Canadians so readily and happily revert in the face of American ignorance. To *think* that a Columbia University professor would sign a petition demanding an end to the Canadian tradition of sending the elderly out onto ice floes to perish!

Doubtless it's funny. And yet an American network could just as plausibly have a reporter hit the streets of Canada asking people to name the capital of Wyoming or explain the electoral college. The only difference would lie in the audience numbers—Americans, lacking that deep-seated need to ridicule those ignorant of all things America, wouldn't bother tuning in.

Besides, they don't know how the electoral college works either.

PROXIMITY AND RELATIVE SIZE would argue that Canada has every right to be on permanent watch against its neighbour, but some Canadians might be surprised to know how deep that impulse runs. We were on guard, it might be said, from the moment Canada came into existence.

In the fall of 2006, when a letter written by Sir John A. Macdonald in the year of Confederation was auctioned off, its contents demonstrated that even the first prime minister had his concerns. "I sail in four days for Canada with the act uniting all British North America in my pocket," Macdonald wrote on April 9, 1867, to Henry Sumner Maine, an English legal expert. "A brilliant future would certainly await us were it not for those wretched Yankees who hunger & thirst for Naboth's field."

The reference was biblical, suggesting stolen birthright.

In 2004 Amy Von Heyking, who teaches education at the University of Alberta, produced a study of how America was perceived in seventy-five Canadian textbooks published throughout the twentieth century. From one end of the century to the other—with a brief reprieve in the lead-up to and duration of the Second World War—Von Heyking found an undeniable "sense of moral superiority," at first from the conservative elite and finally from the left education establishment.

Canadians, the professor found, "are quite self-righteous."

Where could such smugness originate? The French and British have long been accused of condescension, but ironically, America itself had a hand in it. Many of the Loyalists fleeing the American Revolution and its aftermath saw in Canada a second chance at preserving their values, a place where the class system they treasured would survive, at least for the short term. Their upbringing and high expectations, as well as the money many brought with them—soon to be augmented by compensation from the British government—allowed them to assume positions of political and economic influence in the remaining British colony.

Close to a hundred thousand Loyalists fled the emerging United States, approximately half ending up in what would soon become Canada. They brought with them deeply conservative values, a distrust of revolutionary ideas, and what historian Arthur Lower called a fierce "determination to live apart" from the United States of America.

Another point where the definition of Canadian as "not American" has some merit.

These ambitious new members of the privileged class looked down on the new Republic, particularly those who were so determined to dispel all notions of aristocracy and class. When historian Frank Underhill called Canadians the world's oldest and continuing anti-Americans, he must surely have been thinking of the Loyalists and all they set in motion.

Canada's critical superiority is also rooted in both founding nations, the French so endlessly criticized for arrogance and the English, according to Jeremy Paxman, "in the grip of a delusion that they belonged to a higher order of beings." In *The English,* Paxman backs up his argument by quoting poets from Milton—"Let not England forget her precedence of teaching nations how to live"—to Ogden Nash's little shot: "That to be an Englishman is to belong to the most exclusive club there is."

Yet the Loyalists were not, as is too easily presumed, pure English. They were a diverse group—and included the black slaves of the wealthy and a couple of thousand Native allies who'd fought for the Crown during the Revolutionary Wars. Nor were the English the only British group to have a profound impact on the changing face of Canada.

"Canadians," Ronald Bryden of the University of Toronto once said, "like to see themselves as the Scots of North America: canny, sober, frugal folk of superior education who by quietly terrible Calvinist virtue will inherit the twenty-first century." Scots ran the Hudson's Bay Company,

Scots built the railroads, Scots set up Canada's monopolistic banking system, and Scots were at the core of the early public service. The dominant Church may well have been Roman Catholic, but the dominant creed was, indeed, Calvinism.

Calvinism still persists in the Canadian psyche. It is found in those who say the national bird of Canada should be the grouse. It is found in the disinclination to cheer those who dare stick their heads above the fray. It is found almost daily in the newspapers—so many of them founded by Scots—when the annual stories appear slamming whatever cabinet minister has tallied up the most kilometres in government jets. No one ever seems to consider that these numbers suggest the hardest-working cabinet minister who makes the greatest effort to get about.

When Governor General Adrienne Clarkson was quickly admitted to hospital in the summer of 2005 and fitted with a heart pacemaker, more questions were asked about whether she received priority care under Canada's universal health care plan than about the actual state of her health. The symbolic head of state and commander-in-chief has a heart scare and Canadians want to know if she jumped the queue?

Similarly, when Stephen Harper showed up at his first Grey Cup match—the game that supposedly represents the very unity of Canada—the questions weren't about which team won, east or west, but about whether the leader of the Opposition, soon to become prime minister, took a freebie.

We can be self-righteous, but sometimes we're downright insufferable.

That Canadian self-righteousness has arisen over America's continuing debacle in Iraq, but never let it be thought that this departure in foreign policy is some aberration. The differences in opinion—and, to be fair, differences in opinion even within Canada—were far more vehement back in the 1960s, first over nuclear proliferation and then the war in Vietnam.

The political tension was even greater in those years than in recent times. Prime Minister John Diefenbaker had a massive falling out with President John Kennedy over the arming of NORAD weapons with nuclear warheads. Washington said Canada was obliged; Diefenbaker,

who had earlier agreed, now refused. So virulent was the American response to this rebuff that it's considered a major element in the downfall of Diefenbaker's Conservative government in 1963.

Following Diefenbaker, Lester Pearson's minority Liberals soon clashed as well, even though they were open to nuclear warheads on the BOMARC missiles. En route to an official visit to Washington in 1965, Pearson dropped into Philadelphia long enough to deliver a speech opposing the elevated bombing in Vietnam, earning for himself an angry dressing-down from President Lyndon Johnson. So great was Johnson's rage that he reportedly seized the Canadian prime minister by the lapels and all but lifted him off the ground, as he so often did clutching the ears of his pet beagles.

Beyond the political world the vitriol was often even stronger—and it, too, came from both sides of the spectrum. Conservative intellectual George Grant, a Loyalist descendant, launched a full-press attack on American values in his 1965 book *Lament for a Nation*. Grant would go on to claim that "the American Empire" was now a fact, not a theory, and that its goal was no less than the "ferocious demolition" of other cultures by American technological imperialism. And Canada, in Grant's eyes, was being bombarded every bit as much as Vietnam.

A much more liberal writer of those times, Farley Mowat, claimed in a 1967 essay in *Canadian Dimension* magazine that the United States

has now become the major threat to world peace and, by extension, to the survival of mankind. I am afraid that if there is a third world war—the United States will start it. I, personally, am not prepared to give any further credence to the protestations of the Government of the United States that it seeks peace in the world. I believe it seeks power—world power—and that it will use all means at its disposal, including the greatest and most destructive military machine the world has ever known, to achieve its unstated ends. Those who choose to adhere to Washington, on the principle that it is better to be on the side of the winner than the loser, are deluding themselves. It is the future which threatens us ... there will be only losers.

Few were as strident as Mowat. Bruce Hutchison was acutely aware of the differences between the two countries—he thought the Americans "far more of a nation"—but he was also a lifelong fan of the United States. He particularly deplored those periodic uprisings of Canadian nationalism that so easily devolved into knee-jerk anti-Americanism.

Hutchison never pretended the United States was perfect. It had made mistakes and would continue to make them. Yet, he believed, it had treated Canada better than any other power had treated a vulnerable neighbour. "If we had a choice," he asked, "what different people would we want beside us?"

Nearly four decades after Vietnam and with Iraq now the point of departure, my *Globe and Mail* colleague Rex Murphy rather nicely summed up the Canadian manner of keeping an eye on all matters American. "We are on a jealous watch up here," Murphy said. Canadians examine every interaction between their country and the U.S. with almost fanatical rigour "lest some portion of our statehood, our way of life and identity, be diminished, obscured or even obliterated."

And while the far Canadian left, he argued, fuels itself on contempt for everything from President George W. Bush to the exceptional reach of American pop culture, the far Canadian right—Murphy included the Conservative Party—fairly worships American capitalism and fuels its dreams on the heroes of American republicanism.

"In the middle," Murphy offered, "there is the sane appreciation of the Americans as neighbours and allies, and a reasonable admiration for their undeniable achievements and goodwill. This is coupled with a cautious recoil from the excesses of their sometimes unhinged and shameless culture, even as we mimic its more vapid splendours (witness *Canadian Idol* or the "Canadian" edition of *Entertainment Tonight*) or even export a few of that culture's grossest Canadian exponents: Céline Dion, Tom Green.

"Whatever the Americans do, and sometimes whatever they do not do, as it refers to us, is put to a scrutiny and analysis of rabbinical finesse. "They haunt us continually."

AND JUST MAYBE it's our calling to haunt them continually.

What if Canada is America's Jiminy Cricket? What if little Canada's proximity to such a domineering personality is considered a great opportunity? A Jiminy Cricket conscience that pops up on the giant's one shoulder just about every time a chip appears on the other.

Perhaps this giant, so sure in its aggression, sometimes has trouble knowing what's right and what's not, what's true and what's not. And there Canada sits, speaking up periodically in a small, squeaky voice.

What if Canada's role—whether or not America likes it, whether or not a great many Canadians care for it—is to serve as a frequent scolder of paths already taken and a sincere if somewhat annoying little reminder of alternative routes that could still be taken?

After all, Canadians have what author Douglas Coupland calls an "almost universal editorial-page need to make disapproving clucks." They cluck about all manner of things in conversation, their work, their neighbourhood, their community—but with particular zest about the behaviour and excesses of the United States of America.

Not all Americans, incidentally, see this as necessarily a bad thing. At a Washington conference hosted by the Woodrow Wilson Center's Canada Institute in late 2006, former U.S. undersecretary of commerce and international trade Grant Aldonas seemed to say he actually *missed* Canada's nagging and nattering.

Canada, Aldonas told the conference, had such an enviable reputation for cooperation, for honesty, for openness, that it held the United States to a higher standard—which could only be good for the U.S. When Canada is on its game, Aldonas said, it "always requires the United States to play the game at a higher level. And that has been missing, honestly, in our relationship." Unfortunately, he suggested, recent history had produced a "lack of an articulation of Canada's purpose, both in the world economy and in foreign affairs."

As another senior American bureaucrat asked my *Globe and Mail* colleague John Ibbitson at the same gathering: "Where has Canada *gone*?"

He wouldn't find much disagreement in some Ottawa circles, especially in foreign affairs. What the country desperately needs, says Paul

Heinbecker, Canada's former ambassador to the United Nations, is "a wake up call"; it has to do much more to carry its own weight in this world, from security to the environment. And once woken up, it can again speak up with authority.

And here, in one of nature's more curious symbiotic relationships, is where Canada's Jiminy Cricket volunteer work comes into play. While Canada's well-known inferiority complex makes it hypersensitive to all things American, its lesser-known superiority complex makes it incapable of keeping its mouth shut.

The squeaky voice off to the side? That's Canada.

Eight

Missing, Minor, Middling, or Moral World Power?

IT COULD HAVE been worse.

Flatulence might have been the image Canada presented to the world. And sexual confusion. And self-mutilation.

Mercifully, *The Economist* passed on the beaver back in September 2003 when it threw a moose in sunglasses on its cover and declared Canada a "cool" country with its act together.

In its feature story headlined "Canada's New Spirit," the influential British publication praised Canadian cities as "dynamic, successful," and brimming with new immigrants. It said that Canada was showing the rest of the world "a certain boldness in social matters" as it opened doors to same-sex marriage and the decriminalization of marijuana.

I could vouch for that myself. Earlier in the year, my editors had suggested I head across the country to "take the pulse" on the presumably "hot button" issue of same-sex marriage. I struck out, heading first into Alberta, where I'd been told resistance was highest. I went to gay bars and fundamentalist churches, dutifully reporting the responses, each one completely predictable. High in the Sushwap region of the B.C. Interior I met Don Bogstie, a big retired farmer who happily called himself a "redneck" but who told me he was "honoured" that the two women on the farm across the road had asked him to attend their wedding as a witness. He had only one condition—*"That I don't have to wear a tie!"* I knew at that instant that same-sex marriage was only a hot-button issue if I pushed it. I called the paper to explain this, and we agreed that I should come home and move on to another story.

According to *The Economist,* this impossibility called Canada, so often on the verge of certain collapse, deserved, at the least, a careful second look by a world that either took Canada for granted or never thought about it at all.

Exactly how the moose got to stand in for "Canada's New Spirit" is a bit of a mystery. Moose are hardly unique to this country—they can also be found in Alaska, the northeastern United States, Colorado's Rocky Mountains, Norway, Sweden, Finland, Siberia, even Mongolia. Perhaps only in Canada do they wear surfer sunglasses, though.

The beaver, on the other hand, is far more Canada. It might not be unique to the country, but its symbolism is one of a kind. It has by far the superior claim. The country was founded, after all, on the fur trade— beaver being synonymous with fur for centuries. A beaver was on the first stamp. A beaver is still on the Canadian nickel. The beaver is also the nation's official symbol, thanks to Tory MP Sean O'Sullivan's 1975 private member's bill, "An Act to provide for the recognition of the Beaver (*Castor canadensis*) as a symbol of the sovereignty of Canada."

There is, however, the enduring myth that male beavers will, under stress, bite off their own testicles. On the other hand, a great many male beavers have been found to possess a uterus. Further, a growing scientific argument holds that the beaver and its ponds are nature's biggest producers of greenhouse gases.

Flatulence, sexual confusion, and self-mutilation are hardly the message Canadians would like to see carried on the front cover of *The Economist.* Besides, the beaver is a rodent. Think of the fun Bill O'Reilly and Pat Buchanan and that silly young man in the bow tie would have with that. Luckily, *The Economist* went with the moose.

Canadians loved what the British publication had to say about them. Like small-town clergy, they worry far too much about what others think. "Canadians are so incredibly insecure," actor Donald Sutherland once said, "that somewhere in his psyche every single Canadian has a feeling that people in the United States have some kind of visceral, cultural and life experiences he does not have. If you're Canadian, you think about a person from the States as the brother who went to sea, caught the clap and made a million dollars in Costa Rica or Hong Kong."

They fret over what Americans say, what the British say, what the French say, and seem to fret even more when no one's saying anything at all. But if what's being said is somehow positive they'll clutch it to their breast as notice, at long last, of their great hidden talent.

Those were good months for the external mirror. After *The Economist* pronounced, the *Washington Post* chimed in, saying that Canada's open-minded attitudes toward such matters as legal pot and same-sex marriage were making the States look "fussy, Victorian and imperial." *The New Yorker* added that while it might be cold up north and while Canadians might have "a reputation for paralyzing dullness," they were also rather charmingly enlightened about certain matters. "Good old Canada," the magazine gushed. "It's the kind of country that makes you proud to be a North American."

Canadians, of course, had to deflect all the attention with their usual self-deprecation. "It's like we woke up," Rick Mercer told the *National Post,* "and suddenly we're a European country."

The country *The Economist* described wasn't perfect, of course. It was getting a "free ride" from the Americans in defence. It had a growing urban–rural split that should be of some concern. And taxes, of course, were too high. But Canada—dull old dependable Canada—had something new that was making it cool: that "certain boldness in social matters."

While the United States seemed to be growing ever more conservative, the magazine reported, Canada was becoming ever more tolerant. You want same-sex marriage? Fine, head for Canada. You think possession of marijuana for personal use should be decriminalized? Just follow the smoke. Canada, *The Economist* boldly declared, had become "an increasingly self-confident country."

Ha. Only months later, Eeyore Nation was back in full whine. Where this facile negativity comes from isn't precisely known. Northerners—

Finns, Scandinavians, Siberians—are renowned for their periodic black-
ness, and we have already discussed the enormous influence of the Scots
on Canada. As P.G. Wodehouse wrote in *Blandings Castle*, "It is never very
difficult to distinguish between a Scotsman with a grievance and a ray of
sunshine."

So foul was the sudden mood shift—largely brought on by a growing
scandal involving federal sponsorship money and the province of
Quebec—that *New York Times* correspondent Clifford Krause asked in a
feature story whether something had suddenly gone seriously wrong with
the country to which he'd been assigned or whether it was "just the
weather."

What first caught Krause's attention was a remarkably "down" piece by
an Albertan academic that somehow managed to tie the 2004 Olympic
stumble by world-champion hurdler Perdita Felicien to an overall
"national malaise." University of Calgary historian David Bercuson had
written in a *Calgary Herald* comment piece that "It's not the individual
performers whose shortcomings are on display for all the world to see. It
is the very spirit of the nation and the sickness that now has hold of it that
is at fault."

The notion that the world was actually watching all this and seeing
Canada as a land of shortcomings and failures fascinated Krause. It
seemed more than a stretch. And yet, as he talked to thinkers across the
country he found wide acceptance of the view that the place was in
decline and stumbling—bare months after *The Economist* had been
singing its praises to the world. One leading historian, University of
Toronto's Michael Bliss, told Krause he was "in almost total despair." "You
have a country," Bliss told the *Times*, "but what is it for and what is it
doing?"

"For these people," Krause wrote, "Canada is adrift at home and
wilting as a player on the world stage. It is dogged not only by uninspired
leaders but also by a lack of national purpose, stunted imagination, and
befuddled priorities, even as its economy prospers." All this was most
bewildering to Krause, an American who's made a special effort to
comprehend what it is that makes the country tick. He'd seen Canada as

a "sensible country" in its promotion of peace and social justice abroad, its enlightened tolerance at home, its history of grand projects and, when necessary, its grand effort to protect.

Those he spoke to, on the other hand, saw that greatness as a matter of the past and an embarrassment for the present. Peacekeepers were using equipment older than their officers. Politicians seemed to think greatness could be defined by how much money they spent on things like daycare. Education budgets were shrinking and professionals were continuing the "brain drain" south. Krause noted two tellingly titled recent bestsellers: Jack Granatstein's *Who Killed the Canadian Military?* and Andrew Cohen's *While Canada Slept: How We Lost Our Place in the World.*

So much for the cool moose.

Bliss was feeling particularly bleak around this time. The much-honoured historian was heading into retirement with an essay in the *Literary Review of Canada* asking "Has Canada Failed?" In Bliss's view, yes, pretty much so. National dreams had fizzled, the search for identity had gotten lost, Canadians didn't know where they stood on the fight against terrorism, and they had a convoluted government structure that didn't much work on any level.

Bliss was worried about where Canada was headed. There was economic uncertainty and political confusion. Canada might be "polycultural" but seemed increasingly incapable of finding a "sense of national 'self' or national interest in global affairs." In his opinion, Canada was beginning a "decline into global irrelevance" and becoming socially and politically impossible internally. "It is not," he concluded, "the country its founders hoped to create."

Krause found such thinking epidemic. Curious, he checked back through bestselling books of previous generations and discovered a pattern. George Grant's *Lament for a Nation* was a huge seller in the 1960s and is still studied. Other books, such as *Must Canada Fail?*, were also popular in their day. No surprise that when a people spend so much time examining their belly-button lint, they tend to look down. "Intellectual complaining about the state of the nation," Krause speculated, "seems to be as much a part of the Canadian tapestry as curling and maple syrup."

It's not just the intellectuals, though. Canadians complain bitterly about everything from the weather to the politicians they just voted into office. "Canada's one true national art form," Douglas Coupland wrote in *Souvenir of Canada 2,* "is the indignant letter to the editor."

Such obsessive complaining reached a certain level of absurdity when, in Michael Ignatieff's keynote address to the Liberals' March 2005 national convention, he told the gathering that Canada was coming apart at the seams. Its looming breakup, he warned, would be "unprecedented in the annals of political history." Less than a year later Ignatieff was a duly elected member of the House of Commons and, a few months after that, running for the leadership of that same Liberal Party and promising to lead a unified, confident Canada into a significant role in the world.

Clifford Krause's report on how miserable Canada had become was followed by the release of the "Happy Planet Index," a new international ranking from the U.K.-based New Economic Foundation. The happiest country in the world, it claimed, was the little Oceania island of Vanuatu, where some 200,000 blissful people live on a bare subsistence. Then came Colombia, Costa Rica, Dominica, and Panama. Unhappiest were Berundi, Swaziland, and Zimbabwe. Canada wasn't even within sight of the miserable bottom.

Canadians, according to the Happy Planet Index, are far happier than their neighbours, the United States of America.

Happy, but insecure. It was around this time that the Canadian Tourism Commission became convinced that the world does not quite see Canada as Canada really is. And so the commission set out to "rebrand" the country. After all, everyone else was doing it. Kentucky Fried Chicken was now KFC. Radio Shack was becoming The Source. The Reform Party had changed to Alliance and then to Conservative. A small cup of regular coffee had somehow evolved into a tall latte. Why not tweak Canada?

The commission decided to kiss off the old "mountains, Mounties and moose" motif. So what if *The Economist* had used the moose? That was strictly old school. "Our brand," it said, "had started to fade. People weren't sure what we were any more."

The CTC wanted Canada to move into the modern tourism age. If France, a little country that could be plopped virtually unnoticed into northern Ontario, could haul in 75 million visitors a year, why should Canada be happy with a paltry 17.5 million? We might not have vineyards or the Eiffel Tower, but there was 5 percent beer and the CN Tower, not to mention all that empty space for trekking around in. Canada, the commission determined, needed to compete with Australia and India as a place people headed for to have a great adventure. It even had a new slogan to offer up: "Canada. Keep Exploring."

There was little need to advertise that, at least in this country. Hockey and lacrosse might be the national games, but searching has forever been the national sport.

Around the same time, Darrell Bricker and John Wright released their book *What Canadians Think*. The two Ipsos-Reid pollsters came to the conclusion that Canadians, in the early going of the twenty-first century, were a people under enormous stress. Four of ten felt life to be beyond their control. Four of ten felt life was changing too quickly. Three of four claimed they had less free time today than at the turn of the new century. Four of five believed in God but only one in five went to church. Traffic was unbearable. They didn't like other people reading over their shoulder and they particularly did not like men who crack their knuckles.

Nearly three of every four Canadian women would take a good night's sleep over a good night of sex. More Canadians had faith in angels than in those they elected to office. One in five believed aliens from outer space visit Canada regularly, one in ten thought mandatory name tags an excellent idea, and nearly four of every five couldn't deliver the first line of the national anthem—even though that first line happens to be the name of the song.

Not too long after, the Dominion Institute released another poll on the attitudes of Canadians, who expressed grave concern about the effects of global warming and seemed certain that Canada would one day be attacked by terrorists. Toward the end of the survey the pollster had thrown in the old question concerning the eternal glass. Half empty? Or half full? Fourteen percent said half-empty. More than eight of ten said half-full.

No real surprise there, but perhaps it's necessary to be Canadian to understand this. I am, at one and the same time, a constant griper and a constant optimist. I find as much pleasure in poking at the country as I do in celebrating it. Canadians may be the only creatures on earth capable of shaking their heads and nodding them at the same time.

"We're doomed!" Bob Hunter shouted out during a 2004 talk at the University of Toronto. "It's obvious that the world is going to hell in a hand basket—*as usual.*" Hunter, the Canadian co-founder of the Greenpeace movement, thought of himself as a "committed apocalypicist." He'd spent a lifetime warning about fisheries and the environment. He'd stared down a Russian harpooner. He'd made a stand on a dangerous ice floe to prevent a sealing ship from getting to its prey. He'd argued that global warming is merely "the slow-motion equivalent of nuclear war."

And yet, in that familiar, wonderfully mystifying Canadian inconsistency, Hunter said he could sense change coming, sense people changing, sense the world finally coming to its senses. He saw hope for everything, *The Globe and Mail*'s John Barber reported, including the future prospects of the endangered three-toed salamander.

Hunter was sixty-three years old and dying of cancer—he would not last six more months—and wanted one final opportunity to speak to the people of his country about the world they're about to enter.

"The only thing incurable about me," he said, laughing, "is my optimism."

ONE SUCH OPTIMIST is *The Globe and Mail*'s John Ibbitson, who recently published a book called *The Polite Revolution: Perfecting the Canadian Dream.* In a seeming slap to the perpetual doomsayer's face, he begins with the surprising proposal that "Some time, not too long ago, while no one was watching, Canada became the world's most successful country."

Canada works, Ibbitson argues. In part through luck. In part by intent. Whatever the reason, Canada stands at the forefront of a fundamental world change. Ibbitson further contends that it is Canadian history, with its very lack of dramatic confrontation, that makes this country unique.

The legendary politeness of Canadians, he says, is hardly accidental; how else could the French and English have continued after 1759? Such polite accommodation would go on to serve Canada wonderfully well as wave after wave of immigrants—first from France, Britain, and Western Europe, then from Eastern Europe, southern Europe, Asia, Latin America, the Caribbean, the Middle East, and Africa—transformed it from a country of two founding nations into one nation in search of not only its identity but a purpose higher than collecting taxes and issuing passports.

Ibbitson—who comes from Gravenhurst, a small town in central Ontario that has also produced Dr. Norman Bethune—sees a Canada that is increasingly colour blind and that will one day be colour blended. His Canada is urban and ethnically diverse. It has a strong economy and good social programs. Of course it has its problems, from homelessness to unresolved Aboriginal issues. All the same, it works. Canada, he would argue, is already the world's first truly cosmopolitan society.

"The result," Ibbitson said in a subsequent *Globe* article, "is nothing less than a miracle." Canadian cities no longer have one dominant race. They're places where equality rules, where gay and lesbian couples and communities are accepted, where people even remember to pick up their dog poop in the parks. "This has never happened anywhere before," he writes. "Not like this."

There's nothing accidental about politeness in this country, he believes. Others might joke about it, but politeness stands at the very core of how this country operates. "It is the means by which we accommodate each other. It is the secret recipe for a nation of different cultures, languages and customs, whose citizens all get along." Politeness is what led to the social revolution that modern Canada exhibits to the world, a country that he sees as "young, creative, polyglot, open-minded, forward-looking, fabulous."

It might sound Pollyanna-ish, but Ibbitson is hardly naive. He knows the Aboriginal situation is untenable. He deplores the deterioration of

Canada's military over the past decades. He thinks foreign policy has become "a mess"—not the least of which is the strained relationship between the two countries that claim Sweetgrass on one side of the razor wire and Coutts on the other.

Where he separates himself dramatically from those who similarly worry about Canada's place in the world is his view of the past. He advises Canadians to adopt "ahistoricism"—to move away from the past of Riel, Conscription, Quebec sovereignty, the national energy program, and Meech Lake and embrace instead the country as seen through the eyes of those recently arrived. History, Ibbitson claims, dwells too much on misery, brings up little but old resentments. Besides, the flood of immigrants in recent years has "swamped" the history of the old Canada. Stop picking at old wounds, he advises. Stop acting superior. "The Canada we are becoming is moving past all that. The emerging Canada is nothing less than the engine of the social revolution that, if the world is lucky, will one day overtake the world. You don't think it's possible? Think of where we were a century ago. Think of what we have been through since then, what we have endured, what we have learned.

"Think of what Canada could be in a century, if we don't screw up."

THERE DID SEEM, throughout 2006, to be a new and welcome sense of Canada and the world. Although he didn't win the Liberal leadership race—coming second to Stéphane Dion and then serving as deputy leader of the party—Michael Ignatieff did manage to get Canadians discussing the country's international role, even if it was to disagree with his various stands.

"We are a country of peacemakers," he said during the leadership campaign, "especially because we are also a country of immigrants, many of whom have come to Canada to escape the horrors of conflict. As a nation of immigrants from the zones of war, we have a special vocation for peace, and it is by exercising this vocation that we maintain our unity as a people. We have a voice that other countries listen to. Let us use it."

It was also a year in which Conrad Black experienced a change of heart toward the country of his birth. When he so dramatically renounced his citizenship in 2001 to take up a British title, Black dismissed Canada as an underachieving socialist nation perhaps suitable to "someone just arrived from Haiti or Romania." Then, as his own world began shrinking in an American courtroom, Lord Black of Crossharbour returned to live in Toronto and prepared to challenge the fraud and racketeering charges laid by a federal court in Chicago. He also began his fight to be reinstated as a Canadian citizen.

Speaking to the Empire Club in downtown Toronto, Black followed the traditional toast to the Queen with a stunning reversal of his former position. He seemed remarkably changed by the "deliverance" of a Stephen Harper Conservative Canada. Canada, Black had now decided, "is geopolitically among the ten most important" members of the United Nations, largely due to its immense natural resources and future prospects. "Canada today," he said to the surprised crowd,

> is more important to the world than Italy. Europe is dyspeptic with collapsed birth rates and stagnant economies. The U.S. has little disposable influence in the world, the UN is a shambles, NATO is in disarray, and the coalition of the willing is a fraud. We must not let it go to our heads, but Canada is one of the world's great powers. We shouldn't let that go to our heads. We should get used to it.

But get used to *what?* Just what sort of power, if any power at all, does Canada represent in this first gulp of the twenty-first century? It had come out of the First World War—after the Canadian military's proud performance at Vimy Ridge and at Passchendaele—sure it was a country of substance. It emerged from the Second World War considered a "middle power" by itself and others, a sense enhanced by Lester Pearson's Nobel Prize–winning efforts in helping solve the Suez Crisis of 1956. If Canada wasn't moving up or down the shifting list of military nations, it was seen as standing in the middle in a conciliatory and helpful way.

Its reputation as an international peacekeeper evolved under Pearson and has persisted to this day, even though the Nobel winner, on accepting his prize, rather accurately predicted that the only time the world might actually come together as one to confront an issue would be when "We discover Martian space ships hovering over Earth's air space." He also said, again with great prescience, that "The grim fact, however, is that we prepare for war like precocious giants and for peace like retarded pygmies."

Pearson's legacy has been largely forgotten in today's Canada. Schoolchildren seem little, if at all, aware of his story. He is not generally held to sit among the great prime ministers of the country, even though it was during his years in Ottawa that such matters as medicare and the Canada Pension Plan came into being. He gave the country its flag and bilingualism. As Richard Gwyn once wrote, "We are all Pearson's children."

And yet, a poll published when he left office in 1972 found that more than two-thirds of Canadians couldn't name a single one of his government's accomplishments. Thirty-five years later, a similar poll might find that two-thirds of Canadians couldn't even name him as a prime minister.

I often drive from Ottawa to Toronto and back again. And because my brain tends to grind to a complete halt on the faster, four-lane highways, I usually skip the recommended route and head along Highway 7 before dropping down to the dreaded and dreary 401 heading into Toronto. About two hours along this rolling two-lane highway that cuts through the eastern Ontario bog and the southern reaches of the Canadian Shield, I pass by the turnoff to Tweed—where some people claim Elvis Presley is alive and well—and head east toward Madoc, passing by the Lester B. Pearson Peace Park.

Sometimes I stop. But even on a beautiful day with the smell of pine in the air it's a sad stop, for the Lester B. Pearson Peace Park is one of the saddest sights in all of Canada. It was built in 1967, one of the thousands of Centennial Projects undertaken in Pearson's last full year in office. The park is rundown; a bent gate blocks passage. A hand-painted "No Trespassing" sign hangs from the fence and another sign warns that "violators will be prosecuted."

As a symbol for world peace, it is an embarrassment.

Pearson deserves better. He was, after all, the original Canadian Jiminy Cricket for the United States. When he died, *New York Times* columnist

James Reston hailed him as "a wise and joyful man who told us the truth about America and made us swallow it."

Pearson had a world vision. It came naturally from his long tenure in External Affairs before moving into elected politics. And he knew that, no matter how much wishful thinking might have it otherwise, there was no real separation between Canada's relations with the United States and with the rest of the world. They were one and the same. Always had been. Always would be. And it would be Canada's relationship with the super-power next door, more than anything else, that would define its role in the world at large.

When Pierre Trudeau took over the leadership of the Liberal Party from Pearson in 1968, he tried to bring some needed realism to Canada's self-concept of its place in international relations. "Personally," he said, "I tend to discount the weight of our influence in the world ... I think we should be modest, much more modest than we were, I think, in the postwar years when we were an important power because of the disruption of Europe and so on. But right now we're going back to our normal size ... we must use modesty.... We shouldn't be trying to run the world."

It was a message he repeated in March of that year when he spoke to the National Press Club in Washington, D.C. "I hope," he told the gathered media, "that we Canadians do not have an exaggerated view of our own importance." A year later, in Calgary, he said "You only review your foreign policy once in a generation."

A generation has now passed. The clock calling for review has been ringing its alarm for some time. Allan Gotlieb, Canadian ambassador to Washington during the Mulroney–Reagan years, once accused Canada of demonstrating "bipolar behaviour" in its foreign policy. The country makes visionary pronouncements, endlessly moralizes, and boasts of superior values, but doesn't really do or accomplish much. Gotlieb said Canadians seemed forever "attracted to opposite poles in our thinking about the world." I think he has it right—especially in how Canadians deal with the United States in times of international stress. Then the bipolar behaviour can be extreme.

Back in June 1973, with anti-American sentiment running at least as high over Richard Nixon and the fallout from Vietnam and Watergate as it does today over George W. Bush and Iraq, Canadian radio broadcaster Gordon Sinclair took to the airwaves with a stirring defence of American generosity and abilities. "Our neighbours have faced it alone," Sinclair ranted in a broadcast that became a bestselling recording in the United States, "and I am one Canadian who is damned tired of hearing them kicked around. They will come out of this thing with their flag high. And when they do, they are entitled to thumb their nose at the lands that are gloating over their present troubles."

Now, more than three decades later, such dramatic polarization largely remains. When CBC radio described the rapport between new Prime Minister Harper and President Bush as "the strongest relationship in history," *Canadian Dimension* magazine editorialized, "Really? What about Hitler and Quisling?"

There are those determined nationalists, like publisher and author Mel Hurtig and Maude Barlow, founder of the Council of Canadians, who would have Canada put as much distance as possible between it and whatever lies on the other side of that border, especially the American missile defence plan. Hurtig and Barlow are highly intelligent and deeply concerned about the loss of Canadian resources, particularly future pressures on Canadian water. "Now," says Hurtig, author of *The Vanishing Country,* "not later, now is the time for Canadians to take a firm stand to ensure the survival of the country that we love as a proud, independent, sovereign country." Barlow's concern, as expressed in *Too Close for Comfort,* is that the Canadian government, falling increasingly under control of big business, is committed to a "North American fortress with a common economic, security resource and regulatory and foreign policy framework."

At the moment, Jiminy Cricket has so many different voices to choose from that it's hard to determine the smarter thing to say and the better route to take. There are those who would have Canada involve itself only in United Nations peacekeeping, which began in 1948 and took more permanent form in the Pearson and Trudeau years. And there are those who say the day of the Pearsonian peacekeeper has fallen sadly out of synch with the realities of today's world.

Historian Jack Granatstein is one who believes a rethink is long past due. In *Who Killed the Canadian Military?* he details the long decline of what was once a proud and powerful force, lamenting that such obvious military weakness undermines any reputation Canada might naively think it enjoys around the world. Power, to Granatstein—as well as to a great many others—is hard power. Soft power, whatever it means, is to invite ridicule.

"Does this weakness serve Canada's national interest?" he asks. "Do we even know what these interests are? Or, is Canada such a do-gooder that its interests are irrelevant and the projection abroad of its values—multiculturalism, good governance, respect for human rights and so on—are all that matters?"

Instead, Granatstein says, Canada should pursue its own vigorous policy based on the country's own security and independence, and then, with a rebuilt military, work when required with allies on the more global issues. "Keeping the Yanks happy, or at least not angry," he concludes, "must be a national interest."

ONE FRESH VOICE heard in recent years has been that of Jennifer Welsh, a professor of international relations at Oxford University. She's also a Canadian of Métis heritage who left Saskatchewan with a Rhodes Scholarship and has since become a recognized expert in world affairs.

Welsh has decidedly different views on Canada. She has suggested, for example, that the country could do without provinces—something federal politicians and big-city mayors might rejoice over. But it's in her writings on Canada's place in the world that she's generated the most interest. Her 2004 book, *At Home in the World: Canada's Global Vision for the 21st Century,* is a slim, readable study of where Canada has been and where it should be going. She's been accused of being anti-American in pushing Canada to go its own way, but she counters that "Canadians are, by and large, confident about the unique experiment they have built north of the 49th parallel, and that they no longer have to be anti-American to be Canadian."

For Welsh there is much to admire in United States society, much to be wary of. The message of her book, she has said, "is that we should get to know the U.S. more, not less." More know thy friend than know thine enemy.

Welsh contends that Canada needs to expand its view of North America to include Mexico, and not only the fact of the country itself but the increasing electoral power and influence of Hispanics in the United States. In the name of simple realism she rejects the old canard that America is Canada's best friend. Friendship must be a two-way street, she says, not just one road heading south. She quotes an official in the Clinton administration who dismissed Canada as "the boy who gets all spiffed up to win the heart of his dreamboat, while she doesn't even know he exists."

Given such an attitude, it's hardly surprising that a game show on the MTV network features a category called "Dead or Canadian?" A name is given out and contestants try to guess which description fits. And when *South Park* became a movie in 1999 it featured a song that went on to garner an Oscar nomination. The song? "Blame Canada":

It seems like everything went wrong
Since Canada came along.

Yet in some ways Welsh is much like Pierre Trudeau, who was often perceived as anti-American—his relationships with Nixon and Reagan were not good—but who knew there were times when the mouse had to get into bed with the elephant. She is, for example, in favour of Canada joining the United States in continental space defence. "It is hardly fair to rely on the Americans to protect the West," Trudeau said in an open letter to Canadians near the end of his long run as prime minister, "but refuse to lend them a hand when the going gets rough. In that sense, the anti-Americanism of some Canadians verges on hypocrisy. They're eager to take refuge under the American umbrella, but don't want to help hold it." Welsh would certainly agree.

Her provocative work did not pass unnoticed in Canadian government circles. Paul Martin, having promised a full review of defence and foreign policy, brought her in as a consultant on that review process before his government fell. Welsh herself was once a Young Liberal but has had no involvement with the party or Canadian politics over the last twenty years. Whether her thinking influences current or future Canadian governments is uncertain.

Yet it should not be lost. The Canada Jennifer Welsh sees is a newly confident, multicultural country that could have a significant effect on the world merely by serving as its "model citizen." Not quite a "moral superpower," but something perhaps within the realm of possibility. When he was prime minister, Paul Martin said several times that Canada should "set the standards by which other nations judge themselves." A pretty high order—likely beyond the reach of even the purest—but something to shoot for.

Canada, Welsh believes, could demonstrate tolerance to the world; it could show how a pluralistic society not only gets along but cares for those citizens having trouble coming along. Such values, she feels, would create a "magnetic effect," inducing other countries to draw closer to the Canadian model—and closer, by definition, to Canada itself. Canada would gain influence far beyond its economic or military clout.

In other words, as the large signs inside the bookstores read: "The World Needs More Canada."

Welsh counters those who would dismiss her thinking as naive, her hopes more aligned with Pollyanna than reality. "Model citizens," she says, "pull their weight." Model citizens can use sanctions and even force when necessary. Even, if absolutely necessary, without the approval of the United Nations. She wants Canada to have "the best small army in the world," even if it never fights or wins a battle on its own. "This," she told the *Ottawa Citizen*, "is where I think there's a relationship between soft and hard power. Hard power isn't just military. But hard power gets at the idea that you can only achieve what you want to achieve through a bit of stick."

It's an interesting point. General Roméo Dallaire served as commander of the United Nations Military Assistance in Rwanda during the 1994 genocide that saw as many as 800,000 Tutsis and moderate Hutus massacred. He was there as witness, serving as dutiful conscience to the world, but he had no power to intervene or prevent. He had no stick to stop what was happening before his own eyes.

Welsh's vision for the country of her birth comes from a deep sense of what has worked in Canada and continues to work as the New Canada evolves. "Canadians, it has been said, take other countries as they find them, rather than seeking to transform them," she writes. "Nor are we confident in our ability to transform other societies overnight. Perhaps this derives from our own very gradual experiences of building Canada— a process that we see as ongoing. Part of the magic of being Canadian is the recognition that our country is still a work in progress."

A work in progress. A work that needs work, both inside and out. Canada needs to think about its relations with those who live outside its borders as well as those who live within—in particular the Aboriginal situation that prevents Canada from being considered the tolerant, fair country it so desires to be on the world stage.

Tommy Douglas said that "a country's greatness can be measured by what it does for its unfortunates" and that "by that criterion Canada certainly does not stand in the forefront of the nations of the world, although there are signs that we are becoming conscious of our deficiencies and are determined to atone for lost time." He was speaking in 1946. That's sixty more years of "lost time."

Nothing underlines this better than a cartoon that appeared in the October 16, 2006, issue of *The New Yorker*. A man and a woman are picking through the morning paper. The woman, coffee cup in hand, turns to the man buried in the front page and says it all: "You can't spend your political life hiding behind being Canadian."

Nine

The Invisible Founders

SO, THIS IS what it feels like to die.

I was not alone in thinking this. Later, days after I had used up several of the extra lives that are handed out to stray cats and stupid journalists, I would learn that the three others lost with me that week on James Bay felt exactly the same. We did not, any of us, think we'd make it.

It was late June 1986. I had come to Waskaganish on the Quebec shore of James Bay for the launch of Billy Diamond's new boat. The Grand Chief of the James Bay Cree of northern Quebec had already built a successful regional airline and was now moving into a rather different form of transportation. He'd gone to Japan to meet with the giant manufacturer Yamaha, and by combining traditional Cree knowledge and Yamaha technology they had completely redesigned the famous Hudson's Bay canoe—the accepted, albeit dangerous, method of transportation for the northern Cree for generations. Far too many lives had been lost to freak storms and overloaded boats and hidden rocks. Billy Diamond wanted a new boat.

He'd capitalized on the Japanese fascination with North American Aboriginals by striking an early meeting with Yamaha executives in Toronto. Then he'd gone to Tokyo for deeper discussions, and now, two years later, the first Cree–Yamaha boats—wide, handsome fibreglass craft—were rolling off a brand-new assembly line in the old fur-trading village of Fort Rupert, now reverted to its Native name, Waskaganish. The boat was about to be launched from the docks along the shore of the Rupert River where the freshwater flush from Quebec's Ungava Peninsula empties out into the saltwater flats of James Bay.

Billy Diamond and I had known each other for several years—more on that later—and he'd invited me to witness the launch and perhaps even do a story for the *Ottawa Citizen*. I thought it would be a business story, not a survival tale.

With an Ottawa friend, Doug Sprott, I'd driven the better part of a day up through Maniwaki and La Vérendrye Park to Val d'Or and then caught the regular Air Creebec flight north. Nearly two hours later we bounced down onto the gravel runway and hitched a pickup ride into a village where the residents were so excited they could barely contain themselves. A feast was already in progress—beaver and moose nostrils, spring goose, bannock and smoked whitefish, huge pots of dark tea—and word was that the Japanese were coming by executive jet from Tokyo.

Peter Gzowski would also be calling in the morning. Chief Billy Diamond would go live on *Morningside* for the launch of the most unusual joint venture in Canadian corporate history.

A shipment of advertising posters had arrived on the same plane that brought us in. No boat appeared on the poster, but instead an effective message—"The waters of James Bay are not always friendly"—under a rising, threatening swell of churning water. Already that spring five Crees had drowned on the unpredictable waters of James Bay. This boat, the Crees believed, would put an end to such tragedies.

"You're going out for the test drive," Billy laughed when he met us.

"*What?*"

"It's all set up," he said. "Lawrence and Charlie are going to take you up the coast a bit for some fish."

This trip was meant for work, not sport, and yet what could make a better storyline than to actually head out into the water? Lawrence Katapatuk was Billy's lifelong pal, a nonpolitical Cree who kept to the bush as a trapper and hunter. Billy's older brother, Charlie, was even more old world, a strong, silent man who spoke no English and who lived year round along his traplines and in the family's coastal goose camps.

We set out Monday around noon, the Japanese not due until Tuesday morning when Peter Gzowski would be calling and the boat safely back. Billy thought I could go on the radio with him to back up his claims about the boat's seaworthiness.

Doug and I threw our packs into the vast bow—a propitious move, it would turn out—and Lawrence, also fortuitously, tossed a tarpaulin over the packs and supplies. With Charlie standing Cree-style in front of the forty-horsepower Mercury—straight up, left hand holding the upturned throttle handle as if it were the hand of a child, wind straight into his face—we set out in calm waters under sunny skies into the mouth of the Rupert and then north into the gentle chop of James Bay proper.

"Look at that!" Doug shouted.

I turned from my seat on the backpacks and followed his finger. He'd sighted a most unusual rock formation, a small granite island that popped out of the water like some great prehistoric creature rising to challenge.

I nodded. Charlie shook his head at Lawrence, but neither said a thing. Only later would we be told that the Crees considered it bad luck to point to or even to glance at this dramatic rock at the confluence of the Rupert River and James Bay, that to acknowledge the thing was to invite the wrath of *chuentenshu,* the mighty north wind. Charlie and Lawrence were much too polite to say any of this.

The Cree–Yamaha freighter canoe rode beautifully, sliding over the light chop with grace and speed and an awesome sense of power and indestructibility. We could tell from how often the two Cree hunters changed positions—first one steering, then the other—that they, too, were marvelling at it.

The boat was twenty-seven feet long and deliberately wide for James Bay, where the north wind is almost always blowing and the shallow water can be so easily whipped into a frenzy. Since waves tend to be narrow and tight in such shallows, the boat was constructed so that it would crest three or four at once, virtually *surfing,* the ride as smooth as a limousine on a newly paved city street.

Doug and I lay back, turning our faces to the sun and preparing to let the gentle roll of the ride and hypnotic drone of the Mercury outboard put us to sleep.

Two hours out of Waskaganish our little world did a complete flip.

The wind hadn't built slowly, as it does in the south, but instead suddenly crashed down from Hudson Bay farther to the north. The boat began to slam against the instant whitecaps.

And then, even though we'd set out with light jackets and our faces turned to the warmth of the late June sun, it began to *snow*.

Snow. At first large, rolling flakes like small birds riding above the waves, then icy pellets that stabbed like needles into our faces. We pulled our caps and collars tight and hunkered down.

We were quite far from shore. It had been some time since we could make out land and now, with snow blowing and low, dark clouds moving in, it was difficult to make out anything at all.

Charlie, the more experienced of the Cree hunters, was in control of the boat. He was half kneeling, the boat rocking and slamming too dangerously to do anything else but steer. He was fumbling with his shirt and thin plastic rain slick, trying uselessly to bundle up tighter.

The wind began to howl.

I'd seen this phrase written so many times—even sang along with it at the end of Dylan's "All Along the Watchtower"—but never before had I heard wind like this. Perhaps it would be more accurate to say the wind began to *scream*—a scream filled with terror. The Cree treat such things as wind and water as living creatures, animals, and now I perfectly understood why.

The scream grew so loud it drowned out the Mercury. The wind was so wild and ferocious it began to shear off the tops of the whitecaps, sending half-waves of salty water into our faces and down our collars. Lawrence, Doug, and I tied the tarp down and pulled it over us while Charlie drove on into the storm. The snow was so thick now that Doug and I couldn't see any landmarks. We had no idea whether we were heading toward shore or out into the deeper bay.

Sailors know there are few dangers greater than wide expanses of shallow water and a high, unpredictable wind. The small chop we'd set out in had become huge, rolling waves. The freighter canoe could no longer bridge several crests, as it had been designed to do, and instead would ride up one, teeter—the Mercury screeching as water released its grip on shaft and propeller blade—and then collapse down into the funnel. It was as if every few seconds the boat was pushed out a second-storey window and crashed down on the sidewalk below. The jolts were crushing, our backs so hammered that eventually we had to roll onto our sides each time just before impact and then roll back up.

Charlie, still running the motor, stumbled once, his bare hand now so frozen it would not obey his command to get a fresh grip on the throttle. Lawrence jumped up to take over the steering even though it seemed the only directions out here were straight up and straight down.

We were soaked through. The wind was still clipping the tops of the waves and tossing stinging salt water in our faces. The crashing of the big boat into each coming wave was now hurling water over the bow and onto the tarp and floor. We were bailing, but futilely. The snow was building on the tarp and around the seats and transom.

Hours later, speaking in Cree with Lawrence translating, Charlie Diamond would say it was at this precise point—his hands frozen, the salt water washing over the bow—when, having spent his entire life on James Bay, he became quietly convinced that "We weren't going to make it."

Neither Doug nor I needed to be told any such thing at that moment. Both of us, privately, were preparing for the end. The boat was taking on water. The wind was picking up rather than calming down. The crashing was getting so we had to stifle our own screams each time the modern freighter canoe thudded into the next valley.

The boat was rising so high and falling so far now that water blew in at the top of the rise and poured in at the bottom. And yet the vessel itself was bearing up. A wooden freighter canoe would surely have split in half by now, or flipped in the heavy waves, or sunk altogether. We were bailing, but not frantically. The fibreglass Cree–Yamaha creation never even shuddered. It slammed. It crashed. If we were going down it wouldn't be the boat's fault.

Too bad Peter Gzowski was never going to hear this.

Doug and I yanked on the tarpaulin to free it of snow and some of the surface water. Wet snow and water flew off in all directions, most of it staying aboard.

The boat crashed so hard into the next cliff of water that it seemed, for the moment, as if it might finally fracture and splinter and hurl us all to our untimely deaths.

"Look!"

It was Lawrence. He was pointing off over the bow. Charlie stretched up to look. Doug and I tried to look too but the bow rose and fell so fast we had to hit the floor. Then, when it rose again for the next wave, we shifted to our knees so we could see.

The snow had turned to sleet and was blowing hard, the sheets of wet ice hitting like machine-gun fire on the stretched tarpaulin. Off through the grey-white fuzz of what should have been the horizon was the faintest hint of substance: darker, steady, solid.

It was the prettiest sight any of us had seen in the short lives we'd been about to give up on.

Lawrence turned the freighter slightly and a mighty wave, a rogue wave in the eyes of the Cree, lifted the vessel and spun it sideways, tossing it hard into the next wave that washed into and over us.

"He almost got us there!" Lawrence shouted.

He, the sea. Not that he, Lawrence, had erred by daring to change course, even slightly, but that *he,* the sea, had chosen this moment to attack, the water a full and equal personality in this gaunt world, every bit as alive and with as much right to win as the Cree hunters who were up against *him.*

We headed toward the island, which Lawrence and Charlie knew would be surrounded by dangerous shoals. Up ahead we could see the waves spitting high as they broke and exploded just below the surface. With no passageway to the leeward side we'd have to come in from the northwest.

Lawrence turned and the motor crunched into one rock, then another, the propeller screaming as we rose over the rocks then choking as it settled back. But the sheer pin held and the motor kicked back in.

"We're going to have to head straight out into it!" Lawrence shouted. *"Once we're beyond the rocks, we'll come back in with the wind!"*

These few moments were even more harrowing than any of the last two hours as Lawrence deliberately turned the boat away from our only possible salvation.

The freighter bucked and dropped and rose and crashed as it cut new angles across the fury, but Lawrence held hard to the controls and angled the boat so that it rose up onto one wave and cut across at such an angle that he was able to surf the boat from one wave to the next.

Charlie moved on his knees and reached down under the gunwales to retrieve a long pole. He held it in both hands and stood, groin and stomach pressed hard to the bow, then raised the pole over his head as if he were about to drive it into a whale. He was checking for rocks. As Lawrence turned back he cut the engine to half and Charlie began prodding ahead, signalling as he detected bottom, steering Lawrence always clear of the rocks.

Finally they seemed to have the angle Lawrence wanted. With a wrench of the throttle he turned the freighter so quickly it almost dipped sideways into the next wave. The wave caught, the vessel lifted, the motor screamed like a siren as it cleared the water. Then the freighter settled, the motor settled, and we shot straight over the waves, the wind now at our backs, almost soaring into the sheltered approach to the back of the island.

The water was but a moderate chop here, the freighter canoe once again gliding so smoothly it seemed impossible to imagine that moments earlier we'd all been making our peace with death.

Lawrence headed toward a rough beach, shutting down the throttle and reaching back to hoist the outboard as the Cree–Yamaha freighter canoe sizzled into the sand. Amazingly, the world instantly ceased to roll and rise and drop and shudder. The calm was extraordinary. The feeling when our feet first hit the shallows, then the shore, was as sweet and satisfying as any sensation we had ever known.

I knelt and kissed the beach.

IT HAD TAKEN SEVERAL HOURS to reach shelter at the little island the Cree called Obejiwan, but it had taken years to reach this point in what was to become a lifelong relationship with the James Bay Cree of northern Quebec. Five years earlier I'd been working in the Ottawa bureau of *Maclean's* magazine when a young Cree chief with thick black hair and thick black horn-rimmed glasses showed up at the door and asked if he might have a few minutes of my time. He had, he said, a story to tell.

All Billy Diamond had with him that early spring day in 1981 was a mittful of press releases from the Department of Indian Affairs and Northern Development announcing certain initiatives in the James Bay area that were tied to the 1975 James Bay Agreement, the landmark land claims deal the Cree had signed with the Government of Canada and the provincial government of Quebec. Mostly they involved promises not upheld. Paperwork is hardly the stuff of good television.

I let him talk. It took him a long time to say what he needed to say, but eventually the bare bones were laid out and anyone who'd taken the time to listen would have seen that this story went so far beyond mere paper, and even mere words, that its outrage was almost incomprehensible.

It turned out to be the most compelling story I'd ever worked on: six forgotten Cree villages in one of the most isolated pockets of North America, a people then sixty-five-hundred strong who'd never been given the courtesy of even a heads-up before the Quebec government announced a hydroelectric project so huge that it would rival such engineering feats as the Pyramids, the Great Wall of China, and the Panama Canal. It was also a flooding and river diversion project that would, assuredly, wipe out a way of life that, archeologists believed, had changed little over the last ten thousand years. The flooding of the James Bay waterways and the effect on the Cree population was a story so complicated, so huge and tiny at the same time, that it took the young chief an entire day just to talk it out in my little *Maclean's* office.

He talked about his own life. He'd been born on a trapline in the spring of 1949, Malcolm and Hilda Diamond having tried to get back to Rupert House with their five older children before ice out but becoming trapped on the far side of the Nottaway River as the ice broke and backed up.

Little Bileesh Diamin was born in a temporary shelter, Hilda giving birth with the help of older sister Annie, Malcolm cutting the umbilical cord with the same hunting knife he'd used only hours before to skin beaver.

Billy Diamond had been a child others noticed. He was thick and solid and very loud. He had an insatiable curiosity. Older brother Charlie took to hunting immediately, and the older sisters all turned easily to the traditional duties of food preparation and preservation, along with the curing of hides and the various crafts that in those days made living off the land possible.

Not Billy. He was forever wanting to talk, endlessly racing out to watch the passing floatplanes, fascinated by the little village they returned to each late spring and left each early fall with a full canoe of supplies for the coming winter. He used to talk Charlie into carrying the family's old battery radio—complete with a huge and heavy "Nine Lives" dry-cell battery to power it—into the bush so that when they lay in their camps at night Billy could listen to and wonder about the outside world. Billy was soon learning English from listening to Toronto Maple Leafs hockey games and Sunday morning evangelical Christian shows.

Malcolm Diamond became chief, but it frustrated him to the point where he couldn't bear it. He had three voices of authority telling him what to do—the Indian agent who periodically dropped by, the local French Roman Catholic priest, and the manager of the Hudson's Bay outlet—and Malcolm spoke neither French nor English. And with the rise of Quebec nationalism in the 1960s the Quebec government began coming around, insisting that the chief of Rupert House fly the provincial flag down by the wharfs as well as the Canadian flag. When he refused to raise the flag, they did it for him. When the provincial authorities left, he took it down.

Malcolm had a gut feeling that tough times were coming. The provincial government visited more and more often. The Cree trappers were reporting that they'd seen survey crews and helicopters deep in the bush, always around the various rivers that poured out into the bay. When Billy turned eight, Annie, under instructions from their father, dressed little Billy in the new navy slacks and white shirt the family had bought in the

Hudson's Bay store and walked him down to the docks, where a big black Norseman floatplane was tied up. She handed him a small brown paper bag of candy and a small toy helicopter and told him "You be a good boy, Billy, and grow up to be somebody." Then the Norseman's pilot grabbed the youngster and shoved him inside the plane, quickly slamming the door shut and starting up the engine. With the child crying and scream-ing inside and Annie outside on the docks wiping her tears away, the plane taxied out into the bay and took off. Billy Diamond was off to school.

He hated residential school. He couldn't speak the language in which they greeted him. He was forbidden to speak Cree on threat of having his mouth washed out with soap. He hated the food and hated the authority of the Anglican missionaries. When he got in trouble he had his pants pulled down and was whipped with a leather shoe by a male supervisor. He stole bread from the cafeteria to give to another child in the boys' dormitory who had somehow lost his toque and was being punished by being forced to remain all day on his knees in penance. He despised being penned in by a six-foot fence around the school grounds with barbed wire on top—as if the Cree children were prisoners of war.

But Billy loved the library and even liked a few of the teachers. From Moose Factory he moved on to high school in Sault Ste. Marie, excelling in each grade. Many years later he returned to Rupert House, well educated and ambitious. His intention was to talk to his father about going on to law school—he would become a lawyer fighting for Native rights—but Malcolm would hear none of it. Billy had been sent away, the father told his son, to learn English and to come back and serve the people. There were new issues, not the least of which was a provincial insistence that the small children being taught in the village be instructed in French, not English, the official language of the village, and certainly not Cree, the language of the people.

"You are going to be chief here one day," Malcolm told his young son.

It would happen almost immediately. At twenty-one Billy easily won the election and set out to challenge the authorities in a manner that gained him quick recognition up and down the James Bay coast as a force to be reckoned with. He was newly married to Elizabeth, they had a healthy baby girl, and the spring goose hunt was coming fast. Life seemed both good and entirely predictable. For a short while.

Billy had brought home a new radio from the Soo, a tiny two-transistor with an earplug that took only a single small battery and could be carried in a pocket rather than on a sled. He was sitting, dressed in white poplin behind a snow blind, with the radio on and his earplug in when the first geese of spring arrived, drawn to the blind by Malcolm and Charlie Diamond's *"Ka-ronk! Ka-ronk!"* calls. They shot, geese fell out of the sky and splashed on the melting ice surface, and Hilda and the girls quickly gathered them up.

It was April 30, 1971. Billy listened as Robert Bourassa bounded up onto the stage of the Québec Colisée and announced "the Project of the Century"—a hydroelectric project that would tap into the powerful rivers flowing into James Bay.

"Every day," Bourassa would one day write, "millions of potential kilowatt-hours flow downhill and out to sea. *What a waste!*"

Bourassa's scheme would cover an area two-thirds the size of France. Five reservoirs would be built to create a water surface half as large as Lake Ontario. Eight massive dams, 203 dikes, and 1500 kilometres of roads would also be built. The massive project would create 125,000 jobs and cost at least $16 billion. "The world," Bourassa said, "begins tomorrow."

But it seemed to end for the Cree of James Bay. No one had ever consulted them—yet they'd lived here along these rivers for thousands of years. Their traplines would be flooded. The graves of their ancestors would be washed away. One of the villages would disappear. And no one had even thought to ask if it was all right.

Billy Diamond and Robert Kanatewat, another young Cree leader from Fort George, farther up the coast, tried to mobilize the Crees. Billy obtained maps and Robert made phone calls, and they went to work.

To give some small sense of what they were up against, it's worth knowing that the premier of Quebec was talking about the "Project of the Century" at a time when the Cree had barely managed to coin a new Cree word for this creature called "electricity." They came up with *nimischi-iuskutaau*—literally, "the fire of thunder."

The Crees had never thought to look for a word for "reserve."

The Crees had never signed a treaty with the Government of Canada. Natives hadn't even gained the right to vote in the province of Quebec when Robert Bourassa arrived in office.

To make matters worse, they had no infrastructure at all. They were a people of geography only, sixty-five hundred living among five villages and in the deep bush. They'd never had a meeting in all those ten thousand years. There was no chief for all the Crees, no political structure whatsoever to turn to.

Billy and Robert and a couple of the other young leaders called a meeting in the village of Mistassini. They came by floatplane, by canoe, and even walked. They met in the old schoolhouse, with Billy's maps taped up on the walls and the Crees arguing among themselves about whether they should speak in Cree, for the benefit of the elders, or in English, to allow the younger ones more opportunity to explain to the gathering what was happening.

Billy Diamond got an immediate sense of the challenge in front of him when a hand went up at the back of the hall.

"What is it?" he asked from the front of the room.

A middle-aged Cree stood up, twirling his hat in his hand. "First thing we got to do," he told the crowd, "is buy an electric typewriter."

"Why electric?" Billy asked.

The man looked back, incredulous. "Why *electric*?" he repeated. "Because *none of us know how to type*—that's why!"

The Crees' fight against the Project of the Century has filled other books—including one by this hand—and must not overflow this one. But let it be known that the fight was long and difficult, at times torturous, at times even comical. When village elders were called upon to testify at the court hearings going on in Montreal the government kindly sent a jet to pick them up in Timmins. The elders adamantly refused to board the jet because, as they explained, giggling, "The plane has no propeller."

In the end, the Crees couldn't stop the project, as they'd hoped, but they did get major concessions in the flooded area, a new village to be built to replace flooded Fort George, a $135 million settlement, and control of vast areas of land. They signed the James Bay Agreement with the governments of Quebec and Canada, an agreement that would become the basis for the first self-government experiment in the country. It was hailed as a major triumph for Native rights—and Billy Diamond, now Grand Chief of all the James Bay Crees of northern Quebec, was held to be the Native leader of the moment, perhaps the future.

What brought him to my little office six years later on that day in 1981 was a total breakdown of promise.

The Agreement had been going along just fine. New houses were being built in places like Waskaganish. The Crees who wished to live on the land were being paid a per diem to trap. All seemed perfectly in line until communications dramatically broke down between Ottawa and Quebec City over the usual political issues of jurisdiction and obligation.

The two levels of government were to work jointly in constructing new houses and waste and water systems in the villages. The new homes had been completed and ditches had been dug for the sewer lines, but then, with everything ready for one final push to completion, all work had come to a halt.

It matters not who was to blame. The two levels of government just stopped working together. But for the Crees it was disastrous. Supplies and equipment were still to come in and, besides, the Crees didn't have the training to finish off the work, so it was left. They had to resort to outhouses the first winter of the work shutdown. The outhouses worked fine in winter, but when the spring thaw came the sludge melted and began moving through the thin sands of the northern surface. It ended up, naturally, in the ditches that had been dug. It seeped, by gravity, down to where the main town well had been constructed. The sludge worked its way into the water system.

As Third World women everywhere had been encouraged to do, the Cree women had turned away from breast feeding and were using formula that had to be mixed with water. There were "boil water" orders in effect, but there was also slippage. People began suffering from diarrhea, babies began to get ill.

On August 10, 1980, four-month-old Tommy Wapachee from the village of Nemaska died. Soon there were others. Five more babies were dead. Their little bodies were taken away for autopsies and, the Crees claimed, one had been returned to the families for burial wrapped in a green garbage bag.

Billy and Elizabeth Diamond's fifth child, Philip, had also been sick, so ill that he'd been transferred by air ambulance to Sainte-Justine hospital in Montreal. The diagnosis for Philip confirmed the others: gastroenteritis infection, the Third World Killer.

On October 19, 1980, a call came in from the hospital to Waskaganish that the Diamonds should arrange to get to Montreal as quickly as possible. Little Philip was dying.

Billy and Elizabeth flew to Montreal and raced to the Hospital Sainte-Justine. A priest had already given last rites. The parents were ushered into Room 3616 to say their farewells to the dying infant.

They couldn't even recognize their son. Philip seemed more a red balloon of open sores than a baby. The gastroenteritis had given way to chickenpox and then to meningitis. The infant was continually going into seizures. The doctors wanted to know if perhaps the parents' voices might spark some little hint of life yet in the boy, and Billy was asked to draw close and talk to his son.

Old habits die hard. Billy, by now used to dealing in the white man's language when among whites, began speaking softly in English.

Nothing.

But then, realizing that when he'd first held the boy he and Elizabeth had always spoken in Cree, he switched to his Native language.

"Akaawii pichistaayimh, nipwaayimish. Philip, *chiki chiih ihtutaan waash, akaawii pichistinh,"* he told the child in Cree. "Don't give up, my little boy. Fight. Philip, you have a future. Don't let it go."

The baby's eyes moved—a flicker.

It wasn't much, but enough. The doctors moved in and, instead of letting nature take its obvious course, they tried every imaginable procedure to get the child breathing normally again. They eventually brought the infection under control and the seizures stopped. It took months, but little Philip slowly recovered. After 121 days in hospital, Philip Winston Diamond was released and returned to Waskaganish.

Don't expect much, the doctors quietly told Billy and Elizabeth. Philip would likely never walk, he wouldn't be able to talk. It would not be much of a future.

"We still have no sewers," Billy told me that day in the *Maclean's* office.

I went to see for myself. We travelled by plane, by helicopter, by skidoo, and by boat, and the story *Maclean's* eventually published on the land claim gone wrong and the dead Cree babies ended up tabled in Geneva at the World Health Organization, where it proved a huge international embarrassment to Canada. But it worked. Ottawa and Quebec ceased their feuding long enough to carry in bottled water and medical supplies and complete the sewers.

They fixed the water supply and, in other ways, they fixed Philip. Hilda Diamond refused to accept that Philip would never walk and, with Billy and Elizabeth and other members of the family, they set up a schedule where, for hours each morning and night, they would work on the child's limbs, slowly massaging his arms and legs to build up the muscles and keep him active. Medication brought the seizures down to a controllable level and the youngster grew quickly.

By 1986, when Doug Sprott and I headed up to Waskaganish for the Cree–Yamaha boat launch, Philip Winston Diamond was riding his little bike all through the village. He was walking and he was talking. "We can't shut him up!" his father laughed.

Once summer was over, Philip was going to school.

And not any residential school such as the one his parents had been sent off to, but a brand-new school, built by the federal government under the provisions of the James Bay Agreement that Philip Diamond's father had reached and signed.

WE SPENT THREE DAYS marooned on little Obejiwan Island. It was one of the nicest three days of my life.

While Doug and I walked around the schoolyard-sized island, pushing through the black spruce and the aspen, scrambling over the snow-covered rocks and lichen and watching the tides come in and go out, the two Cree hunters silently went about surviving for all four of us.

Even before the snow had stopped, Lawrence and Charlie had turned spruce poles and the big tarpaulin from the boat into a makeshift tent. They'd found an old forty-five-gallon drum some hunter or bush pilot had once cached his gasoline supply in and, using knives and axe, they'd turned it into as cozy a woodstove as any resort has ever advertised. They found a rusted pail and Lawrence deliberately put his foot through the bottom, instantly creating a flue for the top of the tarpaulin tent.

We had shelter, we had heat. We took off our wet clothes and dried them, dancing nearly naked in the tent while shirts dried on the ends of sticks placed in the ground just beyond the edges of the flame.

When the tide was out Charlie and Lawrence set nets they had carried in their own packs. Wearing thigh-high waders, they went out into the shallow waters off the rocky end of the island and tacked the fine nets onto poles they hammered in between the rocks. Once the tide came in and went out again, they gathered up the little whitefish and monkfish that had been caught by their gills, then cleaned, sliced, and suspended them on sticks over the open fire, the cooked flesh so sweet and tender that it seemed to melt in our hands. We had tea. We had fresh bannock.

The more we explored the island the more we came to realize that years ago it had been the site of a Cree goose camp. We fixed up the old outhouse with a magnificent view of the far shore beckoning in the distance. We slept at night, warm and happy, our sleeping bags tight to our necks as the two Cree hunters lay casually on top of theirs and talked in Cree and giggled, probably at us. Who could blame them?

Charlie fascinated me. He walked with me around the island and everywhere he looked he seemed to find something. A bear skull, which Lawrence said meant we'd have good luck. A couple of stove pipes that, fitted together, took the smoke out of our makeshift shelter. It was almost as if he'd been here before, preparing the island for the shipwrecked.

I loved to watch him walk and work. He never hurried. And when he chopped the spruce for the fire he squatted down, knees to his side, legs back, feet splayed for balance. I'd never seen anyone cut wood like this, and it struck me that he was giving up too much power and leverage. I asked Lawrence about it and he said that Charlie lived all the time in the bush, was usually alone on his traplines, and that one little slip of a sharp axe for a Cree hunter could mean bleeding to death if no one was there to help. The hunters cut their wood this way deliberately because it was safer. How different from the likes of Doug and me, or for that matter old Bruce Hutchison, all of whom would have had a splitting block set up and be swinging away at the spruce as if driving home the last spike in a railroad.

When it partially cleared on the second day Doug and I began searching the skies for rescue planes, but we never saw a plane, never heard an engine, never even saw the high trail of a jet headed for Asia or Europe. Nothing. When I asked Lawrence if they'd be sending out anyone to search for us, he laughed.

"Who says we're lost?" he asked.

True enough. On the third day the storm had passed and the chop had returned to what we'd set out in a lifetime earlier. We cut logs and used them to roll the heavy boat back out in low tide and into water deep enough that we could drop the motor down and start it up again. It took less than three hours to make our way back.

When we turned into the mouth of the Rupert, Charlie at the throttle, we could see that the Waskaganish dock area was thick with Crees, Billy Diamond standing in the centre.

The Japanese had come and gone. *Morningside* had phoned and given up. The boat was missing. And Billy Diamond was laughing.

Wasn't he worried? I asked.

"Why would I be worried?" he laughed. "You were with Cree hunters—on *our* land."

BILLY DIAMOND liked to say that the *Maclean's* story changed the Crees' world—but it also changed me. From that point on I wrote increasingly about Aboriginal issues. For every encouraging story like the James Bay Crees there seemed a dozen discouraging tales of poverty and despair and tragedy, but there was also a sense that a larger awakening was taking place—partly through the courts, partly through the media, partly because reality could not be ignored any longer.

Change wasn't coming fast enough, but at least it was coming.

At the very least, relations between those who were here first and the vast majority who came along later were much better than they'd been in the past. And sometimes it's worth looking back in history to see why working for change, even change so slow it seemed imperceptible, is a necessary goal. It's difficult to believe how it once was in this country that today openly brags about such values as tolerance and fairness and understanding and equality.

George Simpson, governor of the Hudson's Bay Company from 1826 to 1860—a role roughly similar to being ruler, hence his nickname "Little Emperor"—openly despised Indians and would ply them with liquor before trading to trick them into bad deals. He was also known to hang Natives for minor crimes and knowingly let elders starve so they wouldn't be any burden on the trading post. And yet Simpson had a long string of "country wives" and fathered children whose bloodlines—including Oxford professor Jennifer Welsh—are still traceable throughout western Canada. They were the lucky ones.

The Little Emperor, who was later knighted for his remarkable service to King and Queen and country, instructed his post factors to deal with any offspring that might result from his endless assignations. He told them to take care of the offspring only if born "in the proper time and of the right colour."

The unborn of "country wives" faced an uncertain future and, at times, no future at all. The white men who fathered these children were under no obligation to help care for them and would do so only if they were particularly fond of the woman and had the means, which few did. At Fort Vancouver, drastic measures were often the order of the day. According to Nancy Janovicek and Joy Parr in *Histories of Canadian Children and Youth,* there was concern at the Fort that fetuses of mixed blood were larger, particularly the heads, making labour difficult to impossible for small-framed Native women. So a system was devised whereby a crochet hook would perforate the skull of the fetus, drain out the brain, crush the skull, and then remove the dead fetus.

This half of North America didn't have the "Indian Wars" that so dominated the expansion of the United States. By the 1870s Washington was spending $20 million a year in the quest to conquer, once and for all, the American Plains Indians. In Canada, even during a time of festering Métis rebellion in the Canadian prairies, the Mounted Police were spending one-fiftieth that amount, $400,000.

Of course relations weren't always more peaceful in the land that would ultimately be called Canada. There was violence in all directions—Native against Native, Europeans against Natives, Natives against Europeans. The most infamous assault by Natives on Europeans occurred in March 1649, when Iroquois warriors attacked a Huron settlement at Saint-Ignace near modern-day Midland, Ontario, creating martyrs out of the two priests, Jean de Brébeuf and Gabriel Lalemant, whom the Iroquois tortured to death.

There were atrocities on both sides, of course, and though a balance sheet is long past possible, the European—and, later, white Canadian—side of the ledger has little, if anything, to commend it:

1534: Explorer Jacques Cartier, searching for a route to China, comes upon the Stadacona fishing along the Gaspé shores. He erects a nine-metre cross bearing the words "Vive le Roi de France," claiming the new land for France. When the chief, Donnacona, complains, Cartier says it's merely a landmark. Cartier later returns and seizes Donnacona, taking the chief, his sons, and seven others to France, where within a few years they all die in misery.

1611: Henry Hudson establishes the fur trade in James Bay, ripping off the first Indian who comes to trade by demanding twice as many pelts as offered for a mere hatchet.

1685: The governor of New France, Marquis de Denonville, writes that Indians "pass on to us a great degree of what is most malicious in them and take themselves only what is bad and vicious in us."

1763: Jeffrey Amherst, commander-in-chief of British North America, advises his successor "to infect the Indians with sheets upon which smallpox patients have been lying, or by any other means which may serve to exterminate this accursed race."

1829: Beothuks, which once numbered as high as two thousand in 1800, have all vanished from the British colony of Newfoundland. Some were massacred for such crimes as stealing salted fish to fight off starvation.

1830: Sir George Murray, secretary of state, announces in London that the new occupants of America "regard the natives as an irreclaimable race, and as inconvenient neighbors whom it was desirable ultimately wholly to remove."

1841: Governor Lord Sydenham comments that "the Indian ... does not become a good settler, he does not become an agricultural-ist or a mechanic. He does become a drunkard and a debauchee, and his females and family follow the same course. He occupies valuable land, unprofitably to himself and injuriously to the country. He gives infinite trouble to the government."

1873: Prairie whisky traders attack a band of Assiniboine they believed, wrongly, had stolen horses, killing at least twenty men, women, and children and burning down their village in what became known as the Cypress Hills Massacre.

1880: According to the Indian Act, which passes in Parliament, "The term person means an individual other than an Indian."

1884: The Government of Canada outlaws the potlatch—the sharing and gift-giving feast that was at the cornerstone of tribal society in British Columbia. The feast is also considered "govern-ment" for the Nisga'a and various other tribes of the West Coast. Attendance at a potlatch is made punishable by jail terms of two to six months.

1885: Poundmaker, the Plains Cree chief who toured the West in boisterous support of the Canadian government, is thrown into prison for three years. His crime lies in not doing enough to keep young Indians from joining the Riel Rebellion.

1886: Prime Minister John A. Macdonald tells the House of Commons that Indians "are simply living on the benevolence and charity of the Canadian Parliament, and, as the old adage says, beggars should not be choosers."

1905: Indian Commissioner Duncan Campbell Scott predicts Indian "civilization" might be attainable in four centuries. Might be.

1909: Captain Joseph Elzéar Bernier, in claiming one of the Arctic islands, takes his rifle and fires nineteen shots in the air. "I instructed an Eskimo to fire the 20th," he reports back, "telling him he was now a Canadian."

1920: The Indian Act is amended to require compulsory school attendance of Indian children. The plan is to get the youngsters to abandon the "savage" life of their parents and join the "civilization" of white society. As deputy superintendent Duncan Campbell Scott so succinctly puts it, "Our object is to continue until there is not a single Indian in Canada that has not been absorbed into the body politic, and there is no Indian question and no Indian department."

1927: Parliament passes a law making it illegal for anyone, Indian or not, to raise money for the purpose of arguing Indian rights.

1930: An Indian found in a poolroom means thirty days in jail for both Indian and poolroom owner.

1945: Veterans of both World Wars have to sign their treaty rights away to fight for their country. On return, they're not allowed to join the Royal Canadian Legion and are given none of the vast support services offered to other returning veterans.

1951: The law prohibiting potlatch ceremonies is finally lifted after sixty-seven years.

1961: Aboriginals are given the right to vote in federal elections, several decades after Canadian women fought for and won the same right.

IN 1975, the same year Grand Chief Billy Diamond signed the James Bay Agreement on behalf of the Crees of northern Quebec, the country's minister of defence talked about Canada's Aboriginal population in a *Maclean's* magazine profile. "What did they ever do for Canada?" James Richardson asked. "Did they discover oil? They didn't even invent the wheel. Why, when we came here, they were still dragging things around on two sticks."

Such thinking, common then, only slightly less common now, gives some sense of the world Billy Diamond was up against. It must have seemed an impossible task to challenge such formidable forces as the federal and provincial governments and international hydroelectric developers. The surveys had been done, the big machinery was already in place, dams were being constructed, work camps were in full force, and the first world oil energy crisis had both the government of Quebec and the government of Canada looking most favourably upon alternative sources. Particularly such renewable sources as the untapped potential of the rivers pouring into James Bay. As Premier Robert Bourassa said, "What a waste!"

The 1970s were a time of increasing confrontation, mostly verbal, between Native and non-Native forces. Some of the nastiest exchanges took place in the early days of Justice Thomas Berger's long inquiry into the social, environmental, and economic impact of the proposed Mackenzie Valley Pipeline. A landmark ruling by the Supreme Court in the Calder case had opened the door to an explosion of land claims, with the newly formed Dene Nation of the Northwest Territories among the most confrontational and, ultimately, persuasive. When Berger finally reported in 1977 he recommended that land claims be settled before any northern development began. Then, with the energy crisis slowly easing, the competing companies eventually pulled out and forgot all about the Mackenzie Valley Pipeline for the next thirty years.

One of the Alberta Natives who testified before that inquiry in the spring of 1976 was Nelson Small Legs Jr. Like Billy Diamond, Small Legs was considered to be on the leading edge of the emerging new generation of Aboriginal leadership. Two days after he testified, however, Small Legs took his own life. He left behind a suicide note: "I give my life in protest to the Canadian government for its treatment of Indian people for the past 100 years."

Nelson Small Legs Jr. also left a second note, this one demanding a full investigation of the conduct of the federal Department of Indian Affairs.

The first note became a rallying cry for increasingly confrontational young Aboriginals. The second note was ignored.

More than a dozen years after Aboriginal rights were headline news during the James Bay court battles and the Mackenzie Valley Pipeline hearings, two events put Aboriginal issues back on the front pages and evening news.

Meech Lake and Oka.

IT WAS ELIJAH HARPER JR., a forty-one-year-old Cree from Red Sucker Lake, Manitoba, who effectively killed the Meech Lake Accord that was supposed to bring Quebec into the constitutional fold and fix Confederation once and for all. The federal politicians who pushed the accord, as well as much of the media that supported it, insisted on placing the bulk of the blame for its failure on one premier, Newfoundland's Clyde Wells. Wells had taken power two years into the accord and become increasingly critical as final ratification approached on June 23, 1990.

Wells's rising concern was pivotal. His eloquent arguments against the devolution of so much power to the provinces had a huge effect on public opinion. But it was Harper who denied unanimity. He killed the accord and knew instantly that Wells would get the blame. What politician—what editorial writer, for that matter—would risk the political incorrectness of blaming a Native?

Harper accepted that the accord offered much to Quebec, but recognition of Quebec, one way or the other, had nothing to do with his decision. Meech Lake, in the opinion of many Native leaders, offered absolutely nothing—zero—to the Aboriginals of Canada. Quebec might have been left out of the 1982 Constitution Act because it refused to sign, but Natives also felt their interests had been largely ignored during the years leading up to repatriation. They had launched several unsuccessful protest trips to London in an effort to get the British Parliament and the Queen to ensure that the British government still had a responsibility for Canadian Aboriginals. Their fear was that the "sacred" rights of the 1763 Royal Proclamation would never be properly protected in the new Constitution if those obligations were to rest with Canada rather than the

United Kingdom. As it turned out, the Constitution Act did recognize those rights, and time would suggest that the Charter of Rights and Freedoms will ultimately prove the best protection of all. At the time of Meech, however, Natives felt that, once again, they were being left out.

In *Reflections of a Siamese Twin,* John Ralston Saul writes that from the middle of the sixteenth century to the middle of the nineteenth Natives were held to be equal to European immigrants and that neither the French nor the English could have done without their assistance and cooperation. To him, Natives make up a "triangular reality" that is Canada.

Meech Lake not only contained nothing for Aboriginal Canadians, it increased provincial powers. And Aboriginals believed they had every reason to fear such a shift.

Between June 12 and June 21, 1990, New Democratic member Elijah Harper had said "No, Mr. Speaker" eight different times to deny the unanimity required to table the accord for ratification. On June 22, with only Manitoba and Newfoundland outstanding, there would be one final chance before the houses rose for the weekend for both provinces to come on board. Failure to do so, politicians and most of the media were saying, would mean the end of Canada. The pressure on Harper in Manitoba and on Wells in St. John's was almost unbearable.

The national media, naturally, flew off to both provincial capitals for the showdown. Manitoba was expected to go first, and if the accord fell in its legislature, whatever happened in the Newfoundland House of Assembly would be academic. If Harper buckled and Manitoba approved the accord the pressures of the entire country would fall on Wells, who was balking and insisting on hearing first from his people.

I was dispatched to Winnipeg. But so, it seemed, was everyone else. Not only was the national media taking over most of the hotel space around the legislature, the Prime Minister's Office had sent an entire team of legal arm-twisters to try to talk some sense into Harper. The shy, ponytailed Native must not be allowed to destroy the country over some minor point—Aboriginal inclusion in the Constitution—that could easily be cleared up at a later date.

Trouble was, no one could find him. Native leaders from across the country and Harper's own extended family had also descended on the capital, and they had ensconced Harper in a place where no one could reach him.

That's where Billy Diamond came in. I called Billy in Waskaganish and he put in a call to Ovide Mercredi, who was then with the Assembly of First Nations. Mercredi in turn contacted Phil Fontaine, the Manitoba leader in the AFN and a close friend of Harper's. I was lying on the carefully made bed of my hotel room, wondering what I might write about with absolutely no access to the main story, when the telephone rang.

It was Phil Fontaine.

"Meet us here," he said, giving me directions to a downtown corner.

I was met by two Native leaders and a white lawyer. We shook hands and they walked me to a hotel several blocks away from the legislature. We got in the elevator and rose to a high floor with a huge, multi-roomed suite in one corner.

There, sitting in a chair by the window, holding an eagle feather in his hand while reading quietly from a black Bible, was Elijah Harper.

"You can stay the night," I was told. "No one's going to get any sleep around here."

It was a remarkable experience. The man who—some were saying—held the very future of his country in his hands was holding the feather of a bird, periodically spinning it. He sat quietly, though the large room was anything but quiet. There were leaders like Fontaine and Chief Gary Potts of the Bear Island band in northern Ontario, cousins and brothers of Harper, Crees down from Red Sucker Lake, national leaders, lawyers, friends, and the curious.

The only ones missing were the federal negotiators, who kept calling and demanding a meeting they never got, and the mainstream media, with one lucky exception.

There was room-service food and coffee. Elijah Harper, who spoke so softly it was sometimes difficult to hear him, was interested in talking about anything but the pressures and the accord, and so we talked about residential schools and hockey and his own fascinating life.

Harper, like Billy Diamond, was born on a trapline in the winter of 1949. He was the second of thirteen children Allen and Ethel Harper of Red Sucker Lake would have, so many children that Elijah was raised by his grandparents, good and quiet people who clung to the "heathen ways" of the Cree traditional teachings.

At age eight, again like Billy Diamond, he was sent off to residential school; but for him it didn't much take. He lasted eight unhappy years and then returned to Red Sucker Lake to take up what he believed would be his life calling: trapping.

Like so many who'd gone through the experience of residential school, he found he was straddling two worlds, the footing unsteady in both. Like the others, he believed, wrongly, that he was alone. It is the mark of his generation to feel that way and only later to discover that others, of similar experience, are much the same. They have a special bond.

The story of the residential schools in Canada is one of shame and of sexual and psychological abuse. Billy Diamond, who would say he had one of the better residential school experiences at Moose Factory, told me that "I lost my foundation years as a child. I was forced to develop into manhood without parental guidance. I lost everything as a Cree child for thirteen years and those years were filled with loneliness and isolation, with punishment and torture and forcible confinement." And he, remember, was one of the lucky ones.

It is, therefore, somewhat just that these same schools would educate a generation of smart, worldly, uncowed Native leaders who would one day lead the fight for retribution. Almost all the young Aboriginals who would become pivotal to advances made in the last quarter of the twentieth century and the early years of the twenty-first came out of this experience: Nellie Cournoyer of the Inuvialuit, Georges Erasmus of the Dene Nation, Jim Antoine of the Northwest Territories, Fontaine, Mercredi, Diamond, Harper.... The list is long, and impressive. Many, like Phil Fontaine, had a hideous, abusive experience, but all took what they could use from the books and teachers to move on to legal careers and leadership roles.

At the end of 2006 an estimated 80,000 former residential school students became eligible for compensation that averaged $24,000. The

12,000 to 20,000 who suffered more extreme abuse, both physical and sexual, could collect an additional $5,000 to $275,000. The settlements showed that one lesson learned at these schools was to fight back.

Elijah Harper had quit his horrendous residential school experience and decided to live as a trapper. But school, without his even realizing it, had opened his eyes to other possibilities, and he grew so upset with conditions back on the reserve that he decided to head back to school with a new attitude and new ambition. He would get an education, and then he would return to Red Sucker Lake and work to improve things for the small band.

He took courses and was eventually accepted by the University of Manitoba, where he linked up with another angry young Native, Ovide Mercredi. Their ever-widening circle would include the likes of Phil Fontaine and Moses Okimaw, who would also end up in Winnipeg in the third week of June 1990.

Together, this group formed a Native association and was soon engaged in battle with the university itself. The engineering students ran a satirical newspaper that in one week published nothing but photographs taken of drunken Natives in downtown Winnipeg—and the association immediately demanded an apology. The young Natives got it, but fell short when they set out to impeach the university president for allowing it to happen. Still, they were a force to be reckoned with, and would remain so for years.

One winter in the late 1960s the group ran into a blizzard driving home from the University of Brandon, where they'd gone to organize a similar organization for its Aboriginal students. Cars and trucks were in ditches. The others wanted to quit, but Mercredi and Harper refused and took turns running out in front of the headlights so that the driver could stay on the pavement. The police and stranded truckers yelled at them to give up, but they believed that if they just kept plugging away eventually the storm would lift. They ran for thirty kilometres before it did lift, but they made it when no one else had managed.

The sheer stubbornness of that bond would pay off twenty-two years later when they hit another bad patch.

Three years before they gathered in Winnipeg, the Meech Lake Accord had been passed in secret by eleven first ministers who couldn't spare a thought for Aboriginals and their standing in the Constitution. Native leaders—First Nations, Inuit, and Métis—had fought against this omission for three years without success. A parliamentary committee looking into the accord had recommended that it be opened for their inclusion. Various politicians, including all three Manitoba party leaders, had called for a change to accommodate Aboriginals, but nothing had been done.

The official contention of the Prime Minister's Office and its legal minions was that the accord held no "egregious" errors and could not, and must not, be opened under any account. The door was slammed.

The same gang that had gone up against the University of Manitoba in the 1960s was now going up against the federal government. But they were no longer kids. Mercredi was a lawyer and deputy chief of the Assembly of First Nations. Moses Okimaw was a lawyer. Phil Fontaine was the head chief of the province of Manitoba. But only Elijah had the clout to actually do anything about it.

Elijah Harper had gone home without his degree. He had worked and then become chief of his band. He'd been one of the Canadian chiefs who had travelled to London to ask the Queen to ensure that Aboriginals be treated fairly if the Constitution was repatriated, as the Trudeau government intended to do. The Queen did nothing.

In 1981 Harper became the first treaty Indian to be elected to the provincial legislature. He was elected again in 1982 and served briefly in Howard Pawley's cabinet. That same year he received a formal invitation to attend the Parliament Hill ceremony when the Queen came to Ottawa to sign the Constitution Act into law. He refused to go.

It was not an illustrious political career for Elijah Harper. He got in trouble instantly when, on election night, a man with no patience for Harper's noisy victory party tried to put his fist through the new member's nose. He got in financial trouble. He was arrested for failing to take a Breathalyzer test. His marriage faltered. His four children suffered. His party was tossed out of office, though he held his own seat.

But then, around the beginning of the Meech Lake discussions, Harper began to pull himself together. He quit drinking and started planning how he might somehow stymie this runaway train called Meech. Georges Erasmus, then also with the AFN, says that Harper had been talking about this very moment for the past two years, though no one thought it would ever prove as controversial and as dramatic.

The moment Harper saw the full details of the final Ottawa deal he called his old friend Gordon Mackintosh, now a lawyer but once clerk of the legislature. A procedural expert, Mackintosh helped refine Harper's motion to block the deal. They discovered, much to their delight, that the Gary Filmon government had incorrectly introduced the Meech Lake motion, meaning they'd have to reintroduce it until the chamber unanimously agreed to consider it or until time ran out, whichever came first.

For all those days in June that Elijah Harper kept saying "No, Mr. Speaker," he held an eagle feather in his right hand. It became the symbol of his defiance, a feather that could appear in the backdrop of an editorial cartoon and instantly remind readers that, somewhere out in Manitoba, one lone "Indian" just might have the power to derail the whole thing.

The feather had been found by Elijah's older brother Saul, a trapper who quietly follows the traditional ways. Saul believed he was being told to walk out to a clearing not far from his home in Red Sucker Lake. When he got there the eagle feather was lying in the very centre of the clearing. He gave the feather to his younger brother Darryl, who took it down to Winnipeg, where he gave it to Elijah for strength to get through this difficult month.

In the middle of this pivotal final week, the Red Sucker Lake band went back to the clearing where Saul had found the feather. There they held hands and formed a circle while asking the Maker to give Elijah strength.

"Look," Chief John Harper, a cousin, cried, pointing to the sky.

High above, circling slowly in the drafts, was an eagle.

"The eagle is on Elijah's side," Chief John Harper told the gathering. "He's going to win."

While we were sitting in the hotel suite talking, Darryl Harper began flipping through the Bible that Elijah had been reading and opened it to the Book of Isaiah, chapter 40. He read the section quietly to himself, then aloud to everyone gathered there.

Though youths grow weary and tired,
And vigorous young men stumble badly,
Yet those who wait for the Lord will gain new strength;
They will mount up with wings like eagles,
They will run and not get tired,
They will walk and not become weary.

Later that long night, when Elijah Harper finally decided to try to get a little sleep before the day of decision, he took the eagle feather, placed it over these words, then closed the Bible.

The following day, at 12:24 P.M. Manitoba time, the feather was once again in his right hand as the motion was made and Elijah Harper killed the Meech Lake Accord with a single word.

"No."

LESS THAN THREE WEEKS LATER, on June 11, 1990, more than a hundred Sûreté du Québec officers, armed with assault rifles, concussion grenades, and tear gas, took up positions around a Native blockade near Oka, Quebec, a village until then known for the excellent local cheeses sold by the Oblate brothers' religious order.

The blockade—mostly downed trees and bulldozed dirt—had stood since March without incident. It had been set up by the Mohawks of Kanesatake, a reserve bordering the picturesque tourist village just to the west of the city of Montreal. The Mohawks were against the expansion of the local golf course, which they said was going to turn Native sacred burial ground into tees and greens and cart paths.

Among those Natives buried in the little cemetery was Kanawatiron, also known as Joseph Gabriel. In 1911 Kanawatiron had been part of a group of forty Iroquois daring to protest against a railway being built across their land. Armed with sticks, axes, and a few shotguns and revolvers, they blocked the railroad navvies from further construction. A peaceful settlement was reached.

The Mohawks of this part of the country had risen up against white oppression several times before. Joseph Swan, a Mohawk who was sent to France to study for the priesthood, returned to lead his people against white laws, which at one point in the nineteenth century included a ban on gathering firewood. White villagers insisted the wood be for their use only. There had often been skirmishes, but real violence was rare.

This time, however, there would be no peaceful outcome. The municipality had petitioned Quebec's Superior Court and the court had ruled that the blockade over the golf course must come down. When the Mohawks refused, the mayor of Oka asked the Sûreté, the provincial police, to enforce the injunction.

The police surrounded the nervous protesters near the top of the hills where the white pines stand tallest. Someone fired first—it has always been disputed just who—and almost instantly there was smoke and screaming and chaos and more shots ringing out. When it was all over, one officer, Corporal Marcel Lemay, was dead of a rifle wound. The police retreated, leaving behind cars that were burned and trashed and overturned by the furious Natives.

The blockade, the Mohawks defiantly declared, was not coming down.

The standoff continued on into summer. A second blockade went up on the Mercier Bridge over the St. Lawrence, erected by Natives on the nearby Kahnawake reserve out of sympathy for the Oka Natives. The obstruction infuriated commuters from the south shore trying to get into and out of Montreal and was marred by violence, mostly thrown bottles and stones. The tension mounted daily on Premier Robert Bourassa until mid-August, when he asked for military backup to put an end to the crisis.

It marked the first time Canadian soldiers had come up against civilians since the October Crisis of 1970. Tensions ran even higher once the soldiers arrived. The Mohawks gave no indication of backing down, no matter how much military might showed up.

Given that Native power had only weeks before brought down the Meech Lake Accord, there was a new swagger to Aboriginal activists.

There was something about the new leadership, about angry, determined young Aboriginals, that seemed to catch the rest of the country off guard.

Two years earlier, Georges Erasmus, then Grand Chief of the Assembly of First Nations, had delivered a warning about land claims and Native rights, telling the country: "We want to let you know that you are dealing with fire. We say, Canada, deal with us today because our militant leaders are already born. We cannot promise that you are going to like the kind of violent political action we can just about guarantee the next generation is going to bring to our reserves."

Such talk had often been heard before, but this was the first time in memory that words were followed by action. "I never thought it would go so far," said John Ciaccia, provincial minister of Native Affairs. "Nothing had prepared me for what would happen."

The army moved in on August 14, the blockade grew larger, and a delicate standoff began that would run through the remainder of that hot summer. Along with other reporters, I was sent down from Ottawa by the *Citizen*. One reporter, Ian MacLeod, managed to get behind the barriers before the army moved in and would remain there, mostly sleeping in his car, for the full standoff. The rest of us lumbered down the 417 and Quebec route 40 in a forty-two-foot custom camper trailer and set up in an Oka-area campground. We'd spend our days poking around the blockade, attending army briefings, making calls to Natives inside the blockade, and then heading back to the campground to barbeque lamb chops and drink beer.

Somehow, given that the Canadian army had been called out over a golf course, it seemed to make sense.

Our camper wasn't the only thing that seemed surreal. Television no longer just covered the news, it made the news. Oka came along just as all-news channels were coming into Canadian homes. CBC's Newsworld was at Oka twenty-four hours a day, often broadcasting raw footage that both fascinated and shocked.

Oka became, in large part, a War by Scrum. The tough-talking camouflaged Natives—complete with facemasks, rifles and knives, and code names like "Lasagna"—severely rattled the country. The young, fresh-faced soldier, jaw jutting out defiantly, standing face to face with the fierce-looking, camouflaged "Warrior" became the image that defined that summer of 1990. Inspired by Harper's victory, Natives across the country took up the Oka cause.

One day I ran into Frank and Rick Thomas, who had decided to walk down St-Michel, Oka's main street, just to get a look at the famous barricade. Rick, having asked for a few days off from his job at a basket works in St. Stephen, New Brunswick, had jumped into his old 1977 Chrysler and driven three hundred kilometres out of his way to pick up his cousin Frank from the Shubenacadie Reserve in Nova Scotia. They'd driven through the night to reach Oka.

"It all begins with Elijah Harper," Frank Thomas said in his "Custer Had It Coming" cap.

"Someone had to take a stand for us," added Rick. "After what happened over Meech Lake every Indian in the country knew we could stand together and win. We knew it in our hearts."

John Ciaccia later told the CBC that bringing in the army was precisely what the Oka Warriors wanted, "because then they could say they were fighting nation against nation." If so, they seemed to belong to two different planets. One side said the battle was about rights and sovereignty; the other side said it was really about the Natives' right to sell untaxed cigarettes. One side thought themselves warriors; the other side called them criminals.

To appreciate the enormous contradictions so often at work in this assemblage called Canada, consider that on one side of the roadblock, the white side, Joseph Brant would be seen as the greatest Native hero in Canadian history. He is the Mohawk chief to whom this country has erected statues, named towns after, and honoured in school textbooks as the wise chief who stood by the British during the American Revolution and eventually led his people to peace and prosperity on the Six Nations land in southwestern Ontario. On the other side of the Oka roadblock, the Native side, Joseph Brant would be known as Thayendanegea, the opportunist who sold out his people's lands in New York state and then the Ohio Valley, who tricked his followers onto a reserve where he himself refused to live, and who later killed his own son who had attacked him as a traitor.

Two weeks after the army arrived, the barricade on the Mercier Bridge came down. But not until September 26, two and a half months after the gun battle on the hill, did the Warriors surrender. The leaders were arrested and chainsaws and front-end loaders moved in to take down the infamous barricade.

The blockade was down. But Oka was not yet over.

IF MEECH LAKE LED directly to the formation of the Citizens' Forum on Canada's Future, then the Oka standoff can be credited with bringing about the Royal Commission on Aboriginals. The commission had been promised by the Mulroney government but then rescinded, and now it was again in the works. Georges Erasmus was to be one of its two chairs and the other would be Justice René Dussault. Aboriginal leaders were most encouraged.

The commission would meet across the country and take five years to complete its report. It would eventually cost $51.2 million—a figure that outraged the Canadian media—and be tabled in the late fall of 1996 under Prime Minister Jean Chrétien. There were high hopes, as Chrétien had once been a sympathetic minister of Indian Affairs.

The final four-thousand-page report was all about change. Its 440 recommendations included the creation of an Aboriginal parliament, the formation of a completely independent tribunal to rule on land claims, and the establishment of an "adequate land base" for the most forgotten of the forgotten people, the Métis. Erasmus believed it would give Natives equal-nation status within Canada, providing full self-government to approximately sixty Aboriginal nations with jurisdiction over a wide range of powers.

Aboriginals, Erasmus said, would be citizens both of their own nation and of Canada. Federal government obligations would be directed to these nations, not individuals, and Ottawa would provide for each nation its own economic base within Confederation. The critics said it would be impossibly costly and would only increase most Aboriginals' reliance on federal funds. Others said the Aboriginal parliament would never work and that if Natives were to be given "special status," what about Quebec? What about what had been promised in the Meech Lake and Charlottetown accords?

In the end, the Royal Commission on Aboriginals report was placed side by side on the same shelf as Keith Spicer's report on the Citizens' Forum on Canada's Future.

EXACTLY NINE YEARS after the standoff began, I returned to Oka to see what, if anything, had changed. It was a dull July day, raining off and on. I went up the hill where the tall white pines still stand and wandered through the little graveyard that had started the fight. For those who knew where to look, bullet marks remained in the trees and in the boards of the flaking lacrosse box.

The grave of Leroy Gabriel, Warrior, was in the very ground that was to have become a golf course, but instead of a ball washer there was an antler stuck into the grass. From the antler hung a small carved eagle, symbol of wisdom, of knowledge, of truth—and high above, hammered into a pair of magnificent white pines, two tattered warrior flags swung softly in the eerie still of a wet, muggy day.

Leroy Gabriel stood with "Lasagna" and "Spudwrench" and several dozen other Warriors who kept their faces behind bandanas and their weapons visible to all as they stared down the hill at the Canadian army for more than two months. It was as close to civil war as this peaceful country has come in modern times.

The Mohawk held the ground that was to be turned into a golf course as sacred. They said that for more than a hundred years their people had been buried there and that the deep wood behind the highway was theirs for future burial. Once the standoff was over, the government promised the Mohawks control over the territory.

Leroy Gabriel couldn't wait. He'd never recovered from his weeks as a Warrior. He drank far too much, and eventually an accident with a hunting rifle ended his pain before he reached the age of thirty. His friends decided not to wait for any government permission and brought him here, wrapped him in buckskin, and gave poor Leroy a traditional Mohawk burial beneath the very pines he had fought for: victory his, forever and ever.

There were now ten graves in the disputed territory. Control of the land was handed over to the Mohawk Council of Kanesatake, but not the deed, much to the disappointment of many Natives in the area. The municipality of Oka received $230,000 for the property, even though Mohawks still claim that the land had never belonged to Oka in the first place and had no need to be purchased.

But now it was theirs, for keeps, deed or no deed. It had been cleared and was beautifully kept, carefully gardened and passionately guarded. Woe to the outsider who dares enter without first asking permission. And even then visitors are asked not to get too close to the gravesite of Leroy Gabriel, hero to many, troublemaker to many—for the winds of Oka had never really stopped blowing through this spectacular plot of land they call the Pines.

"There are still growing pains," Barry Bonspille told me. The local historian worked for the Kanesatake Mohawk Roundtable and lived only a few houses from where the battle took place. His home had been virtually destroyed by vandals during the standoff but had since been rebuilt and refurbished. Even so, nine years later, hardly a day went by that the events of the summer of 1990 were not recalled by someone.

"We get along fairly well with the town now," said Bonspille. "But there's still a feeling that efforts were made to appease the town."

The town got money for the land. Town businesses received some compensation. A new ferry was put into service, the waterfront improved, and the exquisite local park improved.

Native businesses received nothing for their losses. Barry Bonspille paid out of his own pocket to repair his home.

The surface changes in Kanesatake had been vast: council was now elected, policing was now all Native, and municipal employment had mushroomed since the Mohawks began delivering their own programs. The issues that Oka raised, however, are always simmering in the background.

The Mohawk community at this point in 1999 counted some eighteen hundred members, yet only five to six hundred lived in Kanesatake; the remainder were off-reserve, with full voting privileges. Political issues had become centred on such matters as taxation, even though the minority actually living there continued to demand that land claim settlement take precedence. The fight over the cemetery lands had been but a small portion of a larger claim to lands from Mirabel airport to Montreal itself.

"It's kind of ironic," Bonspille said, "but the thing we fought for in 1990 is last on the list of priorities."

THIRTEEN YEARS to the day after Elijah Harper held his eagle feather and said no to Meech Lake, we met again in Ottawa.

He was still recognized wherever he went and often treated as a hero. He had received tens of thousands of letters. When he checked into hotels he'd be given the presidential suite. When he visited schools, children would walk up and touch him just to make sure he was real. On one flight half filled with German tourists they lined up in the aisles to ask for the autograph of Canada's "most famous Indian."

"My life changed," he told me, "but I stayed the same."

He had for a while, but not by the time I saw him again. The familiar ponytail was there, but the heavyset man was a shadow of his former self. He was now in his mid-fifties, still recovering from a mysterious illness that had struck not long after he switched from the Manitoba provincial NDP to the federal Liberals and won a seat in the House of Commons in the 1993 general election. He'd lost seventy pounds and had often been in such pain he wished he could die. Unable to function well enough to campaign in 1997, he had lost his seat. Since then he'd worked as a consultant, living mostly in Ottawa. He had grown somewhat bitter about the inability of federal politicians and the Canadian media to give credit where credit was due—or, as some others would see it, blame where blame was due.

That Clyde Wells, far more than Harper, had borne responsibility for the accord's demise can be explained in part because he was a premier who inherited his province's initial agreement but questioned it. In part it was because Wells was eloquent, articulate, and outspoken, whereas Harper essentially restricted his comments to a single word. And in significant part it was because Clyde Wells was white and Elijah Harper was not.

"We know the truth," Harper said.

In his opinion, Brian Mulroney had made a scapegoat of Wells for political reasons. "He had to portray what had happened as rejection of the accord by English Canada," Harper said. "Besides, he couldn't blame us because everyone knew that we were morally right."

After that moment, he said, Aboriginals would never again be taken for granted by any level of government in Canada. "When we said no to Meech Lake, we said no to the entire relationship."

Much has happened, and much has not happened, in the years since. On the positive side, the Charlottetown Accord—even though it was turned down by the Canadian people for other reasons—gave Aboriginals the accommodation that Meech denied. The land-claims process has been taken seriously, even if it moves at a snail's pace. Natives in the Northwest Territories, where most land claims are now settled, have been offered a one-third ownership by the major resource companies in any Mackenzie Valley Pipeline that might, finally, be built to carry natural gas and oil to southern markets. From the James Bay Agreement in 1975 to the tough negotiations thirty years later with the Deh Cho of the Mackenzie Valley, there has been an increasing acceptance that claims are legitimate and agreements are necessary.

Over Canada's long history, before and following Confederation, there isn't much to commend the various governments for their approach to Native affairs. And yet, for all the paternalism and betrayal, there is undeniable change—even if it's only what John Ralston Saul calls a "halting acceptance" of some return to the very early status of mutual dependence. And for that small change, that "halting acceptance," Aboriginal Canadians have Elijah Harper to thank.

On the negative side, the events of Oka still resonate periodically in places like Burnt Church, New Brunswick, and Caledon, Ontario. The tragedy of the James Bay babies shows up again on the Kashechewan reserve on the Ontario side of the huge bay, where tainted water in the spring of 2006 led to the evacuation of the entire village of eighteen hundred. The nearly hundred thousand Natives who live off-reserve remain as ignored and, by and large, as impoverished as those living on Canada's most isolated and poorest reserves.

Racism, while never as explicit as Commander-in-Chief Jeffrey Amherst and his smallpox-infected blankets, has continued unabated, and on both sides. Former AFN head David Ahenakew was stripped of his Order of Canada after a 2002 interview in which he slammed immigrants and expressed great admiration for Adolf Hitler, claiming that if Hitler hadn't "fried" six million Jews they "would have owned the goddamned world." As Ahenakew himself had told a parliamentary committee nearly twenty years earlier, "Racism is as Canadian as *Hockey Night in Canada*."

Despite Ahenakew's unfortunate outburst, however, attitudes have been somewhat shifting—again on both sides.

In late September 2006 I happened to be in Fort McMurray, Alberta, at the same time as a conference on Aboriginal economic development was being held. I dropped in on the morning the gathering was opened by Chief Clarence Louie of the Osoyoos Indian Band of British Columbia's Okanagan Valley.

"I can't stand people who are late," Chief Louie scolded as he stood on stage, the PowerPoint presentation on the screen behind him temporarily halted. He'd been scheduled to begin speaking at 10:00 A.M. He himself had shown up early and was decidedly unimpressed by the straggling in of so many, even revered elders who'd been invited to begin the session with the appropriate ceremonies. "'Indian time' doesn't cut it," he told them, only partly tongue-in-cheek.

Clarence Louie had been chief for twenty years. He'd taken over a troubled, impoverished band that, after running a deficit of $221,000 in 1990, had been declared insolvent and placed under third-party management by Department of Indian Affairs officials out of Vancouver. Louie was re-elected and within a year managed to get the deficit erased. He led the negotiation of two specific land claims and slowly turned matters around to the point where Ottawa returned control to the small band of 430 Osoyoos.

In 2000 Chief Louie and his council set themselves the goal of becoming self-sufficient within five years. And they did—though not without a few toes being stepped on, noses put out of joint, and the creation of more than a few critics. Inspired by Billy Diamond's argument that "economic development is the key to extending Native rights," Louie led the band in several acquisitions and new developments. Today the Osoyoos have their own vineyard, winery, golf course, tourist resort, and construction company. They're also significant partners in a nearby Baldy Mountain ski development. In 2005 the Osoyoos contributed $40 million to the area economy.

As Chief Louie told the tale of his little band's success he sprinkled his talk with comments—some original, some taken from other sources and often delivered humorously—that no Native leader would have dared deliver in previous years and no non-Native could possibly deliver.

My first rule for success is "Show up on time." My No. 2 rule for success is follow Rule No. 1.

If your life sucks, it's because *you* suck.

Quit your sniffling.

Join the real world—go to school or get a job.

Get off welfare. Get off your butt.

Our ancestors worked for a living—so should you.

WHEN PEOPLE ASK Clarence Louie how he is, he tends to answer "I'm busy," having no interest in "wasting time with the usual social BS" and wanting to get right down to business. "People often say to me, 'How you doin'?" he said at one point during the morning session, pausing for effect before answering: "Geez—I'm working with Indians—what do you *think?*"

He addressed the perception of "the lazy, drunken Indian." It might be unfair but it exists, he said, and the best way to deny it is not to complain but to demonstrate otherwise. Develop "business manners," he said, and stick to them. "Create a climate for success." His idea of a business lunch, he told them, is "drive through"—and right back to work. And real work, he cautioned: "The biggest employer shouldn't be the band office."

He wasn't against tradition, but he was also all for reality: "You're going to lose your language and culture faster in poverty than you will in economic development." He told them the time has come to "get over it." No more whining about hundred-year-old failed experiments. No foolishly looking to the Queen to protect rights. "I have no faith in the Queen," he said. "She wasn't there for us a hundred years ago. I can guarantee that she isn't going to be there for us now."

"Blaming government? That time is over."

IN THE EARLY SUMMER OF 2003, Paul Martin's minority Liberal government was sworn in at Rideau Hall with a full Ojibway smudge ceremony. He had, he said several times during the campaign, two main priorities he wished to deal with quickly: Western alienation and Aboriginal poverty. Within eighteen months the West would respond to his overtures by bouncing him out of office in favour of a Western-based leader and party, Stephen Harper's Conservatives. And the Aboriginal population would be left wondering what would become of the one significant achievement the Paul Martin government had managed to pull off—almost: the Kelowna Accord.

The $5.1-billion accord had been signed in the fall of 2005 by the Government of Canada, the ten provinces, the territories, and the various Aboriginal leaders. It was, as Martin said at the time, "a historic breakthrough." The accord was intended to significantly improve education conditions throughout the country—to bring an end to the all-too-familiar story of Kashechewan.

It had its critics, of course. The Conservative Party obviously didn't care for it, and even some Native leaders were wary. Chief Clarence Louie, for one, thought "the government as well as the First Nation leadership needs to be 'spanked' for not making economic development a priority." There was money for economic development, but the vast majority of funds would go toward social spending, which some, like Louie, considered "a hundred-year-old failed formula."

And yet an argument can be made for both. Economic development is the story of the James Bay Cree, who reached another agreement on more hydroelectric production in 2006, a $5 billion project that will flood land around the Rupert River. While a minority of the James Bay Cree opposed the new deal, the majority were convinced that an arrangement that will pay them $70 million a year in royalties over the next half century is the only way they can survive and even thrive so far north.

The Cree had finally been able to switch on lights and televisions without having to rely on the gasoline-driven generators that roared constantly in the small villages. They built their own transmission lines from the big power plants that had come out of Robert Bourassa's Project of the Century. "Finally, after thirty years," Billy Diamond told me in early 2007, "we have electricity from the largest hydroelectric project in North America—and a Cree had to hook it up. What irony!"

Economic development has also been a success for the Osoyoos of southern B.C. and for numerous other bands located in areas where resource development or simple good fortune has provided some manner of financial base to build on. Most Aboriginal situations, however, are not so lucky. As Phil Fontaine said upon his 2006 re-election as Grand Chief of the Assembly of First Nations, the cost of poverty is "the most important social justice issue faced by this country."

The Accord, however, seemed to have become lost in the election and in the changeover from one minority government to another. A federal government that would soon brag about a $13 billion surplus evidently couldn't live up to its commitment of less than half that amount to do something significant, even historic, about its impoverished Aboriginal population.

Then, in the fall of 2006, the Canadian government joined Russia, the United States, Australia, and New Zealand to deep-six a United Nations Draft Declaration on the Rights of Indigenous Peoples. The resolution, twenty years in the works and once supported by Canada, was to have affirmed the rights and liberties of Aboriginal people wherever they might live on the globe. "Indigenous peoples," article 26 of the draft declared, "have the right to own, develop, control, and use the lands, territories, including the total environment of the lands, air, waters, coastal seas, sea-ice, flora and fauna and other resources which they have traditionally owned or otherwise occupied or used." And if those lands have already been taken away, there should be appropriate compensation.

Canada said no.

The blockade may have come down at Oka. But a great many barriers still remain in Canada.

Ten

Pier 21 to Pearson

WELCOME TO CANADA.

I was in Halifax, with an afternoon to kill on a late fall day. It was unseasonably warm, as it would continue to be well into the early weeks of "winter" 2006–07, the water bathtub-calm in the harbour, the wharf filled with workers taking their lunch break in the sunshine. I walked from one end of the harbour to the other, my mind drifting despite the lack of wind as I tried to figure out how anyone could ever make sense of the sheer size of this country and the vast changes that had come to it over the years.

And then I saw the sign: *Welcome to Canada.*

But that was only the top lettering over the fading coat of arms on the weather-worn notice. There were other languages down each side:

Serdecznie Witanny w Kanadzie.

Willkomman in Kanada.

Benvenuto a Canada.

Bienvenue au Canada.

Welkom in Canada.

One was even written in the Cyrillic alphabet, and while unreadable to these eyes and impossible to type for these fingers, easily translated to this page by simple deduction: *Welcome to Canada.*

At the furthest end of the Halifax docks, just where the wharfs give way and the harbour begins opening its mouth toward the Atlantic, I had stumbled upon Pier 21, Canada's national immigration museum. Our Statue of Liberty. Our Ellis Island.

For eight dollars I got to spend a good portion of an excellent day seeing how this empty country began to fill with people. Pier 21 is a museum carved out of what was once a massive warehouse for shipped goods and then, for decades, a holding, sorting, and moving warehouse for human goods. More than a million Canadians arrived here between 1928 and the day Pier 21 closed in 1971. Another 494,000 military personnel passed through during the Second World War, their return at the end of the war to be followed by more than 50,000 war brides and their children.

There are displays here of old and cracked steamer trunks, purses, dolls and teddy bears, crinkled black-and-white photographs of lost and found families, scribbled notes and carefully handwritten letters and typed orders. The faded Immigration Identity Cards tell the story of Canada in the fewest words and numbers possible: Di Sano, Alfredo, July 13, 1948; Bezkorowajny, Katrina, October 17, 1951; Tonn, Gotlieb….

They came as full of hope as they were of fear, many unable to speak the language. But no matter how they said it, their intention was the same: to make a better go of it here than there once they received the treasured red-ink "Landed Immigrant" stamp.

There's even a song for Pier 21 that some of the war brides aboard the *Lady Rodney* composed in the days before their landing at Halifax:

Where ere we go from east to west,
We want you all to know,
We'll make the best Canadians,
No matter where we go.

War brides came from Britain to start a new life in Canada, as did British Home Children—orphans and the "extras" families could not afford to keep. From 1870 to 1957 some hundred thousand Home Children were shipped to Canada under the British Child Emigration Scheme. They came to work as indentured farm hands and domestic servants and labourers, often under despicable conditions. They arrived, terrified, in a country they'd never heard of, sent by a country that wished never to hear of them again. Remarkably, an estimated five million British Home Children descendants live in Canada, making it the country of the abandoned.

Immigrants came through Pier 21 from England, Scotland, Ireland, Wales, Germany, Denmark, Iceland, Italy, Greece, Spain, The Netherlands, Belgium, Scandinavia, Finland, Russia, the Middle East, Africa, and Eastern Europe. Exactly fifty years before I came to these gates from the other direction, thirty-eight thousand Hungarian refugees had passed through them.

Canada is a much more multicultural country than its closest neighbour, though both have taken in immigrants from around the world. The Americans like to say their immigrants come to a melting pot, all ending up Americans over time; Canadians have called it a vertical mosaic, with hyphens allowing those who come here to maintain a strong identity link with their origins. According to social scientist Michael Adams in *Fire and Ice,* "Whereas 11 percent of Americans are foreign born, the figure for Canada is 18 percent. Moreover, a large proportion of America's foreign born are from Mexico; in Canada they are drawn from virtually everywhere on the planet...."

The great Canadian suffragette Nellie McClung saw her country as a distinctively different version of the United States. Newcomers to this country, she believed, would not be met by a Statue of Liberty proclaiming "Bring me your tired, your poor, your huddled masses yearning to breathe free," but by a Canada standing with arms open wide saying, "Come to me, for I am the Land of the Second Chance. I am the Land of Beginning Again."

McClung believed her country was "too young a nation to have any distinguishing characteristic." But it could create one, she thought, and in 1915 offered up her own *Vision of Canada:* a land of fairness, where race and colour and creed have equal chance at success, where no one can "exert influence," where no one's past will hurt them, where no crime goes unpunished, no debt unpaid, where honest toil guarantees an honest living.

"The Land of Beginning Again" indeed. Utopia, by any other name. The popular Canadian concept is that we're the most tolerant and welcoming country on earth, but history—as Walter Stewart and others have pointed out—is filled with counter-arguments.

The first immigrants Canada tried to restrict were American. Following the War of 1812 laws were passed preventing Americans from holding land unless they had already been in Upper Canada for at least seven years, in effect barring those who might have wished to join the rush to open up good farmland between Lake Ontario and Lake Simcoe and beyond. Instead, the government encouraged the immigration of poor British, many of them Irish fleeing famine and many of them from the English countryside, London officials having perceived the North American colony a good "dumping ground" for the unwanted and the indigent.

"Reduced to pauperism by the results of centuries of plundering, extortion and exploitation of the ruling class at home," Gustavus Myers wrote in his *History of Canadian Wealth,* "these emigrants were herded in foul ships and packed off to Canada under the most inhuman and horrible conditions." Between 1815 and 1839 more than 430,000 immigrants landed at the port of Quebec, and, as Lord Durham once sadly noted, had they known what difficulties awaited them most would have declined to come. Those who survived the voyages often did not long survive the landing. Once *The Voyageur* landed in early June 1832, its cargo of deadly cholera spread quickly, killing some four thousand people in Quebec City and Montreal. Quebeckers formed an organization that offered new arrivals five shillings just to keep on going. They even had a motto: "Welcome Anywhere—Anywhere But Here."

Fear of disease is one thing; fear of difference is something quite apart. During Canada's greatest years for immigration, from roughly 1896 to the beginning of the First World War in 1914, the official most responsible for bringing new blood to this country said he was looking for "peasants in sheepskin coats." He didn't have to explain: Central and Eastern Europeans. Whites.

Blacks were especially undesired, it appears. *Saturday Night* magazine, published in Toronto and supposedly the voice of the more educated and cultured classes, was particularly virulent, claiming in one 1911 issue that the Negro is "indolent, prodigal and shiftless. In other words, he is by nature unfit for carving out for himself a home in the wilderness." A year later, an article in the same magazine called American boxer Jack Johnson a "black baboon" and "impudent nigger" for marrying a white woman, saying he should be lynched and she was obviously a "pervert."

Saturday Night, Walter Stewart pointed out, was at least an equal-opportunity hater, running an article entitled "No Jews" and suggesting that Canada would be unwise to allow any into the country. "Without them," the establishment magazine contended, "there will be no filthy slums, in which they now teem, and without them our courts and our jails would have some measure of relief." It makes one wonder if a comment that appeared in the *Toronto Daily Star* during that decade was intended as ironic: "Canada consists of 3,500,523 square miles, mostly landscape. It is apparently intended for the home of a broadminded people."

The most disturbing test of early Canadian openness came in 1914, when the *Komagata Maru* sailed into waters off the B.C. coast carrying 376 Sikhs. They had come from another part of the British Empire to start a new life. They were well dressed and stood on the decks waving and smiling to the crowds that gathered along Victoria's harbour to see what had come in. No one waved back. They might be British subjects, but they weren't *like us.*

As Stewart recounted the tale, the ship wasn't allowed to land and was sent to anchor in Burrard Inlet, where police boarded and placed guards on the deck. It sat for two months while the province steamed. "We must keep this country a white man's country at any cost," huffed an editorial in *British Columbia* magazine, "and a British country if possible."

At one point the Sikhs had to fight off an army of police and immigration officers—and even a local member of Parliament—who planned to take over the ship, install a Japanese crew, and haul it out to sea. Finally, when a navy ship pulled up alongside and trained its firefighting hoses on the stunned passengers, the Sikhs decided they might just as well give up and set sail again. No one seems to know whatever became of them.

When Bruce Hutchison was writing his famous book on Canada in 1942 he reflected prevailing attitudes in words that would be most politically incorrect today. Hutchison thought the Japanese enjoyed an advantage over regular white B.C. businessmen in that they were willing to live at a standard no white could tolerate. For him "Oriental" immigrants would never be assimilated; whites could hope only that they would eventually "lose some of their fertility and will adopt our standards of life."

Hutchison was, of course, writing at a time of great fear, the Japanese having attacked Pearl Harbor on December 7, the year before his book was published in the United States. After the Allies declared war on Japan, Canada used its War Measures Act to relocate more than twenty thousand Japanese Canadians, many of whom had been in the country for generations, from the coast and into detention camps far from the sea. Though none were ever charged with any count of espionage or sabotage, the orders stood. They lost their businesses, their fishing boats, their farms, their homes. Worse, they were charged $7.50 a month for the privilege of living in what were essentially prisoner-of-war camps. Four years after the war ended, Japanese Canadians still endured severe restrictions, prevented from travelling far from home without a permit and barred from voting or, for that matter, studying to become a lawyer.

TIMES CHANGE, as Bruce Hutchison discovered—and, we have to presume, the author of this book will also discover should this effort prove fortunate enough to survive even a fraction as long as Hutchison's—but times change very slowly when it comes to attitudes toward immigration. The Canadian government eventually apologized to the Japanese, among others, but apologies don't erase what happened.

Though more than three million people arrived in Canada over the four decades from 1925 to 1965, a mere seventeen thousand were black. In the mid-1950s Immigration Minister Walter Harris was still saying that those from tropical climates found it next to impossible to adapt to Canadian "climactic conditions." Around the same time, although twenty thousand applications for visas were completed in India, immigration quotas for Indians were set at only 150 a year.

The immigrants who suffered most at the hands of Canadian intolerance were likely the Chinese. Between 1881 and 1884, fifteen thousand Chinese workers were brought in through British Columbia to dig in the coal mines and build the railway Confederation had promised. And then they were expected to go back to China. No one ever thought, or expected, they might like to stay.

"These coolies were, to all intents and purposes, slaves," Walter Stewart wrote in *But Not in Canada*. "They were sold under contract to white railwaymen or miners." Stewart also cited an 1885 royal commission on the conditions in which these Chinese workers lived. The commission concluded that Canadians would never "feed their dogs upon the food consumed by the ordinary Chinese labourer."

The Chinese immigrant story is a difficult one. Like Native Canadians, they were not considered "persons." They were made to pay a head tax of $50, later raised to $500, just for the right to work. So adamant were some members of British Columbia society to keep them out that a law was passed requiring applications to be written in a "European" language. Little wonder, then, that by the early 1920s Chinese immigration had fallen to practically nothing. In the 1935 general election the Liberals published an advertisement in one of the Vancouver papers that claimed: "A Vote for any CCF candidate is a vote to give the CHINAMAN and the JAPANESE the Same Voting Right that you have! A Vote for a Liberal Candidate is a VOTE AGAINST ORIENTAL ENFRANCHISE-MENT." Canada didn't get around to apologizing for the head tax until 2006, at which point the vast majority of those who had paid it, or suffered because of it, were long since dead.

While covering the 2004 federal election I spent a day with Shirley Chan, who was then running—unsuccessfully, it would turn out—as the Liberal candidate in Vancouver East. She took me to her ancestral home on the edge of the city's famous Chinatown and gave me a crash course on how one Chinese immigrant, Lee Wo Soon Chan, came to this strange foreign country and made it her own.

The home is almost exactly as it was when Shirley Chan was growing up in the late 1950s and early 1960s. Same kitchen cupboards, same sink, same green Formica table around which the family would eat. In the basement of this strangely preserved home is a small shrine to Shirley's mother, Lee Wo Soon Chan, who was known to everyone in the Chinatown district as "Chun Tai" and whom the Vancouver media often referred to as "The Mayor of Chinatown." Photographs of Chun Tai are everywhere—leading marches, campaigning, being cheered in parades, meeting with dignitaries, helping out the less fortunate, posing in her flamboyant hats and pearls and signature dark sunglasses. There's even the chair she sat in when she held court.

Chun Tai had died eighteen months earlier at age eighty-six. She had been, as they say, "larger than life," and now, in this private basement room, she was larger than death. Her daughter had carefully laid out her life story, and Shirley wanted that story preserved. To her, and to a great many other Chinese Canadians, Chun Tai was the one who had saved their distinctive community.

Lee Wo Soon Chan had been a schoolteacher in China and suffered greatly during the long civil war. She was able to get out of the country and made it to Canada, where she found work in a factory. But she was also, her daughter says, "a one-person social agency service." She was bright. She learned English easily and could read and write it. Family and neighbours turned to her to fill in their papers, to sort out their immigration problems, to help them find jobs. She increasingly became an activist in the Chinatown area and was soon known all over Vancouver as a formidable political force.

When Vancouver city council decided that the only solution to its growing traffic problems—problems that persist to this day—was to level the shabby Chinatown area, it was Chun Tai who took on City Hall and won. She organized the people, led the rallies, and convinced the media of the value in reviving this historic area—an area that today is one of Vancouver's most popular tourist attractions.

Shirley Chan had been helping her mother fight City Hall since she was eight. She was a young university student when, with her mother's blessing, she stood in front of a moving bulldozer and refused to budge until it came to a stop inches away. That was the day the city backed down. To no surprise, Shirley grew up to have a successful career in city and provincial politics.

At one point she asked me if I noticed anything unusual about the many photographs set around the shrine.

I looked carefully. The sunglasses? No. The hats? No, but close.

"What then?"

"You won't find a single one, even when she's on vacation, where she's not wearing a high collar."

I looked, not sure what, if anything, that meant.

"It's deliberate," Shirley said.

During the civil-war years little Lee Wo Soon Chan, who was tall and athletic, had been taken out of school and forced to run supplies between villages. She carried them tied to the ends of a strong wooden pole placed over her shoulders. She carried day and night, often under cover of darkness, and she did it so often it changed her appearance.

"It left her with a huge callous that never really went away," Shirley explained, "and my mother didn't want anyone to see it." As she spoke she rubbed the back of her own neck, as if the callous had somehow been passed on.

And of course it had, in the way all children of immigrants carry the past with them.

THERE ARE DISPLAYS at Pier 21, and even a short film featuring performers who enact the tears and joy of those who arrived here and were made welcome ... or *Willkomman* ... once their ship reached Halifax. It would be wrong, though, to think of this place as entirely one of happy endings. A great many hopefuls were turned away for reasons that could be as trivial as eyesight. "Imbeciles," prostitutes, and communists were all denied entry. After the Second World War began, five hundred to a thousand children from France, all with Jewish parents, should have been brought through here to safety, but the Canadian government dithered so long that when final approval came through it was already too late.

There are, indeed, also happy stories of babies being born here and of families being reunited, often with members they had given up for dead.

"I saw my first apple in Halifax," a woman wrote. Others burst into tears at the sight of something as simple as an egg.

It is difficult, no impossible, for a Canadian born and raised here to comprehend what it was like for most of these landed immigrants. Their sense of alienation, of confusion, of fear even, would be so profound as to forever engrave the early days of arrival in memory. "Every act of immigration is like suffering a brain stroke," Toronto psychiatrist Vivian Rakoff, himself an immigrant, once told Peter Newman. "One has to learn to walk again, to talk again, to move around the world again, and probably most difficult of all, to reestablish a sense of community."

At Pier 21 you can see the photographed faces of such people; the shock and bewilderment undeniable. You can sit in a facsimile train car and, thanks to fake windows and video feeds, feel as if you're travelling across the country with those who left the pier for other parts, so uncertain of where they were headed or what would become of them. Their stories are as moving as the train is meant to feel.

Sitting in those small cars, watching video of the countryside flashing by and hearing the recorded thoughts of those who came through these gates only to move on through the rest of Canada, you quickly realize just how immigration has changed over the years. Not only the people, but the destination. The early arrivals all seemed headed into the countryside, but later, even by the time Pier 21 shut its doors in 1971, increasingly to the towns and cities. The business of immigration was shifting away from ports. Today's immigrants land at Dorval and Pearson and Vancouver international airports. And they head, almost exclusively, straight for the cities.

THE NOTION of the hyphenated Canadian has long been of concern to those who'd rather see the hyphen deleted. Richard Gwyn, one of the country's most astute political observers over the past forty years, has said that only one identifiable group, the British Canadians of long heritage, immediately considers itself as coming from one country known as Canada. Everyone else, it seems to Gwyn, has allegiance to two or more nations, whether it be the independent Quebec he fears coming or the old countries whose hold never seems to loosen. In his recent book, *Nationalism Without Walls: The Unbearable Lightness of Being Canadian,* he worries that Canada's sense of self is so weak it might just "slip away" one day, scarcely noticed.

The Liberal governments of the Trudeau era made multiculturalism a policy that overtly encouraged the sustaining of previous ties. No melting pot for Canada. Back in 1971, when visible minorities made up less than 1 percent of the population, the federal government began pushing bilingualism and multiculturalism in tandem. Prime Minister Trudeau said at the time, "National unity, if it is to mean anything in the deeply personal sense, must be founded on confidence in one's own individual society." A fine sentiment, even if critics often argued that the true purpose of promoting multiculturalism was to build the Liberal base among newcomers. But now that visible minorities make up fully half the population of such large cities as Toronto, Gwyn and others warn that the small walls once encouraged by multiculturalism can quickly become tall and impenetrable, as evidenced by Great Britain and various European countries today. A 2006 report written for Statistics Canada by University of Toronto sociologist Jeffrey Reitz and doctoral student Rupa Banerjee confirmed that visible-minority immigrants feel more excluded than white immigrants; second-generation visible minorities also feel less identification with Canada than whites do.

And this, Gwyn argues, makes for an increasingly fragile political culture. Unless those walls come down over time, he fears, the "centre cannot hold." "If we ceased to be a community," he writes, "others would notice and would regret the passing of a distinctive idea about how different people can live together."

In my experience, those who most readily see themselves as Canadians first live in the centre: Ontario. There's more demarcation between, say, those living in Newfoundland who think of themselves as Newfoundlanders first or those in Alberta who think of themselves as only Albertans than there is in generations who see themselves as Italian Canadians or Lebanese Canadians.

Perhaps that's just how the human mind handles Confederation. After all, history would seem to suggest, year in and year out and against better logic, that the centre does hold. Those born in Canada to immigrant families might use a hyphen and others will often force a hyphen upon them, but it's worth remembering that the grammatical purpose of the hyphen is to join, not separate.

A few years ago I stood at the corner of Centre Street and 6th Avenue in Calgary on an early July day and watched the Stampede parade pass by. In a crowd estimated at 300,000 I found myself standing beside a young Sikh, Amritpal Singh, and we began discussing how they were managing to keep an air-filled, four-storey-high plastic bear from blowing clear of the parade in all the wind gusting between the office buildings.

I happened to say that it was the first time I'd ever been to the famous Stampede, which he found astonishing.

"This is the biggest religious celebration of the year," he laughed. "This is my twenty-sixth parade. I'll be twenty-five at the end of the month— but I was at my first one two weeks before I was born. I never miss."

ON ONE WALL at Pier 21 is a plaque to honour a very small baby who arrived here and grew up to become Lt.-Gen. Roméo Dallaire. On another wall are testimonials from such landed immigrants as CBC commentator Joe Schlesinger and writers Denise Chong and Peter C. Newman.

Chong, author of *The Concubine's Children: Portrait of a Family Divided*, was born in Canada but has written about her ancestors who came here from South China at the turn of the nineteenth century. Her grandparents found Canada "inhospitable," yet chose to stay. And for that, Chong considers herself most fortunate.

"In all our pasts are an immigrant beginning," she once wrote in an essay, "a settler's accomplishments and setbacks, and the confidence of a common future. We all know the struggle and victory, the dreams and the lost hopes, the pride and the shame. When we tell our stories, we look in the mirror. I believe what we will see is that Canada is not lacking in heroes. Rather, the heroes are to be found within."

In 1940 Peter C. Newman was among the very lucky, a ten-year-old member of a Jewish family who arrived here in late summer aboard the

Nova Scotia. The Neumanns had fled the Nazi occupations of Austria and Czechoslovakia, and the convoy they joined to cross the Atlantic was twice attacked by German U-boats.

Nearly a half century on he wrote about this experience in an essay for *Maclean's* magazine, vividly recalling the first sighting of Nova Scotia from the bow of the ship that carried the province's name. He remembered being tagged and herded into holding rooms with the same bureaucratic regimentation the family thought had been left behind. But it also struck him, as it can strike only the immigrant, how profoundly life had changed.

To get into Canada, his father had to promise the Canadian Pacific Railway that he'd take up a job he knew absolutely nothing about: farming. City dwellers, the Neumanns were headed into the Canadian countryside.

Another of the testimonials at Pier 21 was written by Nobel Laureate Gerhard Herzberg:

In 1935 I came to Canada, a refugee from Germany and the Nazis. I travelled by train across the Prairies on my way to Saskatoon. As we passed through small railway stations, I would see perhaps two or three houses, a grain elevator. Where were the people, I wondered.

But when I arrived in Saskatoon, I found them. These people were curious, kind and friendly, and they had time to listen to me, and my story. I settled into work at the University of Saskatchewan and found colleagues of considerable repute. Canada is really the country that saved me. I have a sort of hunch that Canada IS my country.

In 2006, 800,000 others around this troubled world wanted to do the same: make Canada *their* country. This is the backlog of immigrants hoping to cross through today's equivalent of Pier 21. The figure had risen by a hundred thousand in the previous year alone.

And the country is growing old so fast that, even with Canada surpassing its immigration targets year after year—around a quarter of a million have been arriving annually in recent years—labour shortfalls and retirement realities are on a collision course. The C.D. Howe Institute published a study calculating that the only way the country could keep its retirees-to-workers ratio at current levels would be to take in 2.6 million immigrants a year by 2020 and 7 million by the year 2050—at which point Canada's population would reach 165.4 million.

And though the doors closed on Pier 21 nearly forty years ago, over the next decades other doors are going to have to open as wide as they possibly can.

IN THE SPRING of 2006 I happened across a recent immigrant in what seemed, on first blush, to be a most unusual and isolated setting: Inuvik, Northwest Territories.

His name was Salah Malik, a forty-nine-year-old Sudanese. Like so many of Canada's recent immigrants, he and his wife, Amani, and their two children, five-year-old Mohammed and two-year-old Lana, were fleeing civil war. They had come to Inuvik by a convoluted route that included time in Toronto, Washington, D.C., and Edmonton. Once in Inuvik, Malik found work as a security guard at the local hospital and a second job pumping gas at an isolated station out toward the little airport.

It had been an extraordinary experience for the family. From hot sunshine to bitter cold and long winter days when the sun barely seemed to exist. From huge populations to hardly anyone at all. But also from civil war to civil peace.

They'd been in the Far North for three years, and it had taken some adjusting. But now there were eight Muslim families—Sudanese, Saudi, Lebanese, Syrian, and Libyan—who had created their own mosque in the town. When the CBC launched its comedy series *Little Mosque on the Prairie* it might just as well have been Little Mosque on the Tundra. The children were thriving in school, Malik was making fairly good money, and the family was adapting to the differences in lifestyle.

The greatest shock since they had arrived, Malik said, wasn't the cold, or the dark, or the lack of shopping, but the day his wife called him in a panic. Someone had dropped a caribou head off on the front porch of their little home. They had no idea who had done so or what it meant. Some *Godfather*-type message to get out of town or else?

Worried, Malik contacted the authorities and asked about it, only to be met with smiles and giggles. His Inuvialuit neighbours had been lucky on their hunt. And in true northern fashion, they were sharing their bounty. The caribou head was considered the finest gift they could offer the quiet newcomers from Sudan.

"The people here," Malik told me, "remind me of Africa."

I laughed.

"No, I'm serious. They have the same culture of sharing, of helping out each other. In so many of those other places we lived, everybody was scared of each other. But not here. It reminds me of Africa."

But as much as Malik liked the people of Inuvik and as much as their children were thriving, Amani had made it clear that she didn't wish to stay here much longer. As soon as they had enough money saved the family was heading back south, likely for Edmonton.

And if not Edmonton, another Canadian city.

Eleven

Prairie Ghosts

THERE HAD BEEN WHITEOUTS all along the Yellowhead Highway since I'd left Saskatoon earlier in the day, the small towns along No. 16—Floral, Clavet, Elstow, Colonsay, Viscount, Plunkett, Guernsey, Lanigan, Jansen, Dafoe—fading in and out like the first television set that came to town.

As I turned south on Highway 6 toward Regina, the little towns vanished completely—this time on the map—until I reached the cross-roads at No. 15, a secondary road that follows the old Canadian Pacific Railway line. When the rail went through this part of the West—the tracks that would carry human cargo from Pier 21 to delivery along the prairies—there were so many water stops and grain elevators that the builders evidently tired of looking for original names. Instead, they took to naming stops after the letters in the alphabet: Fenwood, Goodeve, Hubbard, Ituna, Jasmin, Kelleher, Lestock ... Punnichy, Quinton, Raymore, Semans ...

Like an old church sign, some of the letters are missing. Whatever became of M? Where is N? O? ... Why no T?

I come to Raymore often. My wife Ellen's grandparents—John and Ellen Whitlock—homesteaded here at a time when Christmas and birth-day cards arriving from England said "Mr. and Mrs. J.E. Whitlock, General Delivery, Raymore, Northwest Territories, Canada."

They were living here in 1905, when Saskatchewan and Alberta became provinces. They had their first two children, Ted and Flossie, in a sod house, their next two, Rosa and Fred, in a white clapboard farmhouse with green shutters that still stands on a quarter section of rolling land just south of No. 15. Two boys and two girls, both girls heading off to nurse, Rosa to the east, Flo to the west, while the boys stayed on to work the farm. Not an unfamiliar story on the Canadian prairies.

Apart from Fred's war years as a bomber navigator in the Royal Canadian Air Force, the two brothers never left the farm and were still known locally known as "the boys" long after their parents died—both at age ninety-eight, both staying on the farm virtually to the end, in typical Saskatchewan fashion. Ted and Fred were still "the boys" as they hit their sixties, their seventies. When Ted was well into his eighties he became ill with leukemia and died. When Fred hit his eighties he married Virginia, a widow he'd met at the Royal Canadian Legion in Victoria, where he spent his winters, and the two of them drove across the country in a silver Mustang convertible before heading out for a tour of Australia. When they returned, they came back to the farm.

I was going to dinner that cold, blustery night at the home of Don and Marcia Harris, goodhearted schoolteachers who had, over time, become the family Ted had never had. I stopped in at the little Raymore liquor outlet to pick up a bottle of wine.

And that's where I found the missing T.

T for Tate.

There was a bin near the cash register containing special Christmas gift suggestions from the provincial liquor control board. For $29.99 you could purchase a little red ceramic grain elevator filled with ten-year-old whisky and bearing the name of a town carefully stencilled on the side by the clerks of the various outlets. Depending on where the liquor store was, the popular names might be Climax or Eyebrow or Mozart—Saskatchewan leads the nation in place names, Newfoundland a close second—and here, in Raymore, the bin was filled, predictably, with Raymore and Semans and Southey and Wishart and Nokomis ... but also several grain elevators bearing the name Tate.

People in town knew where Tate was—or at least where it *had been*. Just past Semans and, a few kilometres west, turn right and go north to just beyond the railroad tracks. I tried the next day, but the drifting snow made passage impossible. Highway 15 was plowed and open, but the turnoff to Tate hadn't seen a snowplow in years, perhaps decades. It was a place to check out in finer weather.

I came back to Tate, Saskatchewan, on a summer's day when the flax was in magnificent bloom and the Saskatoon berries ripe for picking. Ellen and I came with our children as well as the Harrises and their children, Don carrying an old map he'd found somewhere that seemed to show where things once were in Tate. Through a long, hot afternoon we walked what's left of the streets of this ghost town that once had its own grain elevator, a hotel, Chinese restaurant, hardware store, post office, school, church, cemetery …

A few buildings were still standing, or half standing, a couple with hornets in the eaves and wild-animal droppings over the broken floors. The old post office still had "Tate" on the sign, the town named after D'Arcy Tate, a solicitor for the Grand Trunk Pacific Railway. The whole place was overgrown with caragana and lilac that would have been planted by those who never for a moment imagined their dream would simply disappear. Abandoned cars were in the fields, their model years—1940s, early 1950s—a rusty reminder of when it all began to turn the other way.

Since that summer day we spent walking silently about the graveyard that is now town as well as cemetery, the post office has also vanished, burned down one late-spring evening by local high schoolers during what some say was a "bush party." Now there's hardly any sign at all of Tate.

Not so with Smuts, which can be seen from a distance by anyone driving along Highway 41 running north and east of Saskatoon. Little Smuts came into existence in the 1920s, when the Canadian Northern pushed a spur line through to bustling Melfort and decided to name the key watering spot after a now largely forgotten politician, Colonel Jan Christiaan Smuts.

Smuts was the longtime prime minister of South Africa and has the honour of being the only signatory of both treaties that ended the two World Wars. Canada was obviously once quite struck by him, for there is a summit, Mount Smuts, near where the Rocky Mountains cross the

49th parallel into the United States. And, of course, there was once Smuts, Saskatchewan.

It was another wintry day when I came, in a different year, and the snow was crisp and fresh fallen under blue skies, the odd lasso of loose snow swirling in gusts across the open fields. At one turn in the road a single coyote, grey and sleek, sat on a small knoll of field staring at the traffic going by this winter's day. One car, one driver—we were the only two creatures for miles around.

There's not much left of Smuts. The houses are abandoned, the few storefronts boarded up. Where once the "Red & White" sign invited travellers to turn in off the highway, now the D dangled upside down in the wind. The boards had greyed and dried under the summer sun; locked doors had broken backward from their hinges. The only tracks, it seemed, belonged to the coyote, the deliberate wanderings of a night watchman as he moved from door to door to door in search of rabbits and rodents.

In one home, an old picture album lay on a bare floor, the photographs of a waving young family so faded they no longer had faces. In the old school, half-renovated, then abandoned as a home, a clean blue dress with white polka dots and a red sash was still hanging in a closet, perfectly fitted to a hanger and swinging oddly in the sudden wind that sent snow in through the window and caused the room to sparkle, magically, in the sunlight.

But the magic, like the town, did not last long.

In a far corner, the October 2, 1964, edition of the *Saskatoon Star-Phoenix* lay iced to the floor, the front page warning of Hurricane Hilda slamming into Texas and heading north. In another room the *Wakaw Recorder* of September 3, 1964, leads with "Rainfall continues to hold up harvesting."

The fall of '64—Final Harvest.

Driving back down the 41 toward Highway 5 that would take me back to Saskatoon, I check the knoll for the coyote, but he was gone. According to prairie Native legend, when everyone else has left, the coyote still remains.

Someone, perhaps, to turn out the lights.

WHATEVER BECAME OF the 800,000,000 souls?

That number is correct: eight hundred *million.*

Back in 1887 the Government of Canada, desperate to attract settlers to the Canadian West, dispatched Edmund Collins to New York City to see if he could get the word out that Canada was open for business. Collins certainly did his best. In an address to one of the influential business clubs on "The Future of the Dominion," he offered up the incredible expert opinion that, "Alone, the valley of the Saskatchewan, according to scientific computation, is capable of sustaining 800,000,000 souls."

Tate and Smuts would have settled, in the end, for one soul willing to stick around.

Collins was hardly alone in his wild ambitions for that part of the country. Sir Charles Tupper, one of the Fathers of Confederation, told the House of Commons in 1879 that "we believe we have there the garden of the world." It was a common theme and remained in use for decades. Before he became premier of the province, Tommy Douglas would tell his Baptist congregation in little Weyburn that they would build a new "Jerusalem in this green and pleasant land." As recently as 1944, the great seer Edgar Cayce was prophesying that rich, fertile, open Saskatchewan "must feed the world" that was surely coming.

But no one saw *this* coming—at least they didn't in the early years. By 1912 Saskatoon was calling itself "the fastest-growing city in the world" and predicting its population would crest two million by 1931. At that point, it was claimed, Saskatoon would join St. Louis and Chicago in the "great family of Western Cities."

Of course it never happened. The Crash of 1929 was followed by nine successive years of drought and crop failure. It got so bad during the 1937 Dust Bowl that, in a small town near Regina, a young baseball player was said to have lost his directions after rounding first and was later found three miles out on the prairie, still looking for second.

Today fewer than one million people live in Saskatchewan, even fewer than there were a generation ago. In most years more people leave than come in, those leaving usually young families and young workers, those coming in often retirees returning for reasons of nostalgia and cost. Some communities have been known to offer lots for as little as a single dollar, livable homes for not much more. There was once approximately a thousand communities in the province, but today for every little Raymore that keeps its hockey rink and gets a high school there's a Tate that vanishes or a couple of smaller communities just down the line—Semans to the west, Quinton to the east—that are fast fading. Only the very large communities—Saskatoon in particular, with its university and high-tech growth and increasingly diverse industry—can be said to be thriving. Everywhere else it's a struggle just to hold steady.

Drive a secondary highway almost anywhere in the grain belt, Roger Epp and Dave Whitson, two Albertan political scientists, wrote in their introduction to *Writing Off the Rural West: Globalization, Governments, and the Transformation of Rural Communities,*

> and the picture that emerges is not one of prosperity. The horizon is bereft of the familiar elevators that once announced towns and villages. The pavement is likely patched or broken. The road is virtually empty save for tandem trucks that spin a rock at your windshield or crowd you onto a shoulder. At strategic points along the remaining rail routes, near towns that survive as service centres in a contracting economy, you can see their destinations: high-volume terminals bearing the names of grain barons like Cargill and Louis Dreyfus, and what were prairie wheat pools before their corporate makeovers.

It's not that money is no longer being made by farming in the Canadian prairies, it's that the money doesn't stay—as a cursory look at most small-town Main Streets will immediately confirm.

Even the familiar landscape has shifted. The iconic grain elevators numbered more than sixteen hundred a half century ago, but today are roughly as many in number as the ceramic ones in the bin at the front of the Raymore liquor outlet. Some have been turned into museums. Most were torn down and carted away as the reality of modern transportation obliterated first the rationale of having one grain elevator or more in every single community and then the rationale of the map-speckled communities themselves.

All that remains the same is the Big Sky—with fewer landmarks on the horizon.

In the great midlands of the United States they call this the "emptying out." The young leave for opportunity, for adventure, for conveniences. Farming, with its uncertainty and its personal pressures, loses its attraction when those who dream of life on the land face up to such matters as international subsidies and competition, crop failures, fickle weather, and the totally unexpected, such as mad cow disease closing down the border to what had been a guaranteed market.

In February of 2000, during a series on Saskatchewan that Adam Killick and I were writing for the *National Post,* we made reference to Eric Howe, a professor of economics at the University of Saskatchewan who happened to call his beloved province "the Mississippi of the North." Howe saw a province ill-prepared in both education and skills to deal with the vast changes coming in agriculture. He saw the best minds leaving and the Native population exploding to the point where, some demographers now believe, by the middle of this century Saskatchewan could become the first province with an Aboriginal majority.

The phrase "Mississippi of the North" outraged those who treasure this province. The premier at the time, Roy Romanow, was furious, claiming the series was factually incorrect—Saskatchewan had *more* than a million people and we were ignoring the fact of recent economic growth. By the time the next election rolled around, however, the census had borne out our numbers—the population had fallen to less than a million and the economy had soured. A short while later the economy shifted again, the oil boom elevating Saskatchewan into unfamiliar status as a "have" province that for a time delivered somewhat more revenues to the national equalization program than it was getting back.

The population, however, remained below a million, sometimes shifting up, sometimes down. Saskatchewan was increasingly seen as a province apart, a province of the past rather than the future, a province of the country rather than the city. It became symbolic of a growing urban–rural split in this country, something that many were soon calling "the new Two Solitudes."

At the time of that controversial story, however, angry readers were keen to shoot both messengers and professor without realizing that we felt as fondly about Saskatchewan as they did. When *Maclean's* columnist Allan Fotheringham called this "the most *Canadian* of provinces"— Fotheringham was born in its tiny community of Hearne in 1932—he wasn't being facetious, or sarcastic, or funny. He was simply being accurate.

But Saskatchewan was fast becoming Canadian in a *Canadiana* sense— a province whose fastest rising value was sentiment.

There's always a danger in over-romanticizing the countryside. I myself am often guilty of it and won't deny having a sentimental streak. But you can't go too far. Journalists—despite the privilege of *entrée,* the air mile points, the expense accounts, and even the ridiculous sense of self-importance—are supposed to keep some thin grip on reality. Jeremy Paxman looked at the tendency in *The English,* pointing out that "somehow the English mind kept alive the idea that the soul of England lay in the countryside." But the romance of the far harsher Canadian countryside isn't as simple as Paxman found it in England: wolves instead of hedgehogs, winter instead of mist, lost in the bush instead of wandering through the cowslips by a gentle stream....

Rather than dreaming of being country squires, Canadians tend to dream of having some small place of escape where the soul can be rejuvenated: a cottage, a camp, a cabin, or even a nice campsite on the banks of a northern river. As the late Canadian historian W.L. Morton observed more than half a century ago, the "alternative penetration of the wilderness and return to civilization is the basic rhythm of Canadian life."

Bruce Hutchison found it at his lake on Vancouver Island. "For myself," he once wrote, "the return to my swamp and the whispered welcome of the forest seems like release from a luxurious prison." Millions of Canadians would agree. I certainly do.

There is romance in Canada for summer retreats and canoe trips, but there is no permanence to such notions. A canoe trip in February is not only impossible to imagine but, in most of the country, impossible to execute. There is, however, a great fondness of heart for rural life and rural connections in Canada. As there should be.

But there is also a great respect for reality in a land where wills sometimes have to be carved into tractor fenders, where the railroad can't go through everywhere, and where, if an Inuk hunter lays down a glove while skinning a seal and the wind blows that glove away, the hunter has about as much chance of survival as the hunted.

And the reality of Canada is urbanization.

Twelve

The New Two Solitudes

I FIRST HEARD this phrase—"the new Two Solitudes"—during a 2003 interview with Carleton University social scientist Paul Reed. Reed, along with other academics and statisticians, was talking about a fundamental shift in demographics—a change that had already produced a Canada the likes of which none had ever known and most had never imagined.

In the decade leading up to the 2001 census, Canada's urban population grew by more than three million while the rural population fell by 300,000. Canada had shifted from a country where 80 percent of the population was rural and 20 percent urban to the precise opposite.

The Canada these social scientists saw emerging wasn't marked by the dual languages of novelist Hugh MacLennan's *Two Solitudes*. The new Two Solitudes wasn't about any east–west split. Nor was it a facile way of describing a country with one level of government in Ottawa and the other in the provincial capitals. It was, instead, two solitudes composed of the vast majority who live in cities and the increasingly small minority who do not. Canada, somehow, had gone from being a settler's country to being the most urbanized large country in the Western world.

Even more dramatically, Reed pointed out, the demographic shift had reached a point where more than half of all Canadians, 52 percent, were living in only four Big City regions: Ontario's Golden Horseshoe, the Montreal Urban Community, the Calgary–Edmonton axis, and B.C.'s Lower Mainland. "It's sobering to recognize," added Reed, "that the

Greater Toronto Area would, if designated a province, be fourth largest in population and conceivably largest of all in economic terms."

"Without quite realizing it," University of Toronto political scientist David Cameron, a colleague of Reed's, argued, "we Canadians are in the process of building a new country within the old one. The new country is composed of the large cities, especially the great metropolitan centres of Montreal, Toronto, and Vancouver, the old country is all the rest. Life in the former bears little resemblance to life in the latter...."

LIFE IN THE FORMER can be very good indeed. Of the great metropolitan centres, I happen to live closest to Montreal and, over the years, have covered more ground in Canada's most walkable big city than in any of the other sprawling giants.

The street I love to walk in Montreal is Ste-Catherine, surely the most alive, divergent, sexy, and interesting one in the country. It's a walker's paradise, a single street that's worth a morning, afternoon, or—best of all—nighttime visit. It's also a rare city street in that it feels as if most of those on it have walked here from their homes, something one rarely feels on other main streets in other cities in other provinces.

It's a street of traffic jams, sirens, musicians, beggars, upper-crust shops, dollar stores, eccentrics, double-parked BMWs, artisans, people from every possible continent and every imaginable country. Walkers along Ste-Catherine move at a pace that can be described only as Montreal: neither too slow nor too fast, eye-to-eye contact, even among members of the opposite sex—which tends to rattle visitors from other parts of the country—and a strong sense that there's nowhere they have to be and in fact nowhere else on earth they'd rather be.

No wonder the international travel writer Jan Morris called Montreal "the most interesting city in Canada." No wonder, after a day of poking along streets like Ste-Catherine, she felt compelled to note how often people here smile and speak and engage each other casually. "They are," she wrote, "less numb than their cousins in Toronto or Vancouver."

Mark Twain said you couldn't throw a stone in Montreal without hitting a church window, and there are parts of Ste-Catherine where it seems he wasn't exaggerating, despite the street's also being the main shopping district of the city. There are birds in the quiet, daisy-filled gardens of the Anglican Church of St. James the Apostle and there's an eerie calm inside the doors of the Catholic Christ Church Cathedral that dates from 1857 and feels, once inside, like 1857.

There may be plenty of Christian charity inside these churches, but not enough to go around on the streets where—as in all big Canadian centres now—the beggars sometimes outnumber the begged. "It's tough working this place," a large young man with a Mohawk says at the corner of Ste-Catherine and Montagne. "There's somebody at every corner—and people only got so much spare change."

Harsh realities are found on any large main street. The homeless seem to multiply going west, and by the time afternoon amblers walk down the streets of Vancouver or even Victoria they've become practically oblivious to this modern tragedy. Buskers are also on the streets, but only rarely do passers pretend they do not exist. An older man sitting on a fold-up camping chair plays a lovely accordion solo in front of Ogilvy's; a young man serenades on a saxophone near the corner of Ste-Catherine and University. The Montreal jazz festival may come to town only once a year, but the music of Ste-Catherine is year round, and to the untrained ear, often as satisfying.

Ste-Catherine had always been the "shopping" street—they used to run an electric street car between Ogilvy's and the Bay—but it fell on such hard times during the last recession that, early in the 1990s, *Montreal Gazette* columnist Jack Todd wrote, "You had to hold a mirror to the lips of Ste-Catherine to be sure it was still breathing."

Ste-Catherine, happily, has long since been reborn. The empty spaces for rent have been largely rented out. There are new projects, new shopping galleries, new brand-name outlets. Its walkers, with the same Montreal disdain for traffic lights as its drivers, control this street more than any other in the city.

I have moved along this street very slowly, very quietly—once when following the funeral cortège of Pierre Trudeau, once when following the hearse carrying Maurice "Rocket" Richard—and I have run, breathlessly, along this street to reach the campus of Dawson College following the horrific shootings of September 13, 2006. But I've been happiest on it when there's no place I have to be but here, and for as long as I wish to ramble.

The surprises are endless. On a day before a Stanley Cup playoff game a few years ago I set out alone in search of a late lunch, walking in the spring sunshine along Ste-Catherine and losing myself in the sights and smells and sounds of downtown Montreal. Near the corner of Ste-Catherine and St-Mathieu, a sex shop offered "Pasta Boobs" for sale. Snorkels and swim fins were in the same window, hopelessly confusing a sheltered visitor from Ontario.

The window of another sex shop—not, of course, that I was seeking them out, merely bumping into them—near the corner of Ste-Catherine and Fort was filled with boxes of "Mama Peckeroni: Traditional Style Pecker Pasta." Simply add water, bring to a boil, stir in, let simmer—and watch the penises grow.

I did not go in. I can produce bonded witnesses who will back me on this. I continued on in search of a late lunch that would not, under any circumstance, include pasta.

At the corner of Ste-Catherine and McGill College, if you happen to quickly glance to the north, you will see Bavaria. Or at least *think* you've seen a glimpse of a European castle in the high hills of southern Germany. If you happen to be there when the mountain beyond is green and lush and if part of the McGill campus is in view, you'll think you've been transported to another world.

And if you head up into the mountain, you *will* enter another world.

I TEND TO SEEK OUT sanctuaries in every Canadian city—Signal Hill in St. John's, Point Pleasant in Halifax, the Boardwalk in Quebec City, the Rideau Canal in Ottawa, Centre Island in Toronto, the Forks in Winnipeg, Wascana Park in Regina, Eau Claire in Calgary, the river valleys in Saskatoon and Edmonton, Stanley Park in Vancouver—but there is only one "mountain" you can climb, even in slippery city shoes, and be back before the next meal.

And that is Montreal's Mount Royal.

In the short while it takes to walk up along the leafy, switchbacking trails to Lac aux Castors, it feels as if you've travelled by airline and shuttle bus to reach a distant resort. The noise of the city falls away until the only sounds that even those who try their hardest can hear are the gulls on the shallow lake and the wind in the willows along the shore. It's the sort of place Van Morrison must be thinking of when he sings "There's a place way up the mountainside / where the world keeps standing still."

Sanitas, a columnist writing in *The Gazette* one month after Confederation in the summer of 1867, asked the authorities to "give us a noble park on the top of Mount Royal from whose summit a succession of the most beautiful landscapes can be seen, and where the commons may go with their families to breathe the fresh air." It took a crisis to force the issue, though, with a wicked winter a few years later convincing Montreal politicians that any more such freezes and the mountain might be stripped entirely for firewood.

Montreal city authorities had the foresight to turn to Frederick Law Olmsted, an American who had created New York's Central Park and who would go on to work on such natural charms as Yosemite National Park. Olmsted had been profoundly affected by the nature writings of his friends Ralph Waldo Emerson and Henry David Thoreau, and there's a certain "Walden" aspect to almost everything he touched. His thinking in New York had been positively revolutionary. "Buildings," he told New York planners, "are scarcely a necessary part of a park; neither are flower gardens, architectural terraces or fountains. They should, therefore, be constructed after dry walks and drives, greensward and shade, with other essentials, have been secured."

Olmsted liked the potential of this Montreal assignment and decided to take it on, even though he was, according to biographer Witold Rybczynski, rather underwhelmed by the $5000 offered for his design expertise.

He set for himself three main priorities that could serve today as valid guidance for any Canadian community deciding what to do with a special plot of land that might be preserved rather than developed.

First, take full advantage of whatever natural beauty already exists. Second, keep the costs down as much as possible. And third, in true Canadian fashion, ensure universal access.

Keeping costs to a minimum is why there are simple trails through the trees, the foliage natural instead of planted and groomed. Olmsted gave no credence to such matters as gardens or sculpted terraces or fountains. He had great faith in simple shade. And the more he tromped around the deep woods of the Mountain, the more he became entranced by a beauty unknown in other large centres. Trying to develop it, or trying even to shape it in ways it did not wish to be shaped, he declared, would "only make it ridiculous. It would be wasteful to try to make anything else than a mountain of it."

Those who knew him best, as well as those who paid him, often grew impatient with Olmsted's obsessive long-term thinking. A fountain, after all, can be built before your eyes; an oak tree takes decades just to be noticed. But he had remarkable patience and a belief in the long term. When his young son Rick pressed him for "results," he told the boy he had better be willing to wait at least forty years. He once said: "I have all my life been considering distant effects and always sacrificing immediate success and applause to the future."

Time brought along certain things of which Olmsted would never have approved—distracting communications towers, an ugly 31.4-metre-high illuminated cross, paddle boats on the little manmade lake—but by and large I suspect he'd be pleased. The closest encroachment comes from McGill University and the very rich along the city side, St. Joseph's Oratory on the west, and massive, sprawling cemeteries to the north. One of these, Notre-Dame-des-Neiges, is the largest Catholic cemetery in North America, holding more than a million graves. Perfect neighbours for such a peaceful setting.

Olmsted preserved a "mountain" with extraordinary vistas of the city and the St. Lawrence River, marvellous hiking and jogging and biking trails, and enough hardwood to drive lumber companies to distraction. About eighty thousand trees were damaged here in the 1998 ice storm, and yet today that onslaught is hardly noticeable.

Rybczynski lived some twenty years in Montreal and was always within walking distance of the Mountain. It was a place for picnics and dogs, for tobogganing and quiet, reflective moments alone. It was, he writes in *A Clearing in the Distance,* "like taking a drive in the country"— without ever having to leave the city.

Today Mount Royal remains a remarkable oasis of peace and beauty, much as it was when Olmsted began his work and just as it was in 1914 when British author Arthur Conan Doyle stood overlooking the city and called it "one of the most wonderful views in the world."

Olmsted's "results" after forty years were impressive enough. The results 140 years after Confederation are even more impressive. For in a country that has flipped from rural to urban but still treasures the natural beauty of the landscape, it is places like Montreal's mountain that make Canadian cities so remarkably livable.

CANADIANS, and even some Torontonians, love to ridicule Toronto as "the centre of the universe," but in some ways it is. It's the major centre. It's where the big theatre productions come on tour and sometimes begin. It's where the big international literary and film festivals are held. And it's the perch from which the national media survey the rest of the country, even if at times condescendingly, even if at times cock-eyed.

Toronto serves as a wonderful foil for those who don't live there—*How about them Leafs?*—but in truth it's a remarkable city composed of dozens of interesting neighbourhoods that can be as dramatically different from one another as are the regions of Canada. It's a city of terrible traffic but magnificent ravines, a city that produces violent headlines, particularly Monday mornings, but is considered safe by those who live there and alarming by those who don't. It was once known as "Toronto the Good" but can be very bad indeed. It's large enough today to accommodate almost every imaginable opinion and impression, even the wrong ones.

"I do not pretend to understand Toronto," Bruce Hutchison wrote in *The Unknown Country.* To him it seemed an island apart, the most insular of cities, yet at heart a small town. How curious that today that definition would be embraced by those who live there.

The city, in Hutchison's time, was second fiddle to Montreal. Yet to him Toronto felt more apart, more aloof from the rest of the country. It was a place filled with people far too busy to have time for the likes of him. He found it stuffy and possessed with "a piety here which annoys."

Toronto is well used to being slagged. "Toronto is like a fourth or fifth-rate provincial town, with the pretensions of a capital city," Anna B. Jameson wrote in her 1838 book *Winter Studies and Summer Rambles*. "We have here a petty colonial oligarchy, a self-constituted aristocracy, based upon nothing real nor upon anything imaginary." More than a century later, in 1946, "We All Hate Toronto" was a popular drama on CBC radio. And several years ago an Edmonton group calling itself Three Dead Trolls in a Baggie had a small hit with "The Toronto Song," in which the band dumped on everything from the CN Tower to high rents to the air that's unclean—"And the people are mean!"

Much of this resentment is brought on by the city itself. Toronto, for example, is the heart of Canadian publishing and reviewing, meaning that the very definition of "regional" writing—therefore minor, rather insignificant, sort of like folk art—is any scribbling done beyond sight of the CN Tower. But the resentment goes only so far. As British Columbia humorist—sorry, *regional* humorist—Eric Nicol once warned, Canadian unity "cannot depend forever on hating Toronto." The Toronto of today is not Bruce Hutchison's Toronto, not Anna Jameson's Toronto, not even the Toronto of Three Dead Trolls in a Baggie. It is a city of excellent theatre, fine restaurants, high-end shopping, fabulous island escapes, superb public transit, homelessness, periodic gun violence, pollution, and a waterfront that developers seem determined to keep from the people. In other words, it has become the world-class city its inhabitants once dreamed of and the rest of Canada once ridiculed.

It is also now Canada's largest city by a significant stretch—and, by definition, where people want to live. And especially those people coming to Canada to start a new life.

The Pier 21 of today is Pearson International Airport. And the train that new Canadians take is now a subway or a light rail heading into downtown Montreal, Toronto, Calgary, Edmonton, and Vancouver.

The new coming to Canada go where, for some time now, the old have also been going. To the cities.

CANADA, ALMOST UNNOTICED, became a country of great cities in the last quarter of the twentieth century. Calgary, once laughed at by Allan Fotheringham for looking as if it had just been uncrated but not yet assembled, went from being an oil-obsessed place with little to offer to a fine city with good light-rail access, soaring house prices in the suburbs, and a downtown redevelopment that made the Eau Claire shopping area and river trails the envy of any growing metropolis. Edmonton, with its dramatic ravines and vibrant bar scenes, was suddenly hard-pressed to stay ahead as the provincial centre for culture, a contest that was good for both cities and led to a blossoming of theatre and music. Saskatoon became a city of education, high-tech industry, and economic diversity, no longer the struggling switching yard and supplier to the outlying farm world. Winnipeg, with a new downtown arena, the best ball park in Canada, and the common-sense development of the Forks area by the rivers, became a city where only those who'd never been there chuckled at the cold winds blowing over Portage and Main. Winnipeggers, meanwhile, used their downtown tunnels to shop in bad weather, perhaps taking time out to rub Timothy Eaton's bronze toe for good luck.

In every major centre in the country it was much the same story. St. John's was booming while the rest of the province of Newfoundland and Labrador seemed to be emptying out. Halifax, with its wharf development alongside Pier 21, was a city for poking around in, filled with historic sites and good restaurants and bars featuring the best Celtic music in the country. Fredericton had its world-class art gallery, the Beaverbrook, with its famous Dalis and Turners and Gainsboroughs. Quebec City, despite losing its hockey team, was still a city of extraordinary charm and élan, with the Boardwalk on a warm May day with a vanilla ice cream dripping over your cupped hand perhaps the finest stroll available in this country. As for Vancouver, nothing need be said that hasn't been said a million times. With the mountains in the background and the sea in every backdrop, it may have the most beautiful setting in all of North America. On a clear, warm day there's simply no better city to find yourself in—and not a bad place on a cold, wet day, either.

In the years since Pier 21 closed down in 1971, urbanization and increased immigration to the cities have meant that almost two-thirds of Canadians live in centres with more than a hundred thousand people. And with more than three of every four new Canadians heading for cities, it's a percentage that will only increase in the coming years.

That reality is also being felt in politics. Years ago, then Toronto mayor David Crombie argued that "city dwellers are the only majority group I know that allows themselves to be over-governed, under-represented and ignored." And their situation was far, far fairer at the time he spoke than it is today.

"Somewhere between asylums and saloons," British Columbia's Joanne Monahan, former head of the Federation of Canadian Municipalities, has said, "that's where you find municipal government in the Canadian Constitution."

In the first decade of the twenty-first century big-city mayors began talking of a "New Deal" that would lead, they hoped, to expanded legal powers for cities, among them the ability to tax, or to take a cut of, the massive gasoline royalties being collected by the federal and provincial governments. Reports began to appear, including the Toronto-Dominion Bank's *A Choice Between Investing in Canadian Cities or Disinvesting in Canada's Future,* whose title essentially gives away the storyline. In 2003 the Toronto City Summit Alliance reported that "quite simply, Canadian federalism is not working for our large city regions." The Laidlaw Foundation and the Canada West Foundation said much the same thing.

Canada, it seemed, was in the midst of a ... civic war.

Perhaps the most eloquent of the New Deal supporters was New Democratic leader Jack Layton, himself a former Toronto city councillor and once head of the Federation of Canadian Municipalities. In Layton's 2006 revised edition of *Speaking Out Louder* he detailed the unfairness of the current political structure. Winnipeg, for example, accounted for two-thirds of Manitoba's economy while more than 50 percent of the taxes paid by its residents went to the federal government, 43 percent went to the provincial government, and less than 7 percent went to city government. In Layton's own Greater Toronto Area the numbers were even more striking, with Ottawa netting some $17 billion in residents' taxes while the province's net take (tax revenue less payments back to the city) was $3 billion. "Canada's cities," Layton wrote, "generate enormous revenues for the federal and provincial governments. What the cities get in return is a pittance. Federal, provincial and territorial governments control the spending of over 95 percent of all tax dollars. Municipalities control less than 5 percent."

"We've got the responsibility," St. John's mayor Andy Wells said at a 2002 symposium, "but we don't have the legislative authority and the fiscal tools."

The city mayors warned that they were all facing current and coming infrastructure crises, from potholes to public housing, transit to waste disposal, but with limited means to raise the required money. Cities have to rely almost exclusively on property taxes and are almost totally excluded, by law, from collecting personal, fuel, and sales taxes. Most such capital expenditures, therefore, fall to the provincial governments—and critics say the provinces are woefully underprepared for the coming infrastructure crush.

In the Greater Toronto Area, for example, a 2006 report predicted that within twenty-five years—when the GTA population is expected to reach eight million—Toronto's roads will have to handle a hundred thousand more cars during morning and afternoon rush hours with another fifty thousand transit riders looking for buses and waiting for space in subway cars. "The hard, cold facts of the matter are that today, there is no such thing as a GTA transportation plan," said Richard Soberman, the civil engineering professor who oversaw the study.

According to the Federation of Canadian Municipalities, $60 billion was needed just for necessary repairs and maintenance of cities' existing infrastructures—without even considering the monies required for such future needs as the GTA faced.

Canadians have little realized the extent of urban sprawl in recent years. A Statistics Canada report on "The Loss of Dependable Agricultural Land in Canada" pointed out that, between 1971 and 2000, the amount of urban land increased by 96 percent. This meant, particularly in southern Ontario, that the best farmland was seen as the best housing land. Good agricultural land began disappearing at worrisome rates. It also meant that the greater the sprawl, the greater the transportation needs. Between 1999 and 2003 the number of registered motor vehicles in the country increased by more than one million—the second car by now more necessity than luxury. Urban transportation, including public transit as well as improved roads, became an increasingly important issue—the need far outstripping the available funds.

The same Statistics Canada report said that urbanization over those thirty years ate up the equivalent of *three* Prince Edward Islands. That would be taking P.E.I.—where you can often drive for miles without seeing another car, where the open fields seem to roll on forever—and turning three times that space into strip malls and industrial parks and housing developments where the buildings are packed so tightly together the only way you can walk from the front yard to the back is by turning sideways and sucking in your gut.

Back in 1980, when "the vanishing land" was very briefly a public issue, Environment Canada projected that, by the turn of the century, urbanization would gobble up land roughly the size of the same Maritime province. Critics at the time thought it a gross exaggeration.

THE URBAN–RURAL SPLIT has had several repercussions. Rural Canadians feel increasingly abandoned, increasingly left out of the prolonged economic boom that has centred on the main cities, particularly in Ontario, Alberta, and British Columbia. City dwellers are also irritated whenever they happen to think about the somewhat anachronistic distribution of power in this country that not so long ago was so very rural.

Little Prince Edward Island, for example, has fewer people than many federal constituencies in Montreal, Toronto, and the Lower Mainland of British Columbia, yet P.E.I. is guaranteed four seats in the House of Commons thanks to a 1915 agreement that says no province can have fewer MPs than senators at any time. Put another way, P.E.I. gets four senators for a province with a population considerably less than Sudbury while each of the two fastest-growing Western provinces, Alberta and British Columbia, gets six.

Even so, it's unlikely that any Canadian living in rural Canada feels more significant, or powerful, than any Canadian living in one of the five city centres. Not when the loudest voices in recent years have been the cries of the major city mayors, chief among them Toronto mayor David Miller.

Electoral reform, in whatever form it ultimately takes in this country, will almost certainly give increased powers to the urbanized economic centres. And while a reformed senate—even if it one day approaches the Elected, Equal, and Effective triad once proposed by the Reform Party— is intended to help balance the regions, it would still be urban focused.

When Glen Murray was mayor of Winnipeg he was one of the driving forces behind the search for a New Deal for cities. If the country is 80 percent urbanized today, Murray told me one day in Winnipeg not long before he left city politics for an unsuccessful try at federal politics, it will be 90 percent urbanized by the year 2020. In his view, if the nineteenth century was about empires and the twentieth century about nations, then the twenty-first will ultimately be about modern city states.

He saw "a real immaturity in Canadian political organizations" that would need to be addressed in the coming years. With city power on the rise, provincial power would have to dwindle. "If the federal government treated the provinces the way provinces treat cities," he warned, "there would be civil war."

THE TRANSFORMATION from rural to urban hasn't been restricted to Canada, of course; the United States too has increasingly become a vast hinterland with pockets of virtual city states. David Brooks's recent essay in *The Atlantic Monthly* asked, "Are We Really One Country?" But the American Two Solitudes, if we may call it that, is far more split along political lines, divided as it is between the red states of the heartland, which voted for George W. Bush, and the blue states along the seaboards, which didn't vote for Bush. Brooks perceives a split so profound that the reds have no idea what life in the blue states is like, and the blues no sense of life in the reds.

Red of course stands for Republican conservatism, blue for Democratic liberalism. In Canada, where, conversely, red is the colour of the Liberal vote and blue the Conservative, the elections of 2004 and 2006 demonstrated a similar split, with red prevailing in the cities and blue in the smaller communities and countryside.

A country divided.

And following the January 23, 2006, election even more a contradiction than ever, with a minority Conservative government in charge and the Liberals largely reduced to those city centres that were, in so many other ways, running so much of the country: Toronto, Montreal, Vancouver, Ottawa. Tory blue, however, was solid in Alberta, where oil and gas had turned Calgary and, by extension, mushrooming Fort McMurray in the oil sands into the main economic engines of the country.

Stephen Harper's slim victory in 2006 may have averted yet another crisis in the rolling panic attack that is Canadian unity. Eighteen months earlier, when the Liberals had squeaked out a minority victory under Paul Martin, the West had recoiled in anger. It meant, to them, that Eastern voters—Ontario in particular—had decided to stick with the Liberals despite the ongoing sponsorship scandal and the clear signals from the West that it was well past time for change. The West had the economic power; the West had the growth; but the West felt powerless in determining Ottawa.

I was in Calgary at the end of June 2005, watching in the Roundup Centre as the air went out of the thundersticks the Tory faithful had been holding in anticipation of victory. The anger was palpable.

"There is no Canada!" Elizabeth Craine told me. She'd worked for the Conservative Party since John Diefenbaker's time and had that very day served as a scrutineer for Harper in his Calgary Southwest riding. "There is no Canada," she repeated as supporters and candidates stood around the Centre looking as though they'd just been struck by lightning.

"There's Quebec. There's the Maritimes. There's Ontario. And there's the West. They're all different.

"Let's wake up to reality—it's time for us to form our own country."

She was hardly alone. Western alienation—a distant cousin to Quebec separation—has been around since Riel, since railway route decisions, since Montreal and Toronto bankers controlled farm loans, since Pierre Trudeau brought in the despised National Energy Program, since Meech Lake failed to address the West's desire for senate reform. It flares periodically—Alberta even has its own separation party—and, had Harper not won in early 2006, likely would have blown as dramatically as Leduc No. 1 did back on February 13, 1947.

The rage following Martin's victory was undeniable. A professor in Calgary emailed me to predict that the country would disappear within ten years. Voters in British Columbia began talking about joining with Alberta and putting an end to Canada altogether.

"I'm not a wild-eyed lunatic," Elizabeth Craine told me that night. "None of us are out here. We just want to see things change. And we can see now that it doesn't work and it can't work. This country is never going to be anything but frustration. Why can't we divide it up? Lots of countries get divided up—and they survive."

Canada, of course, did survive long enough for Harper to claim his own minority. The slogan the Reform Party had adopted on its founding back in 1987—"The West Wants In"—was finally a fact. "The West is in," former Alberta premier Peter Lougheed told me when I went once again to Calgary, this time to listen to the thundersticks pounding in celebration. "Even if it's a minority government, it will be a positive thing for Canada."

"National unity and the state of federalism," added Reform founder Preston Manning, "is in better shape today than it was before this election began."

But no one really expected it to last long; it never does in Canada. Another election could just as easily throw power back to the Liberals. And, increasingly, Alberta was coming to resent how much of its oil money was being lost to such matters as equalization. There was also the continuing matter of senate reform, which Harper had promised to address. And then there was the growing issue of the environment, which Harper would need to deal with. The panic attacks might have subsided somewhat, but the nervous twitches, whether talking about the threat of Quebec separation or Western alienation, were a constant.

The West was in, all right, but as one newly elected Western politician put it, this might delight and calm the West but would most assuredly cause "the Central Canadian Sphincter Index to shoot to the top."

One inescapable observation about the Harper victory was that the Conservative seats were almost exclusively away from the big cities, Edmonton and Calgary being obvious exceptions. And within the West itself there were signs of the urban–rural split, with Edmonton, Calgary, and booming Fort McMurray—now being called the "Shanghai of Canada"—drawing thousands of rural Westerners to high-paying jobs in and around the old industry.

It didn't help Saskatchewan that Alberta, with high-paying jobs and the lure of two mighty cities, was right next door. Young workers and young families were quick to follow opportunity. When my *Globe and Mail* colleague John Stackhouse was researching his *Timbit Nation* in 1999 he passed through Yorkton, picked up the local *This Week,* and found the following reference to the fact that twenty-six thousand people had bailed from the province that year: "Once again, Saskatchewan plays the farm team, educating people for the twenty-first-century economy, at the expense of the Saskatchewan taxpayer, and sending them off to build other provinces." It all seemed to underline what Sharon Butala had written in an essay nearly twenty years earlier: "Saskatchewan was only the holding area where one waited impatiently until one was old enough to leave in order to enter the excitement of the real world."

Yet those who come from Saskatchewan, much like those who come from Newfoundland, have a sort of worship for the place—even if the place left behind has vanished, as in the case of Tate down the road from Raymore.

Wallace Stegner, the celebrated American writer, lived with his family on a homestead near Eastend, Saskatchewan, between 1914 and 1920. He called it "Whitemud" in *Wolf Willow*, the novel he wrote of the Canadian prairies, and said that "prairie and town did the shaping, and sometimes I have wondered if they did not cut us to a pattern no longer viable."

Stegner returned to little Eastend after some three decades living and prospering in the southern United States. Places like Eastend, he believed, were not unlike a coral reef in that they were formed by substance built up through the "slow accrual of time, life, birth, death.... The sense of place so rock solid it, at least, never vanishes." He walked about the town that had so formed him, and concluded, rather evasively: "Has Whitemud anything by now that would recommend it as a human habitat?"

By not answering, he answered.

When the Royal Bank of Canada did a study on what has been called "the internal brain drain," it found there were two big losers among the ten provinces: Saskatchewan and Newfoundland.

No one was surprised in the slightest.

Thirteen

The Colony of Dreams

IT WAS IN BONAVISTA, three hundred kilometres up the wild and rocky eastern coast of Newfoundland from St. John's that, legend has it, Giovanni Caboto first set his feet on firm ground on June 24, 1497. Giovanni was a Venetian but also an entrepreneur, so as "John Cabot" he claimed the land for King Henry VII of England and, for his troubles, collected a ten-pound bonus.

Newfoundlanders consider this their first selling out by outsiders, and certainly not the last.

John Cabot was supposed to be searching for the fabled western passage to Asia, but instead he found this massive rocky island at the far reaches of the Atlantic. He sailed along the western coast until he found the deep shelter of Bonavista Bay, where the cod were so plentiful his men had only to lower weighted baskets into the water then quickly haul them back up teeming with glistening fish. He called it "New-Founde-Land" in the language of his new patron, and the name stuck.

There's a statue of John Cabot on the outcropping of rock that stands between the sheltered harbour and the open sea. For years the fishermen of Bonavista would pass under his gaze as they headed out, just as their fathers and grandfathers and great-grandfathers and great-great-grandfathers had done for centuries. But no more—not since the federal government closed down the cod fishery in these parts and obliterated the only reason Bonavista stands here in the first place.

Yet few here, if any, believe the federal fisheries scientists. They've been wrong before—who, after all, foresaw the collapse of the East Coast fishery?—and they say they're wrong again. The fish haven't gone; they're just ... not here. When Newfoundland's Wayne Johnston was seeking a title for the novel he wrote about his home, he didn't need to think long. *The Colony of Unrequited Dreams* could just as easily stand as the provincial motto.

Not long after the most recent fisheries closures, I called in on Bonavista and found Larry Tremblett cleaning up his fishing boat that hadn't left its moorings in weeks. The vessel, appropriately, is called *High Hopes*—and Tremblett certainly had them. He was convinced that Newfoundland remained a land of such untapped potential—the return of the fisheries, the offshore oil and gas—that it could equal Saudi Arabia if only it were managed correctly. "We'd have people coming down here to do our work for us," he told me, pushing back a frayed and faded baseball cap over curling hair.

It's an old refrain and eerily similar to the "New Jerusalem" dreams of Saskatchewan. A half century earlier Newfoundland's first premier, Joey Smallwood, predicted that his stubborn little province would one day emerge as the "new Alaska." It's always something. The New Norway. The New Iceland. The New Singapore ...

Tremblett pointed to the gulls floating on the calm harbour water. He said that the gulls of Bonavista, once so well fed from the constant dumping of cod guts from the plant, wouldn't even acknowledge the boats coming in and out of the harbour. Now they sit and wait for the odd flush of crab waste. "Watch this," he said.

He walked over to his boat and returned with a handful of herring bait. He threw a couple down into the water and then stood, holding the bait high in a Statue of Liberty pose. The gulls swarmed him instantly, an image that was less a gentle East Coast postcard than something from a Hitchcock film.

But Larry Tremblett doesn't need a horror movie to frighten him. There are payments on his boat. And his two boys, who were supposed to join him on the boat, have left the province in search of work. He has no idea if they'll ever be back. "This," he said, spreading his hands over the scene, "is turning us into a senior-citizen town. The young people get out of school and pack up and go—they've got no other choice."

The mayor of Bonavista, Betty Fitzgerald, worries about her town losing its young, worries about distraught fishermen turning to drink, to violence, to suicide, worries about what the rest of the country—which she says she loves—thinks of her and her fellow Newfoundlanders. "You won't find any harder working people in the country," she said, her long, strawberry-blond hair flying in the wind that snaps the flags outside the town hall offices. "We're caring, kind, hard-working people—so why put us down? Because we're such laid-back people who don't speak out? Why? ... This really bothers me, that people would blame us. I don't think of myself as lazy. Tell me that to my face and they'll be sorry."

Fitzgerald puts in eighteen-hour days at a job that pays nothing in an attempt to salvage some future for the little town. The John Cabot statue attracts the occasional tourist, but hardly enough. If the fishery takes too long to recover, or never does at all, towns like Bonavista are as surely doomed as the Tates and the Smuts three and a half time zones west.

The decline of the Newfoundland fishery has spawned as many theories as gulls drifting over the quiet Bonavista Harbour. The only thing everyone agrees on is that bad management played a part—but whether it was Ottawa's or the province's remains open to question.

"In 1975," Michael Harris writes in his powerful 1998 book *Lament for an Ocean,* "there were 13,736 registered inshore fishermen in Newfoundland; by 1980, that number had ballooned to 33,640. There wasn't a politician in the land who was prepared to accept the consequences of restricting entry to the fishery." The federal government brought in the unemployment insurance that made seasonal work more attractive while the provincial government offered incentives and grants. Licences and quotas were easy to get, and so fish plants went up in unlikely places. And the discrepancies between reported and actual catch were never properly addressed. It was clear from the mid-1980s, Harris argues, "that the fishing industry could not support the number of people who depended on it for a living." Harris was simply ahead of the times on this story.

In the fall of 2006 the journal *Science* reported on a massive international study that predicted the collapse of the entire world's fishery by the middle of this century. In the words of lead researcher Boris Worm, a Canadian, "I think we're smart to realize where we're heading, and avoid it."

All the same, it was not hopeful news for those Newfoundlanders who believe that if the cod isn't already back it's on its way soon. The study also found that 29 percent of the fish and seafood species are currently being caught at less than 10 percent of their historical high catches. Canada, Worm said, is already starting to scrape "the bottom of the barrel," opening a fishery for sea cucumbers and hagfish in Cape Breton.

"After that, it is jellyfish—and then no more."

IN THE LATE WINTER of 2005 I drove from downtown St. John's out to Conception Bay and a small community called St. Philip's. I'd come to visit a man called Gus Etchegary. In his home, high on the bluffs overlooking the spectacular bay, the eighty-year-old retired fish plant manager pulled out huge multicoloured bristol-board graphs to demonstrate own theories of the fishery's demise.

"Honest to God," he said while assembling his massive charts, "I hate all the whining and griping. I hate it. But there'd be no need for any of it if our resources had been managed properly."

Joining Confederation back in 1949, he said, was nothing short of a shotgun marriage forced on islanders by Great Britain. The worst part of it, he continued, was the transfer of control over the fishery to Ottawa, not to St. John's. His charts showed massive catches each year from 1 on: decades of consistent 200,000- to 300,000-tonne takes, with another 75,000 tonnes or so going to foreign fleets. And still, year after year, fishery recovered.

After 1949, however, everything began to change. Cod stopped being salted and was instead frozen. European war fleets were turned into fishing vessels, with trawlers and then freezer trawlers moving in to take what used to be caught by jigging with line and hook. By 1968, Etchegary said—thick finger hammering at a spike in the chart—the foreign ca

had soared to 810,000 tonnes. "And that wasn't even accurate. They were underreporting."

The spawning stock shrank, the catches fell year after year, and eventually the fishery collapsed. "The fish," Etchegary said, "never had a chance to recover. Just think of it. A totally renewable resource worth more than $3 billion a year—lost to mismanagement. We should be making a significant contribution to the national economy, not always being criticized for having a handout.

"And here we are, for Christ's sake—we're destitute."

MAINLANDERS TEND TO SEE Newfoundland as forever on the receiving end of equalization payments—and, indeed, roughly one of every three dollars Newfoundland spends today does come from those federal payments. But for Betty Fitzgerald, too many Canadians likely agreed with Stephen Harper when he spoke of a "culture of defeatism" in the East.

Newfoundland, in truth, often led the country in growth in the early part of this century, its percentage increase in gross domestic product rising more quickly than other provinces' in part because it had been so much lower to begin with. That growth, however, is another story in the urban–rural split. St. John's and its suburbs were booming, with housing prices going up, SUVs in the driveways, a thriving university, and myriad new developments in oil and high tech that had nothing to do with the vanishing fisheries.

Those not living on the more prosperous Avalon Peninsula, on the other hand, could feel things slipping away. And yet they were determined to find some catch that would allow them to remain. At one point close to tears herself, Fitzgerald shook with anger: "People call us crybabies— well, I've got news for them. We're not crybabies. We're fighters. And now we're going to have to prove that we're fighters."

Newfoundlanders are tough. You have to be tough to survive here. The history of Newfoundland is filled with shipwrecks and seal hunt disasters and lost fishing vessels. Its early governors used to bail at the first sign of snow until in 1817 orders came from London that the current governor,

Admiral Francis Pickmore, must stay over and thereby demonstrate to the locals that their betters were truly better. In the spring Pickmore headed back to London—in a coffin.

"A person might live to the end of his days," Newfoundland humorist Ray Guy once wrote of the resilience of Newfoundlanders, "and never cease to marvel and wonder, one way or another." The wonder today is whether the province is up to battling what may prove the toughest element of all: economic reality. With collapsing fisheries and few jobs, the small places are shrinking, the people leaving for better opportunities either in St. John's or, more often, on the mainland.

This "emptying out," of course, is also occurring in Saskatchewan, northern and northwestern Ontario, northern Quebec, the rural parts of Atlantic Canada, and isolated pockets right across the country. But only in Saskatchewan and Newfoundland and Labrador is it necessary for those running for premier to talk about stopping the flow and even bringing the young people back. And only in the province of Newfoundland and Labrador—whose half-million people live on a land mass the size of Japan, with the lowest population density of all Canadian provinces—has out-migration become part of a larger story of discontent.

So serious did this become that in 2002 a Royal Commission began conducting hearings on "Renewing and Strengthening Our Place in Canada"—a provincial venting that produced eerie echoes of the Citizens' Forum on Canada's Future a decade earlier. Canadian civil wars, it might be said, are fought sitting down or, in their most physically active form, standing patiently in line for microphone no. 3.

Vic Young, the erudite St. John's businessman who chaired the Newfoundland commission, was fully aware of the growing discontent. "We brought enormous riches into Canada," he announced at the opening session of this $3 million navel-gazing exercise. "Our fishery, our forests, our hydro power, oil and gas reserves, our people, our strategic location. But we find ourselves at the bottom of the ladder. How can there be such a disconnect between what we brought into Canada and where we are today?"

That disconnect had outraged an increasing number of provincial personalities, including James McGrath, former federal fisheries minister in the brief 1979 Joe Clark government ("I wasn't there long enough to do any damage") and former lieutenant-governor of the province. "Why is it," the man with the thick glasses and wild head of white hair asked when I visited him at his "town" home in St. John's, "that we're one of the wealthiest pieces of real estate on the globe and yet we're perceived as the basket case of Canada?"

Newfoundlanders, McGrath said, were fed up with playing the hapless buffoon to the rest of the country, the punchline to so many jokes and, in the fall of 2006, the subject of ridicule in a car commercial for the manner in which they speak. Thanks to education and the sophistication of modern communications, the new Newfoundland, he believed, had finally grown out of its "incredible inferiority complex." "We are," he said, "no longer ashamed of our culture and our accents."

McGrath had come to believe that for Newfoundlanders Confederation was a raw deal that verged on "cultural genocide." Ottawa destroyed the fishery. Ottawa wants its share of oil royalties. Ontario takes the iron ore away for processing. Quebec takes hundreds of millions of dollars a year away in electricity. Those who'd been against Confederation in 1949—and the McGrath family numbered among the St. John's "townies" who opposed it—are back in full voice, joined by a frustrated youth whose province keeps leading the country in economic growth yet cannot offer them work.

"In 1949 we had a $40 million surplus," McGrath argues. "We had no debt. We had the world's biggest fishery. We had untapped mineral resources in Labrador. We didn't even know about the oil and gas off our shores or about the hydroelectricity from Churchill Falls. That's the 'basket case' we were when we came into Canada. And now there's this perception in Canada that Canada would be better off *without* this basket case?"

The growing frustration even led to a province-wide demand for a proper balance sheet that would prove Newfoundland has more than held its own in Confederation. One local newspaper, *The Independent*, concluded that since 1949 Canada has benefited by $53.5 billion, with a provincial return of only $8.9 billion. The federal government, on the other hand, cited other statistics to argue that billions more have flowed into the province than out.

In typical Canadian style, province and federal government were heading in opposite directions.

In early 2005 the new and nervy premier, Danny Williams, ordered the Canadian flag be removed from all provincial buildings. The revolutionary pink, white, and green flag of the original colony went up poles all over the island. Williams also rather brilliantly turned desperate federal campaign promises into a new deal on oil royalties and protection under the absurdly complicated equalization program. There were political and financial victories, but still the out-migration continued—in particular to Alberta and its high-paying jobs in the oil industry.

Newfoundland's toughest question of all—how to keep the young from leaving—was something the Royal Commission left alone. Perhaps it knew the answer and felt it better left unsaid. After all, Clyde Wells had swept to power in 1989 with the help of an impassioned call for jobs that might bring loved ones back from the mainland. One 1999 study even claimed that, at the rate people were leaving, by 2030 the population level would fall to what it was fifty years earlier when Newfoundland first became part of Canada. Another, kinder study done for the Atlantic Institute for Market Studies projected on the basis of current trends that the population in 2036 will equal that of 1960.

Bonavista is typical. Since the fishery went down, the once-bustling little town has lost more than a thousand residents—one in every five—and almost all of them young people who headed off to find their futures in some place that was not Bonavista and did not involve a collapsing fishery. Mayor Betty Fitzgerald was sitting on seventeen different committees trying to figure out how to bring new hope and new work to her little town. There'd been a few nibbles from tourism, but tourism, like the former fishery, is seasonal.

It would never be the magic formula so desperately required.

THE SEARCH FOR NEW IDEAS is nothing new in Newfoundland. Fears that the fisheries alone would never be enough were voiced from the day it entered Confederation. "We must develop or perish," Joey Smallwood told Newfoundlanders. "We must develop or our people will go in the thousands to other parts of Canada. We must create new jobs, or our young men especially will go off to other places to get the jobs they can't get here."

Smallwood created an Economic Development Department in 1950 and put a mysterious Latvian, Dr. Alfred Valdmanis, in charge, paying him the unheard-of salary of $25,000 a year to come up with new ideas. The department built a chocolate factory in Bay Roberts, a battery plant in Topsoil, a glove factory in Carbonear, a leather goods factory in Harbour Grace, a rubber boot factory in Holyrood. There was a knitting mill, a cement plant, a shoe factory—all founded on Valdmanis's ill-founded theory that a war-damaged Europe would never recover its industrial might in time to hold on to its traditional markets. "As from the spring of 1952," Valdmanis confidently predicted, "there won't be further unemployment in Newfoundland."

Valdmanis, of course, failed to recognize the Marshall Plan's effect on Europe's recovery. The projects failed. Doug Letto, the St. John's author of *Chocolate Bars and Rubber Boots,* calculates that over six years the schemes ate up $26 million. Following decades would see the Come-By-Chance oil refinery, the Marystown Shipyard, a phosphorus reduction plant, a scheme to produce hydroponic cucumbers, plans for forest products, iron ore, oil and gas, nickel—all held to be the answer, with some outright disasters, the others never quite answer enough.

As Newfoundlanders themselves often say, "Pigs may fly, but they're very unlikely birds."

"Our young are gone," the mayor of Bonavista said. "There's nothing here for them. Since 1992 it's been a struggle to keep as many people here as you can." The facts back her up. According to a telling chart in the *St. John's Telegraph,* the province's population numbered 570,181 in 1984, among them 52,963 men and 52,520 women in the twenty to twenty-nine age group. Twenty years later the population had fallen to 517,027 with only 33,299 men and 34,955 women in their twenties. It was pretty obvious who was getting out. And with 20 percent of the 2004 population above age fifty-five, it was equally obvious who was staying on.

After touring the province with a microphone open to anyone who wished to step up, the Royal Commission on Renewing and Strengthening Our Place in Canada reported in 2003. "Into it, predictably," wrote my *Globe and Mail* colleague Jeffrey Simpson, "poured a torrent of grievances, a deep sense of unfair treatment and misunderstanding from Canada, and revisionist histories of the good old days."

The report moved beyond any obsessive griping and recommended ways to improve federal–provincial relations and encourage Canada to show a little more federal sympathy for the special needs of Newfoundland and Labrador. Not surprisingly, it called for greater federal spending on such matters as highways, fisheries science, health, and hydroelectric development.

It did not, however, touch on the impossible topic of the emptying out, the decline of rural Newfoundland that proved so disruptive in the years of Smallwood and will only worsen in the years to come. While only 20 percent of Canada's population still lives on the land, Newfoundland has twice that amount and no idea how to keep so many there. Certainly not with the St. John's area thriving and Alberta calling.

The Royal Commission was "stumped," said Simpson, "although of course it did not say so. All it could recommend, for which it should not be blamed, was an 'informed public dialogue on the future of rural Newfoundland' and a provincial strategy.

"At least it did not draw castles in the sky, for which we can all be grateful."

Fourteen

City Elephant, Country Mouse

GERALD MERKEL and Connie Smith are two rural born and raised Canadians who have decided to go different routes. Merkel, who's in his mid-forties—quite young by Saskatchewan farm standards—is remaining as a grain farmer near Raymore, Saskatchewan, and Smith, who's nineteen, has left the tiny outport fishing community of Brookside on Newfoundland's Placentia Bay for the lure of booming Fort McMurray and the northern Alberta oilfields.

One staying on the land; one headed for the city.

On the day I came to visit Gerald Merkel, whom I've known for many years, the Saskatchewan countryside was so spectacularly beautiful it seemed the world should be not slipping away but rushing toward it. The trees and fields were covered with a mid-winter hoarfrost and, in the bright sun of the world's biggest sky, made diamonds and lace of the entire province. I drove up through the spectacular Qu'Appelle Valley and continued north past Raymore toward the Merkel farm. As I left the highway and turned onto the concession roads, three mule deer bounded from one field and, as if on pogo sticks, bounced across the road and over another fence and away into the sparkling tangle of alders and wolf willow.

It would be difficult to imagine a scene more idyllic—or more concealing. Like the Potemkin village that hid reality behind fresh paint, false fronts, and smiling faces, the hoarfrost and the sunlight made it virtually impossible to take in the canola crop that had remained frozen in the fields. The fresh-fallen snow also covered the spot just behind the barn where, earlier in the year, Gerald had accidentally run over his father, George—and not only once, but twice.

Accidents happen, and on the farm far more readily than anywhere else. Gerald had been backing his pickup and an attached fertilizer trailer up to the holding tank and George Merkel had hurried over behind the trailer to help line things up. It moved more quickly than he'd expected, and as he tried to get out of the way he stumbled and went down, calling out for Gerald to stop. The roar of the truck engine drowned out his shouts and the large trailer drove right over him.

Gerald hadn't seen his father go down. He'd felt the bump but put it down to uneven ground. He decided he'd have to adjust his approach and pulled forward again—running the machinery over his father a second time.

As Gerald shifted the trailer into better position he caught sight of something unusual out the side mirror.

It was his father.

"I was sure he was gone," remembered Gerald, a heavyset man with thick hair, beard, and glasses. "He just lay there not moving. When I got to him he looks up and says, "'Don't worry, I'm not dead yet.'"

George Merkel was eighty-two years old when he was run over twice by his son. He had survived the Second World War and he would survive this, but not before spending months in the Regina hospital and then the little Lestock hospital down Highway 15 recovering from a shattered leg, broken ribs, and a punctured lung. He prided himself on the fact that the surgeon who operated on him in Regina walked in one day, picked up George's chart, and shook his head. "You're one tough son of a bitch, you know," the doctor said. George was. He blamed himself, not his son. When you've spent your entire life farming you know only too well how these things can happen.

George Merkel had seen bad times before. He remembered when the banks and government programs persuaded prairie farmers to expand during the 1970s only to have rising interest rates hit them like a year-round frost. He'd already sold off his cattle years earlier and cut back on his planting. He hadn't really expected his son to go into farming but was quietly happy when he did.

Unfortunately, the Merkel farm was irrational by now. Too small to sustain a family, perhaps too small even for a single man living with his aging father. According to Ingeborg Boyens in *Another Season's Promise: Hope and Despair in Canada's Farm Country,* between 1936 and 1996 average farm size in Saskatchewan increased from 400 to 1152 acres and the number of farms dropped from 142,391 to 55,995. In subsequent years that number has fallen even further. The common refrain has been "Get Big, or Get Out."

But Gerald Merkel had neither the capacity to get big nor the inclination to get out. He was stubborn, stubborn as his father, stubborn as generations of pioneers who simply kept believing in next year's crop. He wasn't particularly aware of conventional wisdom and most assuredly not interested in it.

"Some mainstream economists have written off the rural and would say this is the natural death of communities that cannot compete," Alberta political scientist Roger Epp, a Saskatchewan native, told the *Regina Leader-Post.* "What if you are rural people rooted four generations deep in prairie soil and you are attached to that place in ways that don't make sense in the current economy, which tells you to get mobile and find a job? How do you articulate that and how do you defend it?"

Gerald Merkel was determined to defend his right to stay on the land and attempt to make a go of it. He set out to expand to a sensible, workable size. He rented five quarter sections from neighbours and seven quarter sections from Fred Whitlock to the south of town. That gave him 3.5 sections, 2240 acres of good land to work, and he covered his bets by planting an assortment of wheat, peas, canola, and flax.

So far it had worked. His credit line was shrinking, his rental base growing. He supplied most of his own seed. He had his own equipment, his father's equipment, and access to Fred Whitlock's equipment. Still, a year of planting and fertilizing was running him $150,000. He was deep into the Credit Union.

The year began with the accident, but by mid-summer he was convinced things had turned in his favour. He had a wonderful crop, the best ever, and when the flax was blooming sea blue the Merkel and Whitlock farms had never looked better under the big Saskatchewan sky.

But nature, as Thoreau noted so long ago, "is no saint." On August 20, with the bumper crop only two weeks from the start of harvest, Gerald fell asleep while watching television. When he awoke it was 3:00 A.M., and as he made his way to his bedroom he stopped by the window and checked the thermometer.

–3°C.

He stared at it for a moment and then decided there was nothing he could do but head for bed. He didn't even bother to wake his father.

"What was the point?" he said. "We were screwed."

Only a small portion of the crop was salvageable. The canola Gerald simply left in the field, hoping beyond hope that it would cure out enough in spring to still be worth something, however minuscule. With rent due and loans overdue, Gerald Merkel figured he was out $100,000, with no prospects of planting in the coming spring unless enough federal and provincial aid came through to bail out those farmers who trusted more in themselves than insurance.

"This was my worst year," he said. "We've had earlier frosts before, but this year everything was so late. Two more weeks would have made all the difference. Now it just doesn't add up.

"She's beyond crying."

IN 2006 CONNIE SMITH moved from Brookside, Newfoundland, to Fort McMurray, Alberta, from a tiny village to the country's fastest-growing new city. And in Fort McMurray she found everything that little Brookside couldn't possibly provide a nineteen-year-old eager to head out into the world and see what life had to offer.

Smith and her boyfriend, Raphael Murphy, had come to the right place. The oil sands were booming, with nearly seventy projects now producing more than a million barrels of oil a day, roughly half the country's production. One study embraced by the local chamber of commerce was claiming that $125 billion worth of oil sands investment would be coming into the municipality of Wood Buffalo over the coming decade. Smith was in Fort McMurray barely a day when she got a good job as a waitress—$7 an hour and healthy tips in a restaurant with a perpetual waiting line.

The population, thanks to hundreds and thousands of Connie Smiths and Raphael Murphys arriving through the year, had roared past seventy thousand. New houses, new malls, new roads, new bridges were all in the works. Connie and Raphael were already talking about buying a four-by-four pickup now that Raphael was working in the oil sands and bringing home a regular paycheque. They were dreaming about a brand-new home a few more years down the road. What they weren't considering was heading back east. Connie's sister was already here. A brother was elsewhere in Alberta. A cousin was expected to arrive any day.

They had a bit of Newfoundland in this northern Alberta city. There were bars that catered to Newfoundlanders, and a special club that featured bands from Down East. Some estimates had as many as twenty-five thousand Newfoundlanders in the booming city, approximately one of every three citizens, with more on the way. No wonder one St. John's restaurant put a sign up in the summer of 2006 saying, "If you are NOT going to Alberta, apply within."

Connie Smith plastered the walls of her room with photographs of back home. There were pictures of her parents—her mother died several years ago and her father had a new partner—as well as photographs of siblings and aunts and uncles and cousins and friends, all smiling in little Brookside.

"I miss them," she said on a bright September day in 2006. "But I like it here. We're here for the long run."

It was enough to cause tears back home. Her father, Onslow Smith, and his common-law wife, Margaret, had already left Brookside and moved to somewhat larger New Harbour. It didn't really matter where they lived, though; there had been no work for Onslow since the fish plant closed at Marystown. Their children were all now in Alberta. The neighbour children back in Brookside had also left for Fort McMurray. The emptying out had been so profound that Onslow and Margaret found little Brookside, where about thirty families continue to live, just too painful a reminder of what they'd lost.

But Margaret said she understood why it had happened. "I guess I would go, too," she said over the telephone forty-two hundred kilometres away, "if I were younger.

"But if I had my choice, you know, I'd never leave here. Ever."

FOLLOWING A DAY at the Merkel farm I drove up to Saskatoon to see Ashley O'Sullivan, president of the University of Saskatchewan's research-and-development wing, Ag-West Bio. O'Sullivan is among the many, many agricultural experts who'd say that the Gerald Merkels of the prairies are an unfortunate anachronism, well intentioned but out of touch with modern reality. As Wallace Stegner put it, a pattern no longer viable.

"In the last century," says O'Sullivan, "it was called 'farming.'"

The last century, of course, closed out only a very few years ago. What O'Sullivan discussed for *this* century was the "bio-economy," a catch-phrase encompassing scientific research, new technology, and farm methods that bear little resemblance to time-honoured prairie traditions.

O'Sullivan spoke of using genetics to create new value in crop production, of using molecular technology to change breeding as dramatically as the development of hybrids once transformed farm practices. He even saw a future where it might not be necessary to spray for insects and blight. "Fifteen, twenty, twenty-five years from now," he said, "we won't think of farming as farming any more. We'll think of it as capturing value from biological initiatives. We're at the infancy stage here. I call it the Model T stage—we're just starting out. This will be the economy of the future."

Gerald Merkel begs to differ. He believes, because he has no other choice but to believe, that the family farm will always matter in Saskatchewan, will always be at the core of this province. Neither he nor his father blames anything but fate and the elements for what happened to that so-promising crop. A family doesn't spend three generations on the same plot of land and not come to terms with nature's fickleness.

"It happens," Gerald said as we sat drinking coffee in his kitchen.

"If you think too much about it," added George, still wearing a huge brace on his left leg, "you're going to go bugs."

His son stirred his coffee, steam rising and vanishing, and stared out at the snow that was once again starting to fall. "There's always next year," he said, determined to plant again. "It's agriculture, after all—people have to eat."

PEOPLE HAVE TO EAT, and farmers, by nature, have to look ahead. "Hope," Nellie McClung said back in the grim days of the Great Depression, "is still the dominant sentiment out there, after all the tragedy. And where hope is, there you have power. And I believe that Southern Saskatchewan's best days are before her yet."

She could still be right. Eric Howe, the University of Saskatchewan economics professor who caused such a row when he tagged Saskatchewan "the Mississippi of the North," was also oddly hopeful. He wasn't about to back down from his controversial phrase—racism and poverty are easily found in both southern state and northern province— but overall prospects had begun changing as Saskatchewan and Alberta celebrated their centennials. "I think it's going to be very interesting watching this change," Howe said when I spoke to him in Saskatoon.

Agriculture was still profoundly important, but resource development was playing an increasingly key role in the Saskatchewan economy. The oil and natural gas industry and leading-edge science coming out of Saskatoon were bound to transform this province as dramatically as the flood of immigrants had done almost a century before. Only this time, the emphasis would be far more urban than rural.

Some were saying that one day Saskatchewan would turn into a sort of Alberta Lite, but Howe disagreed. "I just don't see Saskatchewan becoming Alberta," he said. "That would require a 180-degree turn, and I don't see that happening."

"The reason Saskatchewan has the place it does in Canada," he continued, "is because interesting ideas come out of Saskatchewan. For the last forty years, those ideas have been all about how to live well poor. You have to have health care, but that means somebody else has to pay for it because you happen to be poor. I think that, just maybe, over the next forty years, the ideas that will come out of Saskatchewan will be about how to live when you're well off."

I also went to see former provincial finance minister Janice MacKinnon. She cautioned that the traditional farm, and its psychological hold on an entire province, is not something that's easily abandoned. "The mistake an economist makes," says MacKinnon, who now teaches history at the University of Saskatchewan, "is to look at the pie and then say agriculture is just not that big a slice. But it's a big part of the psychology."

AND THIS, REALLY, is the point here. Canada may today be *physically* 80 percent urban and 20 percent rural, but sometimes it feels 80 percent rural and 20 percent urban *psychologically*.

Wyndham Lewis, the famous English author and painter, was in fact a "sort-of" Canadian—born in 1882 on a ship moving along the Bay of Fundy—and it was his belief that, no matter how urbanized Canada might ultimately become, it would be forever connected to the vast landscape on which those sprawling cities barely make a mark. "This monstrous, empty habitat," Lewis wrote, "must continue to dominate this nation psychologically, and so culturally."

It's something outsiders certainly notice. British-born Susan Buchan, the wife of John Buchan—author of *The Thirty-nine Steps* and Canada's governor general from 1935 to 1940—found that no matter where in Canada she travelled with her husband, no matter where she found Canadians living, "the wild is always there, somewhere near."

Peter Gzowski once told a story about travelling by train across flat Saskatchewan. An Englishman who also happened to be on-board remarked that the landscape struck him as "the biggest expanse of bugger-all I've ever seen in my life."

Gzowski stared out the same window but didn't see the same thing. It wasn't "bugger-all" at all; it was the landscape. And the Saskatchewan prairie, he thought, "explains a lot about us, from medicare to unemployment insurance, from the railways, the CBC, to our inherent decency and sense of politeness. We have a lot at stake here: we huddle together against the cold."

Margaret Laurence took the connection even deeper in an essay she wrote back in 1971 about her earliest beginnings in the little town of Neepawa, Manitoba:

> Because that settlement and that land were my first and for many years my only real knowledge of this planet, in some profound way they remain my world, my way of viewing. My eyes were formed there.
>
> ... "Scratch a Canadian, and you find a phony pioneer," I used to say to myself in warning. But all the same it is true, I think, that we are not yet totally alienated from physical earth, and let us only pray that we do not become so.

In the summer of 2003 *The Globe and Mail* launched a massive series looking at new Canadians. The idea was to examine, in depth, the impact recent immigrants were having on the country and, by extension, the impact Canada was having on them. As part of that series the paper commissioned a poll that would look at as many aspects as possible of the immigrant experience—which by this time, of course, was almost exclusively an urban story.

When Canadians of all heritage and history were asked to name what was, for them, the defining characteristic of Canada, the result stunned *Globe* editors: 89 percent chose the sheer vastness of the land.

That's nine of every ten Canadians—eight of whom live in cities—choosing the landscape.

Canadians may indeed be the most urbanized society on earth. And yet, for reasons that are sometimes understandable—a distant family farm, Aboriginal heritage, a history that somewhere includes fishing, mines, logging, the railway—as well as for reasons no one can quite comprehend, there remains among all Canadians this enormous connection with the land and water.

No matter what the address or country of origin.

Fifteen

Nous Nous Souvenons

SHE WOULD STAND equal to—if not greater than—the Statue of Liberty, said the man who envisioned her creation. Let Liberty hold high her flame at the entrance to New York Harbour; Madeleine would stand on the banks of the Saint Lawrence, dress rippling in the breeze off the wide river, loaded musket in hand. And while Liberty would stand for the freedom of the individual, Madeleine would stand for the whole, for the good of everyone. "The contrast," said the man who believed so totally in the inspiration of Madeleine de Verchères, "… will be wholly in favour of the Dominion."

The man was an anglophone, Earl Grey.

Not just an anglophone, but a Brit, and as Lord Grey, governor general of Canada from 1904 to 1911, surely the most passionately *Canadian* of all governors general right up to 1952, when the Canadian-born tradition began with Vincent Massey. When Grey left to return to Britain, Sir Wilfrid Laurier said that he'd given "his whole heart, his whole soul, and his whole life to Canada."

He also gave the Grey Cup, which turned a football game into the most unifying annual sporting event the country has ever known.

And he gave, as well, the political push that erected this towering statue of a fourteen-year-old girl along the south bank of the St. Lawrence in the town that bears her family name.

Verchères, one would think, would stand as the most patriotic of Canadian small towns. Its ribbon-like main street, with small shops and boutiques, hugs the riverbank as if town and setting had been matched on a postcard. It was here, on December 28, 1842, that Calixa Lavallée was born, the musician who would go on to compose "O Canada." And it was at little St. Antoine, also in Verchères country, where, on September 6, 1814, George-Étienne Cartier was born. Fifty-three years later, Cartier would be the central francophone force behind Confederation, John A. Macdonald's trusted lieutenant, and the man held most responsible for persuading the French of Lower Canada to join in this curious experiment they would call Canada.

It was George-Étienne Cartier who was so essential to the "great coalition" that pulled Lower and Upper Canada out of deadlock and that launched Macdonald's Conservatives, George Brown's Clear Grits, and Cartier's *Bleus* toward a federal union of all British North American colonies. In his earlier years Cartier had even authored a song, "O Canada / mon pays, mes amours!," that seemed likely, until Calixa Lavallée came along with his patriotic tune, to be adopted as the national anthem of the new country.

John Ralston Saul has argued that it was actually Cartier, far more than Macdonald, who deserved credit for the transcontinental railway that solidified Confederation and brought British Columbia into the fold. In *Reflections of a Siamese Twin* he calls Cartier "the real force behind the idea" and the one who understood what a national rail line would mean to this young country. It would be a line to cut off those Americans still dreaming of North American expansion. It would put the onus on British Columbia to join Confederation. But it would also challenge the nation itself to "demonstrate that it had the energy and the desire to exist." Cartier applied his mind not to how the railway could be built or paid for, but to what it would eventually mean. "It was," Saul writes, "a great creative idea—an act of invention—in the sense that a scientist understands a discovery before proving that it is there."

In his distant past, however, Cartier had been involved in the rebellions of 1837 and 1838, after which he'd been forced to flee to the United States. When he returned he became a ranking member of the ruling class he'd once fought against, even serving as solicitor for the Grand

Trunk Railway. Saul remarks on the irony that Cartier, the early musket-wielding rebel, would later create the Canadian army, the first military in charge of the protection of Canada. So it's understandable how, in later analyses of his life and times, Cartier would come to be seen in different light. Some Quebec academics—including Léandre Bergeron, author of *Petit Manuel d'histoire du Québec*—consider Cartier a classic *chouayen,* a sellout.

Today they call pretty Verchères "The Village of the Patriots." It was here in Verchères that Ludger Duvernay, the founder of the Saint-Jean-Baptiste Society, was born. It's here where Parti Québécois leader Bernard Landry lives along the riverbank, the fleur-de-lys alone snapping in the wind over his drive. And here, of course, is where the statue of Madeleine de Verchères—which Lord Grey believed would one day inspire Canadian citizenship—performs a quite different role.

Today, she stands as the symbol for defiance of the forces that surround Quebec.

ON A LOVELY LATE-APRIL DAY in 2005 I came to Verchères in the hopes of talking to locals about what was then widely presumed to be a fast-coming federal election.

The Liberals had been in power for a dozen years, including three straight majority governments under Jean Chrétien. Those majorities had come to an end amidst a growing scandal over the federal government's sponsorship program in Quebec. The program intended to create a warmer feeling toward Canada after the failed 1995 referendum on Quebec sovereignty was now seen across the country as a diabolical scheme to spread federal tax dollars among a small circle of conspirators, most of them in the advertising industry, a few of them in the federal government. The current prime minister, Paul Martin, had trusted that in calling for a special inquiry he would deflect attention away from himself and his minority government, a strategy that had failed miserably. The daily revelations of the Gomery inquiry had become the national soap opera of 2005—with Martin certain to pay a price whenever the election was called.

I went to the small park dedicated to Marie-Madeleine Jarret de

Verchères and stood for a long while admiring the three-storey-high statue of the heroine of New France, her dress and her bronzed hat seeming to flutter in the wind, her musket ready for the next attack.

There are historical plaques around the statue, but the story is told in much richer detail by Colin M. Coates, director of the Centre for Canadian Studies at the University of Edinburgh and co-author, with Cecilia Morgan, of *Heroines and History: Representations of Madeleine de Verchères and Laura Secord*. Writing in *The Beaver*, Coates tells of the adolescent girl who took charge of the family fort here with only two younger brothers and two aging, frightened soldiers for help and how she somehow bravely held off an Iroquois war party for eight days.

It's a wonderful, inspirational tale—no wonder Lord Grey was so swept away by it—but it's also one that leaves many historians rolling their eyes. Madeleine was fourteen in the fall of 1692, the fourth of twelve children but the eldest of those who'd survived those tough years of high infant and child mortality. Her amazing story, curiously, didn't even come out until some seven years after the event. She was then twenty-one and applying for a small pension for herself. If the authorities couldn't see fit to offer that, she hoped, then perhaps they might consider a better posting for a brother who was then a cadet in the colonial New France army.

To help make her case, she told how, when she was only fourteen, she'd been left in the fort while her parents were away and had disguised herself as a man to fight the Iroquois.

It was a tale dramatically told: the young girl racing for the fort, an Iroquois warrior catching her by the scarf just as she reached it, her spinning out of the scarf just as she slipped through the door and was able to bolt it tight. She put on a soldier's hat as she climbed to the bastion, where she fired off the cannon to warn others of the danger.

She chose to write to the wife of a minister, who was much impressed by Madeleine de Verchères's words: "Although my sex does not allow me to have other inclinations than those demanded of me, nonetheless permit me, Madame, to tell you that I have feelings that draw me to glory as do many men."

The royal court was fascinated by the story, and the King's officials asked the colony's authorities for verification. It came, but without much enthusiasm, according to Coates, though it did speak warmly of her father's long years of loyalty. Madeleine was, in the end, granted a small pension, but apparently more on account of her father than of her incredible tale.

Nearly thirty years later she went after an increase—and this time really spun out the story. Now there were forty-five Iroquois, shots were flying, the old soldiers in the fort cowering. Madeleine took charge "without regard for my sex, nor for the weakness of my age." With the help of the terrified old soldiers and her young brothers she fired the cannon and shot at the invaders until they retreated.

Over the coming days, with the Iroquois surrounding the little fort and periodically attacking, she was able to slip out four different times to complete various and often bewildering acts of bravery. Once she rescued passing canoeists before they fell into the clutches of the Iroquois. Once she risked her life to pick up the laundry that had been left down by the river.

Madeleine got her increase, but not much further notice. After she died in 1747 another century would pass until her story began to be told again and again, with new details added in. It was a time when it seemed the whole world was searching for heroic figures, and the colony, now British, was no different. Madeleine de Verchères answered the need perfectly.

Lord Grey, a great romantic, heard the story when he got to Canada, fell in love with it, and swiftly launched his long campaign to have a statue erected in her honour. In Coates's account, the new governor general dispatched an emissary to meet with Lomer Gouin, the premier of Quebec, and "fire Gouin with the desire to find such money as may be required to signify the great entrance to Canada by the erection on Verchères bluff of a figure which will tell the immigrant that the heroic virtues are the bedrock foundations of Canadian greatness."

Canada's Joan of Arc would be everything, and more, that America's Liberty was. Madeleine, he said, would stand for "the highest ideals of citizenship."

Grey failed to get the provincial government to cough up the required funds, but he did get the federal government to start the work with $25,000 seed money. Famous sculptor Louis-Philippe Hébert was given the commission and—after some admitted struggles to ensure the young girl remained true to her sex and did not become a cross-dresser—Hébert's masterpiece was unveiled in 1913.

The statue hasn't changed since, nor have many of the charming stone buildings of the pretty village of Verchères. But the province itself has changed profoundly since that day.

YOU DON'T NEED to go far to discover this. You merely have to strike up an idle conversation with the young woman planting tulips around the small park in which the statue of Madeleine de Verchères stands staring out defiantly over the choppy water.

Marie-Eve Lainesse, who grew up in Verchères, was twenty-five years old this fine spring day when I happened to stop by the statue. She was born the year of the first Quebec referendum on sovereignty: 59.5 percent voting to stick with Canada, 40.5 percent for going it on their own. She was roughly the age of Madeleine de Verchères when the heroine held the family fort during the much tighter second referendum in 1995: 50.56 percent voting no to sovereignty, 49.44 percent voting yes.

And now, as a young woman of voting age, there was already talk of a third referendum coming as a further possible fallout from the growing sponsorship scandal. Another, more certain response, of course, was the fall of the Liberal government and the collapse of its traditional Quebec base.

Marie-Eve Lainesse went to elementary and high school here, went off to Collège d'enseignement général et professionnel (CEGEP), studied landscaping, and landed a job working for the area parks. She has a wide circle of friends, is very sociable and, contrary to what the pollsters and pundits routinely say of her demographic, is deeply and profoundly passionate about politics. The Gomery inquiry had galvanized her generation.

"We're all upset," she said as she brushed a smudge of planting soil off her cheek. "All very, very angry." She and her friends, she told me, watched the Gomery proceedings as closely as, in winter, they might watch the Montreal Canadiens play. They read the newspapers and talked endlessly about what it means for them.

And what it means, she believed on this fine spring day by the river, is an end to Canada, the last rites for Confederation.

"C'est finis," she said. *"Finis."*

MARIE-EVE LAINESSE knew people her age who, whenever that next election came, would vote for the Conservatives, even though she herself considered Conservative leader Stephen Harper to be merely "George Bush the Second."

She predicted, with surprising accuracy, the coming Conservative blip in the province. When the election was finally called for the end of January 2006, the Conservatives would pick up ten seats in a province where only months earlier it was said they had no chance of even one.

The growing fury toward the Liberals, she claimed, was simple to understand. The sponsorship scandal had the rest of the country looking at Quebec as a province of "criminals and thieves." This stereotype had all Quebeckers with their hand in the till, not just a handful of greedy advertising types in Montreal. It was just one more slight, she believed, to add to the ever-growing list that stretched from the hanging of Louis Riel to conscription, from the unnecessary arrests during the October Crisis of 1970 to the Night of the Long Knives that had duped the province on the Constitution, from the rebukes of the Meech Lake and Charlottetown accords to the sponsorship scandal.

She herself had given up hope for political solutions. The federal parties had all failed her generation, she said, including the Bloc Québécois, which had set out for Ottawa in 1993 with sovereignty association the stated goal and which had, in her opinion, slipped from its goal to its own form of establishment politics. What was the point of relying on the BQ, she asked, "when the rest of Canada does not trust it? Nobody speaks for us. Nobody."

The only political sense she'd heard in recent weeks had come from, of all sources, Alfonso Gagliano, the former federal cabinet minister who'd overseen the tainted sponsorship scheme. The prime minister and his inquiry, Gagliano had said on Radio-Canada, "is going to destroy the party and break up the country." It might not happen immediately, the disgraced minister went on, "but I think at this stage the separation of Quebec from Canada is not stoppable. It's a question of time. It's going to happen."

Marie-Eve Lainesse believed the same. *It's going to happen.* There would be another referendum, she was convinced, before she'd turn much older. Her own parents, who voted "no" in the last referendum, would change their minds in the next. Now they would vote "yes."

Why?

"Gomery."

And how will this referendum, the third one, play out?

Marie-Eve Lainesse stared out over the water, her glance remarkably similar to Madeleine de Verchères's faraway look behind her.

"Cinquante-quatre percent 'oui,'" she said.

The following morning, my own paper, *The Globe and Mail,* would produce with *Le Devoir* a far more scientific survey that would hold precisely the same result: 54 percent of Quebeckers would vote in favour of sovereignty. If, of course, a vote were held at that precise moment.

IF BRUCE HUTCHISON COULD admit to not understanding Toronto, I must confess the same personal shortcoming for Quebec. I am a small-town Ontario Anglo. I studied French in high school and even went off to a bilingual university, Laurentian in Sudbury, and took conversational French, including an "advanced" class. But I haven't the nerve to speak the second official language—except, of course, the moment I step outside of Canada. When I'm in parts of Quebec where the francophones are often unilingual, I can get by—but barely.

It is a common affliction—Hugh MacLennan, who lived and taught in Quebec most of his life, said his inability to speak French was "a constant shame to me, and I recognize it as the severest handicap in my entire life." Personally, I plan to leave whatever is left of my mind to science so that they'll be able to determine what, exactly, is missing in the Canadian Anglo brain to induce such absurdity.

And yet, in other ways, I know Quebec fairly well. I've covered most federal elections since 1979, and each one has taken me much farther into Quebec than my usual quick forays into Montreal. I've also covered several of its provincial elections and—even if the copy might sometimes read like radio signals from outer space—I've talked to people across the province, from the Anglo enclaves of Montreal and the Eastern Townships to the sovereigntist *bluets* of the Saguenay region and the political sophisticates of Quebec City.

I've reported on a decade of hockey in the province, written about the Quebec Carnival, spent months with the Crees of Northern Quebec, been in the Oka standoff, covered the referenda, toured the province with the Spicer Commission, and holidayed in the Gatineau, in Quebec City, and in the Laurentians.

And yet I can't pretend to understand Quebec. The only comfort in this, thin as it is, is that I've never been fully convinced *anyone* does.

It does not take a great mind, however, to notice the delicacy of it all. If Confederation is a cat's cradle where every pulled string compels another string to tighten, Quebec is the scissors threatening from the table—a constant caution, even if never employed, that the game must be played with the utmost care.

I've never been quite sure where the *Je me souviens* of the Quebec licence plate comes from, but it seems to have taken on a sense that throughout the province everything will be remembered at once, as one single political psychic force. It makes Canada, such a polite country, reluctant to use the word "conquest" when referring to the British victory at Quebec City in 1759. Louis Riel, hanged for treason in 1885, may yet have a statue erected in his honour on Parliament Hill, one that might even go so far as to call him a Father of Confederation.

Hard to believe, at times, that back in the 1870s Montreal cigar manufacturer S. Davis & Sons issued a series of outlaw cards that included one of Riel. But that, of course, only underlines how differently he can be interpreted, largely depending on which official language is spoken.

Louis Riel was born in 1844 at the Red River Settlement near present-day Winnipeg. He studied for the priesthood in Montreal and then took

law, working at it briefly in the United States before returning to St-
Boniface when he was twenty-four. The following year, 1869, Ottawa sent
in surveyors to the district, confident that Canada's push to purchase
Rupert's Land from the Hudson's Bay Company would go through with
Great Britain's help.

The Métis of Red River—most of mixed French and Native heritage—
had grown increasingly alarmed at the prospect of coming under Ottawa's
control. They feared, justifiably, that more people and the reality of trains
coming through the West would mean the end of the buffalo they hunted.
They were further disturbed by aggressive early settlers arriving from
Ontario on the understanding that Canada would be taking over and
opening up these fertile prairies. These new arrivals were invariably
Protestant Anglos and usually members of the Orange Lodge—meaning
they had little time for the French-speaking Catholics along the river. The
Métis organized, Riel emerged as a leader, they blocked the survey crews
and, with relatively little effort, captured Fort Garry.

When a number of English-speaking settlers tried to mount a counter-
rebellion they were rounded up and imprisoned. Two were sentenced to
death, and one execution, of surveyor Thomas Scott, was carried out by
firing squad on March 4, 1870.

Ottawa sent word that everything could be worked out. Promises were
made concerning various rights the Métis were demanding and all seemed
relatively in order—with the obvious exception of the fallout from the
Scott execution. Ottawa wanted a quick and quiet solution to the
problem. The Catholic Bishop of St-Boniface was dispatched to Red
River with a federal proclamation of amnesty, the bishop as well as the
Métis convinced it would cover all actions to that date, including the
execution. The bishop persuaded Riel to release the few remaining prisoners and then to head for Ottawa for the final negotiations regarding the
creation of the new province.

This outraged the Ontario Orange Lodge. Instead of punishment for
Scott, its members cried, the Catholic Métis were being rewarded with
provincial status. Manitoba would come into being on July 15, 1870, the
French would have certain rights, including Catholic schools, and a

special land grant of 1,400,000 acres would go to the Métis. There was, however, no official mention of full amnesty. The Ontario Orangemen were demanding that justice be served.

Ottawa dispatched a military force under Colonel Garnet Wosleley to Red River that summer, and Riel, convinced it was coming for him, fled to the United States. Meanwhile, in Ontario, a reward of $5000 was offered for the arrest of Thomas Scott's "murderer," widely taken to be Riel himself, though he wasn't even present at the execution.

So volatile was the situation—Ontario screaming for Riel's head, Quebec calling Riel a hero for defending language and faith—that Prime Minister Macdonald pleaded with Riel to remain in exile. Macdonald even secretly arranged to send Riel money if it would only keep him away. It was as if Macdonald instinctively knew what would happen if Riel came back.

Riel did not stay away, returning to the new province and even running for a federal seat, which he easily won. He reached the House of Commons but they threw him out when Mackenzie Bowell, future prime minister and an Orangeman, tabled a motion demanding his expulsion. Riel ran for office again, won again, but this time didn't even attempt to take his seat in Ottawa.

"Imagine," George Bowering wrote in *Stone Country: An Unauthorized History of Canada,* "how the Central Canadians felt when their disruption in the West, Canada's most wanted outlaw, was sent by his people to Parliament."

The Riel colleague who had actually ordered Scott's execution was arrested, charged, and found guilty. He, too, was condemned to death, only to have the sentence commuted to a short term in prison. It took until 1875 before Ottawa could get a motion through granting Riel his amnesty—but by then Riel had suffered a nervous breakdown, had spent time in an asylum, and was said to be often delusional. He called himself "David" now, and his calling, he told friends, was to establish a new form of North American Catholicism with its own pope.

Since part of the amnesty deal was that he leave Canada for at least five years, Riel returned to the States and even briefly became an American citizen. But in 1884 he came back to Canada when a group of Métis in the Saskatchewan Valley begged him to come and help them fight for their rights, which they felt were being trampled by the flood of new settlers from the East and around the world.

It was at Batoche that the second rebellion took root. Riel by now was far more radical, claiming that God was speaking to him and calling himself the "Prophet of the New World." He declared that a "provisional government" was now in place for the Métis and that it, not Ottawa, would be deciding matters for the vast area that was still part of the Northwest Territories, as Saskatchewan wouldn't get provincial status until 1905.

Concern in Ottawa was sufficient that a second military force was dispatched—this time the newly formed North West Mounted Police, who were able to travel by the new rail system.

There was a profound difference between the 1870 and 1885 uprisings. The first Riel "government" was set up in an isolated area very difficult to reach and, significantly, not even a part of the young Dominion but rather the land of the Hudson's Bay Company. The second uprising was in an area being flooded by immigrant settlers, now easily reachable by rail. Most importantly, Riel was doing it in Canada proper this time. To claim his government was taking over matters was interpreted as treason.

Known as the Northwest Rebellion, this second uprising included Plains Indians who'd been starving from lack of buffalo to hunt. Native leaders like Cree chief Big Bear and Blackfoot chief Crowfoot were furious with Ottawa for what they considered ill treatment of Natives by Indian Department workers. Riel was actually tapping into the first wave of Western alienation—destitute Natives, angry white settlers who'd been led to believe the railroad was going through the area, Métis who felt their rights were being denied—and his ten-point Revolutionary Bill of Rights found wide acceptance. He became president; buffalo hunter and guide Gabriel Dumont his commander. They took prisoners and occupied the village of Duck Lake. The police, bolstered by locals, moved toward the lake only to be met by Dumont's forces. The Mounties retreated, but not until nine volunteers and three police had been killed. Dumont, a brilliant field general, lost five Métis and one Native fighter.

Ottawa sent almost three thousand soldiers by train, most of them Ontario militia, and combined with Western forces they soon counted some five thousand. There were more skirmishes and more deaths, including a dozen men from the North West Mounted Police at Frog Lake. The government cut off rations to Big Bear's people and his band, after which one of Big Bear's followers shot and killed the local Indian agent. The warriors later killed two priests and six other whites. Big Bear had tried to calm matters but it was too late. The army was moving in fast.

Riel and Dumont differed on where they might best make a stand, and Dumont, the more aggressive, won the argument. At the Battle of Batoche, Dumont led three hundred Métis and Natives in a well-organized defence that lasted until they ran out of ammunition and were forced to fire nails from their rifles. More troops were brought in, as well as a gunboat to attack Batoche, and fighting soon broke out again. The bolstered Canadian forces finally overran the rebels, claiming to have killed fifty-one of them, and on May 15 Riel surrendered and Dumont fled the country.

General Frederick Middleton, who had led the Protestant volunteers from Ontario, sent off a note to Big Bear in early June, claiming, "I have utterly defeated Riel at Batoche with great loss, and have made Prisoners of Riel, Poundmaker, and his principal chief." He called for Big Bear to surrender. "If you do not, I shall pursue and destroy you, and your band, or drive you into the woods to starve." Big Bear fled for a while, but, acutely aware that his starving people could not last, surrendered.

Riel's trial for high treason was held in Regina. His lawyers argued insanity and said he was delusional—his secretary had won acquittal by reasons of insanity—but Riel's remarkable address to the jury made many wonder if he could possibly be dismissed merely as a madman. On September 18 he was found guilty. Poundmaker and Big Bear were given three years, while other Natives received various sentences. Eleven were tried and convicted of murder for the Frog Lake massacre and eight were eventually hanged.

While the jury in Regina did convict Riel of treason, they did not wish to see him hanged. "We, on the jury, recommend mercy," the foreman told the court. "The prisoner was guilty and we could not excuse his actions. But, at the same time, we felt that the government had not done its duty. It did nothing about the grievances of the Métis. If it had, there would never have been a second Riel rebellion."

Quebec certainly didn't wish to see Riel hanged. He was a hero in French Canada now, defender of Church and language. Ontario, however, felt a little differently. "Strangle Riel with the French flag!" the *Toronto News* called in an editorial. "That is the only use that rag can have in this country."

Pressure was enormous to have Scott's execution avenged, and after various appeals and despite a medical report in which one physician found Riel "insane" and the other two "excitable," Macdonald's cabinet decided in favour of hanging. The Church in Quebec was outraged.

Macdonald showed surprisingly little understanding of how Riel would continue to play out in the country that Macdonald himself had had such a large role in creating. Having helped put together the coalition that allowed French and English to work together for Confederation, more might have been expected of him. But no. "He shall hang," the prime minister said at one point with rather great prescience, "though every dog in Quebec bark in his favour."

On November 16, 1885, the rope was placed around Louis Riel's neck and the trap door sprung.

He is still twisting.

ON THAT DAY the noose would also tighten around Macdonald's party. From then on the Conservatives would have, at best, a fragile and complicated relationship with a Quebec they had once taken for granted. Sir John A. Macdonald, writes Bowering, "was feeling the fires that would threaten to scorch every prime minister from now on—the heat provided by friction between Quebec French and Ontario English."

The effect of Louis Riel on a country that wouldn't even let him take his seat in Parliament was, and remains, extraordinary. Wilfrid Laurier, perhaps the greatest prime minister of all, launched his career by passionately denouncing the federal government's decision to let Riel hang. Quebeckers by and large switched their allegiances from Cartier's Conservative *bleus* to Laurier's Liberal *rouges*. And, of course, the Riel incident still reverberates in the West, among Natives and Métis who feel their rights have never been upheld as promised and even among many non-Natives who continue to feel Ottawa treats them as a colony that, every once in a while, needs some discipline.

All traceable to one man who called himself "The Prophet of the New World."

One begins to see how Margaret Atwood saw this great French–English dichotomy in her *Two-Headed Poems:* that we aren't strangers to each other so much as a "pressure on the inside of the skull." And that pressure periodically flashes into a full-bore migraine. The trigger can be major— as it was in the Conscription Crisis, in the demise of Meech Lake, and in the October Crisis.

The October Crisis of 1970 was the culmination of years of ferment. In 1963 five bombs exploded in mailboxes located in anglophone neighbourhoods. In 1967 French president Charles de Gaulle, on a state visit during Centennial Year, shouted *"Vive le Quebec Libre!"* from a balcony and won himself a quick invitation from Prime Minister Pearson to exit the country and a lasting place in the heart of sovereigntists.

By 1970 the Front de Libération du Québec had been blamed for more than two hundred bomb blasts and five deaths. That fall the FLQ captured British diplomat James Cross and Quebec cabinet minister Pierre Laporte, who was later found murdered, whereupon Prime Minister Pierre Trudeau called out the army and instituted the War Measures Act. New Democratic leader Tommy Douglas, who voted against the use of the act, told the House of Commons that "the Government is using a sledgehammer to crack a peanut."

Cross was found alive, the FLQ cell proved far smaller than believed, and the War Measures Act was dropped. Six years later, on November 15, 1976, René Lévesque's Parti Québécois, committed to the separation of a sovereign Quebec from the rest of Canada, defeated the Liberal government of Robert Bourassa. Civil unrest by a minority had evolved into political statement by the majority.

At other times, the issue that starts the temples pounding is somewhat less dramatic, even minor. The sponsorship scandal, while hardly minor, involved very few people and relatively little money. "The notion that

Quebeckers would separate from Canada because of the $100 million sponsorship scandal in Ottawa is ridiculous and, frankly, galling," said a *Globe and Mail* editorial at the time. "Countries do not throw themselves onto a sharp knife over such things. Ethnic cleansing, slavery, oppression, battles for scarce land, denial of the right to self-expression—these are what tear nations asunder."

But Canada does often throw itself onto a sharp knife over such things.

In 2006 an event occurred in Montreal that seemed as far removed from provincial politics as it was possible to get: the September shootings at Dawson College. It was a stunning tragedy, a gun-crazed young man deciding to go out in a blaze and take several innocents with him.

It could have been so much worse. Policemen happened to be at the English-language CEGEP on another matter when Kimveer Gill—who called himself "The Angel of Death" on his personal website—parked his vehicle, got out, and marched into the campus cafeteria firing a semi-automatic rifle at will. The police, fortunately, stopped him from more damage, but even so, one young student was dead and nineteen injured, some seriously, before Gill fatally shot himself in the head and the rampage was over.

It was a shocking but seemingly straightforward story. It was compared to other such school assaults. Much was made of the Goth underworld Gill so admired and the hatred found on his website. The entire country appeared to embrace Montreal at this time of such distress.

The shootings took place on a Wednesday afternoon. On Saturday *The Globe and Mail* ran a detailed re-creation of the tragedy by senior writer Jan Wong, herself a former Montrealer. She happened to muse about the origins of Gill's enormous anger and tied his fury to that of previous Montreal killers: the Concordia University engineering professor who'd shot four colleagues to death in 1992 and the infamous December 6, 1989, attack at l'École Polytechnique that left fourteen young women dead at the hands of another young man wielding another automatic weapon. All three killers, Wong noted, had a relatively recent immigrant connection. And then there were Quebec's long-controversial language laws.

"What many outsiders don't realize," Wong wrote, "is how alienating the decades-long linguistic struggle has been in the once-cosmopolitan city. It hasn't just taken a toll on long-time anglophones, it's affected immigrants too."

She did not for a moment claim that the killers weren't disturbed. "But," she said, "it is also true that in all of these cases, the perpetrator was not pure *laine,* the argot for a 'pure' francophone. Elsewhere to talk of racial purity is repugnant. Not in Quebec."

In a column, that might have been fair comment, though not many columnists would care to tie such furious violence to language. Wong's piece, however, was a news feature. The explosion was intense.

L'Affaire Wong led to calls in the House of Commons for an apology to the people of Quebec. Premier Jean Charest wrote an angry letter to *The Globe and Mail.* The prime minister himself wrote in to say that Wong's interpretation was "patently absurd and without foundation." The paper apologized.

It shouldn't just be people who go on stress leave—sometimes countries need it too.

Not long after, Liberal leadership front-runner Michael Ignatieff happened to say on a French-language television program that, in his opinion, Quebec was a "nation." It wasn't an unusual statement—other candidates had at times said much the same—but he said he would stand with a resolution coming up through the party ranks from the Quebec wing calling for a vote at the party convention.

Again, in a matter of hours the fragile egg that is Canada seemed on the verge of rolling off the stove. Ignatieff was widely ridiculed for calling for Quebec to be recognized as a nation within a province within a country—sort of a Canadian version of Churchill's famous description of Russia as a riddle wrapped in a mystery inside an enigma. It was a misstep that, weeks later, surely contributed to his coming up short in the Liberal Party leadership race.

Ignatieff, seemingly unaware of having done so, had just pushed one of the country's most-wired hot buttons. His error, it seemed, lay in having been outside the country during Canada's torturous constitutional

wrangling and the heated debates over Meech and Charlottetown. He
would have read about those years, studied them, and even written about
them. But what he seemed not to comprehend was that this wasn't an
intellectual issue—a great many feel Quebec can think of itself as anything
it wishes, within the context of Canada—so much as it had become a
purely *emotional* one in the years following Meech. There was no appetite
for constitutional talk, no stomach for even its consideration.

The Bloc Québécois, unsurprisingly, considered Ignatieff's remarks
a gift horse, and party leader Gilles Duceppe promptly introduced a
motion in the House of Common calling for just such recognition. The
panic was instant. The country, the doomsayers shouted, was back in
the handbasket. The sky was falling. The end was nigh.

A few days later Prime Minister Harper finessed the Bloc by introducing
the government's own motion recognizing the Québécois as a "nation within
a united Canada." The shadings were obvious: not the province of Quebec
but the Québécois people, not within Canada but within a united Canada.

It worked. The House voted 266 to 16 to endorse Harper's motion
with the fuming Bloc forced to vote with the government.

The country would live for another day. Until the next panic, anyway.

AFTER LEAVING VERCHÈRES and Marie-Eve Lainesse to her tulip planting, I headed east beyond Quebec City and then in a wide loop came back
along the North Shore of the St. Lawrence and turned north at Montreal,
eventually ending up in the small village of Saint-Lin on a rainy, windy
afternoon.

It was here, in this small village that lies in the heart of the farming
region of Lanaudière, that Carolus Laurier once farmed a small property
and where in 1841 a rather sickly child called Wilfrid was born. There is
a small museum here in honour of the prime minister who believed the
twentieth century would belong to Canada. And since no one appeared
about the wet streets to talk to, I went in and spent a happy hour walking
around the artifacts.

Laurier was forty-five years old before Canadians outside the province
really began to take note of him. He'd come to some national attention

during the Riel debates, but it was during a trip to Toronto in December of 1886 that he became widely recognized as the powerful speaker he was. Those who came to hear him thought he looked sickly enough to be headed for an early grave—not someone with thirty-three years left in him and three consecutive majority governments yet to claim.

"Below the island of Montreal," he told the entranced crowd,

> the water that comes from the north, from the Ottawa, united with the waters that come from the western lakes, but uniting, they do not mix. There they run parallel, separate, distinguishable, and yet are one stream, flowing within the same banks, the mighty St. Lawrence, and rolling on toward the sea, bearing the commerce of a nation upon its bosom—a perfect image of our nation. We may not assimilate, we may not blend, but for all that we are still the component parts of the same country.
>
> We may be French in our origin—and I do not deny my origin, I admit that, I pride myself on it. We may be English, or Scotch or whatever it may be, but we are Canadians: one in aim and purpose.

Reading these powerful words reminded me of the George Étienne-Cartier statue that stands in Quebec City, its base bearing a chiselled quotation with similar sentiments:

> In a country like ours
> All rights must be protected
> All convictions respected.

The most encouraging words I found in the little Laurier museum, however, came from one of his darkest moments. Laurier had finally lost his majority and his government in 1911 when Ontario suddenly turned against him over trade issues. He was finished, they said. He would, in fact, never again be prime minister.

"We are making for a harbour," he wrote, "which is not the harbour I foresaw twenty-five years ago. But it is a good harbour. It will not be the end. Exactly what the course will be, I cannot tell, but I think I know the general bearing, and I am content."

Words worth repeating today.

And again tomorrow.

AT MASSON, a village on the Quebec side of the Ottawa River down-stream from the capital, I checked the odometer of my rented car as I waited for the ferry to return from the Ontario side.

Trip: 1125.6 kilometres.

Odometers don't lie—at least not until the expense forms are filled in—but still, it didn't seem like that much. I had spent most of yet another week poking around the country's most fragile province. Not a single road travelled twice. Chatter at every stop. And yet I'd barely scratched the surface of this vast and complicated region.

The Masson ferry that would take me across the Ottawa River to Cumberland was slow in coming, and as I waited I had to wonder if it was only during spring runoff that the distance seems wider than normal. Certainly after that difficult week, after listening to fine young people like Marie-Eve Lainesse say *"C'est fini,"* the gap seemed wider than ever.

I had, as always, been treated magnificently in the province of Quebec. I've never understood those outsiders who claim they were snubbed or that people who could speak perfectly good English refused to use it or even insulted them in a language they don't understand. It has never happened to me. Nor do I expect it to, despite my obvious shortcomings.

And yet, one older man, Fernand Boirier, had spit in the village of Joliette. Not at me, but at the Liberal government in Ottawa and what the Gomery inquiry had taught him about this government. Another man, this time in Boucherville, had told me a story of sailing solo across the Atlantic, the greatest experience of his life, and how all that time for reflection had only served to convince him that it was time to go solo out of Confederation.

I talked to the Masson ferryman for a while.

Maurice Bourbonnais's family has been connecting Quebec to the Rest of Canada and the Rest of Canada to Quebec since 1939, his father, Eugene, taking over from his maternal grandfather, who started with a little barge that held three cars and charged fifty cents.

Today, Maurice's two sons, Alain and Luc, have joined the business, marking four generations of Bourbonnais ferrymen, and the traffic has risen to 600,000 vehicles a year at considerably more than fifty cents a crossing.

The link is pivotal: federal government workers heading for the capital, travellers looking for a more interesting route between Montreal and Ottawa, vacationers heading both ways summer and winter—winter ferrying made possible ever since they put in an air bubble system and bought an ice breaker.

The certainty of this connection between the two is also pivotal to Maurice Bourbonnais's personal health. He's worked through two frights before—the 1980 referendum and the 1995 referendum—and waited both times for traffic to recover and stabilize.

Since the 1995 referendum business had increased until, ten years later, it not only was back but had surpassed earlier levels. Life had been good, right up until the Gomery inquiry and the latest talk of yet another referendum on the way. "We don't want to see that, for sure," he said as the ferry pulled out. "None of us want to start back on that again. But what you see today at the federal level—well, it doesn't help, I can tell you that."

Maurice Bourbonnais's great dream had been to build a bridge from Masson to Cumberland. It would be another bridge over the Ottawa to permanently connect the two largest provinces, but one with a toll gate controlled by the Bourbonnais family. "It wouldn't cost taxpayers any money," he said. "And I could be ready to go in two years." He'd already spent $500,000 on a feasibility study and was convinced it would work—providing, of course, traffic patterns remain as they have been.

With Gomery and the fallout that followed, however, had come the decision to "put the project on hold." He'd wait and see if this crisis passed. He hoped it would. They usually do. No, in fact, they always do. Until, of course, the next one.

"I really think the majority of the people would not go for separation," he said as we talked about the nervous-making polls of the moment.

It's not just the ferry engine that churns on a day like this. One poll frightens; the new poll comforts; the next poll will be in the morning paper, results unknown. The talk shows babble, the newspapers scramble, the street talk bounces from side to side like a car that has slipped loose of its emergency brake.

No one could argue, on this spring day when the rain was pelting down and the runoff was in full force, that the distance between Quebec and the Rest of Canada was wider at the moment.

Nor would anyone say that the water was anything but muddied and swirling—at least for that moment. Just as it had been so many times in the past. Just as it would certainly be—luck holding—in the future.

AT THE CUMBERLAND SIDE of the crossing, a new and very large blue and white sign is now the first thing you see as you leave Maurice Bourbonnais's ferry.

"Welcome to Ottawa," it reads. "Shaping Our Future Together."

Or so we hope.

Sixteen

North of Summer

"CARE TO SIT UP front for a bit?"

Major Ian Searle looked like a happy-face sticker in uniform: round glasses, round face, grin a semicircle as he repeated himself after first indicating I should pop out one of the red and yellow military-issue earplugs.

"Want to sit up front?"

I'd been hoping for days to sit up in the cockpit of the Twin Otter, and if I tossed out any more hints, I feared, the Department of National Defence pilots wouldn't ask me up front for a look so much as send me back for a jump.

I believed I was stepping into the co-pilot seat. I had no idea I was walking into a revelation.

WHAT THE MOOSE is to the Canadian landscape, the bright yellow Twin Otter is to Canadian air space. Like its smaller and equally recognizable yellow cousin, the single-engine Beaver, the de Havilland Twin Otter is noisy, cramped, and not particularly comfortable, yet so remarkably reliable that neither Searle nor the pilot, Captain Dominique Lassonde, was even born when the newly unified forces took possession of the aircraft in early 1972.

It was mid-June 2005, and Lassonde and Searle were flying the governor general from Base Alert on the northern tip of Ellesmere Island to the Eureka weather station to catch a larger plane heading back, eventually, to Iqaluit, the capital of Nunavut, Canada's newest territory. It was to be

Adrienne Clarkson's final trip to the Far North before her tenure in office ran out, and, while there, she intended to make a political statement on Canada's sovereignty claims. *The Globe and Mail* had sent me along to cover the story.

We'd been flying south along the east coast of Ellesmere when, a couple of hours into the long trip, we turned inland to follow Archer Fiord as it stabs deep back into the huge island. From Archer Fiord we headed into the mountains, caught the path of the Dodge River, and finally reached one of the great ice fields of the High Arctic.

There are no words to describe such scenery, but since so few have been there, it is necessary to try.

It was a perfect, sunny day—though we were so far north in mid-June it could just as easily have been a perfect sunny night. The shadows were sharp, the cliffs dramatic, and the ice below blue and white and, from time to time, that incomparable polar azure that comes when bright sunlight falls on the melting ice that lies over pockets of water.

The pilots chose the lowest flight path they could safely travel, though at times it seemed as if the towering black cliffs of the fiord were so close that, had my father been along with one of his Player's roll-your-owns, he might have stuck an Eddy match out the window to scrape it along the rocks for a light.

The passengers were all hooked up by intercom—a necessary safety feature in the noisy aircraft—so they could not only hear messages coming from the cockpit but also exchange comments among themselves. The outbursts of incredulity proceeded to steamroll over each other as the plane rose and turned and twisted over the river path, mountains rising sharply on both sides.

But then, an hour into this extraordinary flight—with me now giggling in the co-pilot's seat, enjoying the ultimate in Mordecai Richler's *entrée*— Captain Lassonde suddenly pulled back on the controls and the plane rose, like a leaf on a high wave, up out of the river valley and up, up over a spreading plateau of white.

The commentary mounted as we did:

"*So beautiful!*"

"Outstanding!"

"Extraordinary!"

And then we all went silent.

We'd risen over a world so deep and distant and white that bare eyes couldn't bear to look at it. The plane, which had somehow seemed significant as it twisted over the gorges and above the riverbed with its fractured ice and blue reflections, now took on an *in*significance that was then unexpected and remains inexplicable.

The plane seemed to shrink, little more than a mosquito flying over a gigantic white shoulder of a country with more faces than even Statistics Canada can keep up with—but not a single one of those thirty-two million-plus faces here on this vast spot. Perhaps there never had been anyone here.

No one in the plane spoke. No one dared speak, each passenger and crew struck with his or her minuteness in a land so large and diverse not even the imagination seems capable of capturing it.

I had no idea where I was. I had never dreamed such a place existed on the entire earth, let alone in my own country. The sense of ... *ignorance* ... was almost overwhelming.

I'd thought I knew this country. Now, in an instant, it seemed such an impossible conceit, such foolish arrogance.

Perhaps you could never know it. Perhaps it was unknowable.

AL PURDY CALLED the Canadian hinterland "north of summer," and in the late springs of 2005 and 2006 I took two very long journeys into that northern hinterland, first with the governor general into the eastern Arctic of Nunavut all the way to the polar ice cap, then, on my own, into the western Arctic of the Northwest Territories, all the way to the Beaufort Sea. After thirty years of travelling through the ten provinces I was really just beginning to grasp the sheer size of Canada. So vast is this northern land mass that the only way I'd ever see it all was to leave Canada altogether and head for outer space.

But the landscape was only part of the revelations that came out of those two extensive trips north. The people were equally surprising. And in their own way, just as breathtaking.

The next summer in Behchoko, a small Dogrib community in the Northwest Territories, I sat one long afternoon and watched as eighty-year-old Elisabeth Chocolate scraped the fat from beaver pelts using a traditional tool fashioned from the leg bone of a caribou. Then her son-in-law, Patrick Adzin, stretched the pelts for drying by nailing them carefully to plywood sheets. The pelts would bring in $25 a piece, but he couldn't care less about the money. The following day Patrick was off to another rotation as a heavy-equipment operator for one of the diamond mines. Trapping beaver—the job of his father, his grandfather, his great-grandfather, and so many generations back he couldn't even count—had become his hobby, his … *golf*.

The territory was booming, with diamond mines opening up, plans being laid for a gas and oil pipeline down the fragile Mackenzie River Valley, talk everywhere of new roads, bridges, and jobs, jobs, jobs. It seemed as though, nearly a half century on, John Diefenbaker's great "Northern Vision" was coming true, at least in the Northwest Territories.

"Sir John A. Macdonald opened the West," Dief told a Winnipeg crowd in February of 1958. "He saw Canada from east to west. I see a new Canada—a Canada of the North!" His government would build new roads into the North to reach the rich resources. It would create hundreds of thousands of jobs for Canadians. It was, he promised his cheering supporters, "A new vision! A new hope! A new *soul* for Canada!"

The Globe and Mail, in a Valentine's editorial that followed the speech, said the new prime minister had "struck a note which has not been heard since the completion of the transcontinental railways." It gave him his majority government. But a few years later this great Northern Vision amounted to a partially paved road that headed north out of Yellowknife toward the Barrens, soon petered out into gravel … and then vanished altogether into the tundra.

Diefenbaker never won another election, and the "Northern Vision" faded for more than a generation—suddenly to rise again in 2006. There was new vision, all right, and new hope. But there was also great concern for the old soul of Canada.

In Dettah, another Dogrib community, this one within sight of Yellowknife, I met with ninety-three-year-old Michel Paper, who could talk about the first time he ever saw a white man, and how they were so terrified of each other that they ran in opposite directions. He'd never seen a shovel before either, and the day he was shown his first one he began twenty-six years of working with it at the nearby Giant gold mine.

"A shovel," he laughed. "I didn't know what it was used for. I could hunt. I could snowshoe. I could run a dog team. I could fish. I could trap. But I didn't even know how to hold a shovel."

He used that shovel to help poison his own land, the mines and their tailings leading to arsenic in Great Slave Lake. "We lived so good before the white man came," he told me. "Nobody ever got sick. We got our food from the land. We got our fish from the lake. We drank water from the lake. Then after 1934 people got sick. There's no animals here any more. Big animals are all gone. I don't know where they've gone. We're scared to eat the fish now because we're told they're all poisoned. We're told not to drink the water."

Michel, who grew up in a world where he could chop a hole in the ice or lie down on the warm rocks and drink the ice-cold waters of Great Slave Lake, now lives in a world where water comes in large jars accompanied by an $80-a-month bill.

Today, North of Summer is under siege from sources other than gold mining. The greatest concern comes from beyond, in the form of gases that bring temperature changes that threaten to change the entire world—but nowhere so dramatically as in the North.

There are magpies now in Yellowknife, something never before seen. But then, too, there are grizzlies that arrived from the opposite direction, also never before seen. Territories premier Joe Handley says he's looked out his office window and seen coyotes running across the ice of Frame Lake. Coyotes have never been known to be so far north. Same with white-tailed deer, now often sighted. Polar bears are in danger of having no ice on which to hunt. In some places caribou populations have dwindled to the point where hunting has been suspended. Wood bison are getting closer and closer to Yellowknife. There are new plants showing up.

The winter temperature in wide parts of the Far North has been eight degrees above average. Robins have been sighted in Iqaluit.

In May of 2006 an American big-game hunter shot and killed an animal they're calling a "grizlar"—half grizzly, half polar bear—on Banks Island in the Arctic Ocean. The hunter and his guide had presumed it was a polar bear, having white fur, but the head and the eyes and the neck and even the claws looked wrong. Somehow the two breeds, from decidedly different habitats, had come together to produce the first hybrid ever recorded in the wild.

There are many serious issues in the magnificent north of this country. There is poverty. Assaults and sexual abuse are far above the Canadian mean. Infant mortality rates are triple the national rate. There is widespread alcoholism and easy access to drugs. Gasoline sniffing is an epidemic among the young in some communities. Suicide rates soar far beyond the averages found in the rest of the country. The education system sorely needs repair. There are few jobs in Nunavut and, so far, limited prospects for the resource projects that are flooding into the Northwest Territories and Yukon.

But nothing compares to the threat coming from environmental change—change that could mean the end of certain northern species and that threatens the very way of life for the Inuit and Inuvialuit and First Nations and Métis.

There are still deniers out there, but their numbers are declining faster than the polar bear population—and faster still, had any of them travelled with us to Tanquary Fiord on the far northern edges of Ellesmere Island. There, hiking in the northernmost wilderness reserve in the world, Canada's Quttinirpaaq National Park, we stared in awe at "The Hand of God"—a massive glacier shaped, eerily, like a long forearm reaching down into the fiord, thumb and four fingers tightened as if it were a giant hand seeking purchase on earth. The rangers have photographs taken over the years that show the arm shrinking, the fingers appearing to tighten … the grip slipping.

"The world can tell us everything we want to know," Quitsak Tarkiasuk of James Bay told a workshop organized by the Canadian Arctic Resources Committee in the late 1990s. "The only problem for the world is that it doesn't have a voice. But the world's indicators are there. They're always talking to us."

The world might find it easier to talk than the people themselves do. The Inuit have no word for such things as the robins and barred owls and even hornets they've been seeing in recent months. During the winter of 2004–05 officials in Nunavut brought together twenty Inuktitut and Inuinnaqtun interpreters and elders to see if they could find ways to talk about all the baffling changes that have come their way in the last few years.

They came up with 131 new words, many of them variations on *hila,* a simple word for that most complex of northern realities, weather.

For "climate change," they now say *hilaupaalannguqtirninga.*

For "global warming," they will say *hilaupuunnakpallianinga.*

And *nunguttut*—a word they hope is never used—will stand for "extinction."

In the words of Sheila Watt-Cloutier, chair of the Inuit Circumpolar Conference from 2002 to 2006, "If you can protect the Arctic, you save the planet."

"Everything is here, you know," Michel Paper said that day I visited him at his home in little Dettah. "A lot of gold. A lot of diamonds. A lot of oil and gas. The Creator did so many things for us. He put fish in the water and we took the fish out and He never asked us for anything. The white man asks for everything. I sometimes think the white man has more power than the Creator."

The old man shrugged. He began absent-mindedly shuffling the cards that sat on top of a well-worn cribbage board. "He's not going to go away, you know."

Who?

"The white man. He's not going to go away. All my life I helped whites. Whites need to help me now. You're not going to go away—so we should work together."

ON THE LONG TRIP through Nunavut we spent time in Iqaluit, Pangnirtung, Pond Inlet, Resolute Bay, Grise Fiord, Eureka, and Alert. Seven small specks on a huge map.

But that, perhaps, may be what makes this country different from any other. You might *see* England, and you might *tour* Europe—but it is impossible in Canada. It is a country you can only taste. And for a good many of us, all that does is increase the appetite for more.

My experiences in the Far North were all new. I put a borrowed snow machine through the ice in Resolute—*Sorry about that!*—and met a man in Iqaluit, Adamee Itorcheak, who was determined to bring wireless internet to every single community.

At the impossibly spectacular community of Pangnirtung I found the Pang Golf and Country Club, open twenty-four hours a day and with no twilight fee—there being no twilight during the Nunavut golf season. There's just the one hole, but if it were part of the PGA Tour it would make the seventeenth of Sawgrass or the eighteenth at Pebble Beach look like so many straightway, no-frill mini-putt holes.

Late one "night" I watched while children as young as seven and those in their twenties lined up to take their turn on the most challenging hole in all of golf. They teed off on the only flat surface of rock along the shore. Arctic Ocean and ice floes were out of bounds to the left, steep hill and more rock formed hazards to the right. And if you teed off straight down the middle it could be even worse—solid rock to bounce the shots off into nowhere, puddles and bog to suck the ball down into a trap that would terrify Tiger Woods.

A makeshift flag marks the hole that has been dug out of the dirt, and beyond that sits the Pangnirtung Visitors Centre, a small display case just behind the main window holding a number of artifacts from early exploration days. One treasure, found in an old Scottish whaling camp, is an ancient golf club, a rusty niblick.

The white man, as Michel Paper said, obviously did not go away.

At Grise Fiord—site of the world's greatest white-knuckle landing strip—I spent a day with Larry Audlaluk. While he skinned a ring seal down by the water I knelt and watched and listened to his remarkable story: a people torn from their roots and forced to move thousands of kilometres north to make do in a land whose animals they didn't recognize and hadn't a clue how to hunt; a people so miserable that some, like

Larry's own father, died from heartbreak that first cruel winter; a place so dark and desolate that the people themselves decided to move across the bay to catch just a little more sunlight each day when there was sun; a place where, the day Larry came back from this bay carrying an Arctic char, his mother broke down and wept at the memory of how food she once knew tasted.

More than fifty years had passed since Larry Audlaluk came here as a very young boy. He talked about the hardships and the unfairness and how, over time, the horrible dark and cold place where his people had been sent by the government became something quite unexpected. "People have to move on," he said. "The young have grown up here. This is their home.

"It's my home now … I love it here."

LARRY AUDLALUK'S HOME in Grise Fiord, Nunavut; Betty Fitzgerald's in Bonavista Bay, Newfoundland; Clarence Brazier's in Sprucedale, Ontario; Gerald Merkel's in Raymore, Saskatchewan; Elizabeth Chocolate's in Behchoko, Northwest Territories; Connie Smith's in Fort McMurray, Alberta; Marie-Eve Lainesse's in Verchères, Quebec; Shirley Chan's in Vancouver, British Columbia; and some 32,146,547—and counting—other Canadians' homes in St. John's, Halifax, Charlottetown, Fredericton, Quebec City, Montreal, Ottawa, Toronto, Sault St. Marie, Thunder Bay, Winnipeg, Regina, Saskatoon, Calgary, Edmonton, Prince George, Vancouver, Victoria, and in thousands of towns and villages and crossroads across five and a half time zones and stretching from the boardwalk at Point Pelee to the runway at Alert.

And such a home, too. A home so many say they love, as Larry Audlaluk does, but a home, too, that seems forever in danger of some imminent collapse over some threat or other, whether real or perceived.

Some prefer to stick to the doom and gloom, the true northerner's sure bet. I prefer to think Peter C. Newman got it right in his memoirs, *Here Be Dragons,* when he neared the end, sighed deeply, and wrote that after half a century of recording all the mistakes and twists and crises of the country, he could conclude only that "Canada takes a lot of killing."

But the Bumblebee Nation, somehow, remains afloat, its flight plan determined by whatever wind happens to be blowing, by pure whim, by good luck, by some unknowable genetic command to keep going, no matter what.

Perhaps this country's true genius does lie in that line down the middle of the road that a highways worker stumbled on back in 1930. It certainly isn't perfect—accidents will happen—but by and large it works well enough to keep things moving in all directions.

What we cannot know—what we really don't even want to know—is which direction that line is headed.

And what, pray, lies around the next corner.

And the next ...

TOWARD THE END of that long trip into the Far North we reached Canadian Forces Base Alert on the most northern tip of Canada's most northern point of land, Ellesmere Island. Beyond this shore there is only frozen ocean between Canada and the northernmost tips of Norway, Russia, and Alaska.

It is so far north that if you hold up a compass it will point to the north magnetic pole—to the west and *south* of where you're standing in this land of endless contradiction.

Here, on a bright early June day in 2005, with a sharp wind gusting in off the ice, Governor General Adrienne Clarkson and her husband, author John Ralston Saul, set out to build a stone cairn. They chose a point at the very end of the long Alert runway, right where the loose stone and gravel drops down fast toward the jumbled ice of the frozen Arctic Ocean.

Right where Canada ends. Or where Canada begins, depending on which direction you might be travelling.

Clarkson herself chose this spot so that it might stand as a statement of proprietorship at a point where, on a clear day, you can spin in your tracks on the loose gravel and make out the United States Mountain Range to your lower left, the British Empire range to the lower right, and the high cliffs of Greenland to the far right and know that, straight ahead across the choppy ice, Russia sits somewhere beyond the slow pale curve of the horizon.

It would stand as a stake. Proof of ownership at a time when, increasingly, ownership is coming into some dispute.

This year, 2007, marks a full century since Norwegian explorer Roald Amundsen found what had defeated so many others: the Northwest Passage. It was a storied search that had eluded Martin Frobisher himself, who once called the passage "the only thing left undone whereby a notable mind might be made famous and remarkable."

Frobisher missed his Northwest Passage fame by reaching only Baffin Island, far to the south of this spot at the end of the Alert runway, but the charming former pirate didn't exactly vanish from history's record. He grabbed a few unthreatening Inuit and filled his hold with black, mica-flecked stone before heading back to England, where he put the poor Natives on display and somehow persuaded an alchemist to tell potential investors that the strange black rock held gold. It was the first Bre-X scandal, as historian Charlotte Gray has called Frobisher's scam, yet he still managed to inveigle a knighthood out of his good friend, the lonely Queen Elizabeth I.

Frobisher led a charmed life. Not so another of the more famous explorers who came in search of the passage, Sir John Franklin. He too might have received a knighthood, but he's remembered only for leaving behind one of the North's greatest mysteries—the fate of his 1845 voyage in which 129 men, including Franklin himself, vanished and could not be found again despite some forty search expeditions launched in the following decade alone. It wasn't until 1986, more than two centuries on, that three bodies were discovered and found to have alarmingly high levels of lead. Franklin believed he'd found not only the secret to the passage, but also the secret to survival: food preserved in tin cans and sealed with solder. What killed them first? The cold they found? Or the poison they brought?

There is hardly a historical account of the North that doesn't leave the head spinning. Henry Hudson set out in 1611 convinced he'd discovered the secret passage, only to realize he was stuck fast in what would be called

Hudson Bay, his crew about to mutiny and send Captain Henry and his son John off in a lifeboat, never to be seen again. Samuel Hearne tried it overland in 1770, sure that if he didn't find the elusive passage he'd at least find copper. He found no mines. He lost his toenails. And so it goes— each story a fable in what might forever have remained a fantasy had Amundsen not finally figured it all out.

What brought the governor general north that day was a growing realization that, once again, Canada's sovereignty over isolated land was being challenged. The United States has never recognized Canada's claim to sovereignty over the Arctic archipelago of North America. In 1909 American explorer Robert Peary announced that he'd made it all the way to the North Pole and claimed "all adjacent lands" for the United States. Some people—and not all of them Canadians—say he was nowhere near the actual Pole. His "all adjacent lands," for all anyone knows, could have been nothing more than a huge ice floe.

In 1969 the SS *Manhattan,* an American icebreaking tanker owned by Humble Oil, set out to plow through Amundsen's passage without bothering to ask Canada's permission. It was a deliberate omission, the unspoken a statement on the American disdain for the Canadian claim. As can happen only in the world of Canadian politics, the *Manhattan* then got stuck in heavy ice and had to have the Canadian icebreaker *Sir John A. Macdonald* come to its rescue. The *Manhattan* continued on through the passage, the United States thereby dramatically defying Canadian sovereignty with the helping hand of its good neighbour to the north.

For decades such incidents were held to be nothing more than mildly amusing. But as the twenty-first century got under way everything changed. The Arctic melt was moving so quickly that a number of nations, not just the United States, began looking at the Northwest Passage through the eyes of Frobisher and Franklin: a new, open, and workable transportation route to and from China, now the world's fastest-expanding economy.

Only months before Clarkson set out for Alert, little Denmark had raised its flag over Hans Island, a tiny, uninhabited barren rock that lies in Nares Strait between Ellesmere Island and northern Greenland. The flag-raising was taken as a provocative act, though hardly worthy of anything but launching stiff words in Denmark's direction.

Canada rather naturally felt a proprietary interest, since Canadians alone make up what very little human presence there is on Ellesmere and points north. The most northern community in all North America is found here at Grise Fiord, Larry Audlaluk's home—though it might be advisable, under the circumstances, not to mention that Grise Fiord was created out of thin and very cold air back in the early 1950s by the Canadian government shipping in unsuspecting Inuit from farther south. Still, Grise Fiord had survived and now stood as a significant symbol in the vague, slightly throat-catching northern statement that all this empty white space at the top belongs to *us*.

Saying and showing are, however, quite different matters. Apart from the Alert base and a small weather station at Eureka, the only military presence in the area was the two-man Royal Canadian Mounted Police station at Grise Fiord and the Canadian Rangers, a charming but rather ragtag Inuit force composed of mostly older males wearing red tams and jackets and carrying worn .303 Lee Enfield rifles passed down from the armed forces, some of the rifles dating as far back as the First World War.

Clarkson had come north inspired by Vincent Massey, the first native-born of Canada's many governors general. Nearly a half century earlier, in 1956, Massey had made his own statement concerning who exactly owned exactly what when he flew on military transport over the North Pole and, on the way back to base, had the co-pilot pop the window a moment to drop out a metal canister containing his vice-regal flag.

Naturally, the canister instantly vanished from sight into the white reflection of permanent day—but at least the sentiment was there.

Massey's disappearing canister had given birth to Clarkson's dream, only she wanted something that could be found again, if necessary. Surely the most passionate about the North of any governor general—a passion largely fed by her husband's insatiable curiosity about Inuit life— Clarkson had decided to build a rock cairn similar to those built by past Inuit generations, many of which have withstood the elements for centuries.

Rather than a directional guide or a food cache, however, Clarkson's cairn would contain evidence of the country's head of state at this spot in mid-June of 2005. It would stand as a statement for all who might later challenge either Canada's right to the incredible riches that lie under the Beaufort Sea and Arctic Ocean or its control of the passage between Europe and Asia that might prove the single benefit of global warming.

With the sun shining and the afternoon wind picking up, volunteers from Base Alert had pitched in to help build the cairn. They carried boulders and small rocks and, under instructions from an army engineer who must have played with such material as a child, they built a solid cairn at the far end of the runway.

When it reached the height of John Ralston Saul, the tallest man in the group of a dozen or more workers, they paused before setting the large finishing rocks over the top. Then they took a small green ammunition case and opened it up to place within it their statements on Canadian sovereignty over the Far North.

No one remarked that a Canadian Armed Forces ammo case stamped "EMPTY" on the side was its own ironic statement.

Governor General Adrienne Clarkson placed her vice-regal flag in first, copying what Vincent Massey had done forty-nine years earlier with his canister. Clarkson and Saul then added their own personal notes, handwritten and folded to keep each message to itself. Everyone who worked on the cairn then signed another piece of paper and it was carefully folded and placed inside the small steel box.

But there was still room.

If people truly deplore a vacuum, this was proof. One man placed a business card inside. A woman put a small pin in. A Mountie took his badge, RCMP Nunavut, and dropped it in. Someone found an expired fishing licence to put in—causing another man to shout out: "I sure wish I had my wife's credit card here!"

They were about to seal the box when Julie Verner, a fair-haired, bespectacled soldier, stepped forward and asked them to wait a moment. The forty-five-year-old warrant officer had something to add.

She surprised herself by asking the others to wait, but there was something about the cairn that had her thinking. She'd hiked out to see another, older one, farther along the bay, and it had struck her that such constructions last forever in the Arctic.

It never occurred to Julie Verner that she might stand for something. But she did. She came from Sault Ste. Marie, pretty much the midpoint of the Trans-Canada Highway that runs from one side of the country to the other. She was the child of a francophone father and an anglophone mother and had married a man whose heritage was neither. She was also the mother of four young children, the elder two now able to talk freely to their Poirier grandmother in Rouyn-Noranda who spoke no English at all.

"I remember thinking," she told me months later, "here we are on the top of the world and you could never put a flag up that would last very long. But this cairn could last forever—maybe even longer than Base Alert will be there. I thought about someone opening up this cairn hundreds of years from now and there not being a Canadian flag there saying this is *our* place."

And so, very carefully, with her eyes beginning to sting, Julie Verner reached up and tore the small Canadian flag off the shoulder of her uniform. She rolled it over once in her hand and then dropped the tiny flag in and turned away, tears now freely flowing.

Taken one way, it looked like disrespect to the uniform. Taken the right way, it was merely a soldier serving her country.

Canada, a country that so often makes no sense at all.

Canada, a country that, every so often, makes total sense.

Roots and Rocks

THESE ARE MY ROOTS.

I can feel them with my bare feet; I can grab them with my hands; I can find them with my eyes shut; I can even swing from them along the rock cliffs that ride high over the pine-needled trail that runs out to the far point where they brought me to stay when I was all of three days old.

"Roots and Rocks," we called it back then—so very long ago that the photographs are black and white and the magnificent two-storey log cabin that stood high on the point is long since gone. But if you know where to look, you can still find the trail in from the highway. And hints of what once was.

We played Roots and Rocks from the time we could walk. The rules were as simple as life itself seemed back then: you can step only on roots or rocks; miss a step and you're dead. Now some of the players really are dead. Now no one lives here any more but ghosts.

We ran races back then. Roots and Rocks up to the Big House, Roots and Rocks down to the kitchen cabin, Roots and Rocks all the way out along the cliffs to the highway, Roots and Rocks to the icehouse, to the spring, to the outhouse. There was a time when the four of us—three brothers and a sister—and a half dozen or more cousins could fly along these roots and rocks as if they held both a magnetic field to catch our bare feet and a spring to throw us to the next safe landing … and the next … and the next.

To a passing canoeist, we must have seemed a wilderness camp for children having to learn to walk all over again; to us, we were always one step away from death and, it seems looking back, never quite so alive again.

Apart from the disappearance of the log house and the three small cabins, the outhouse and the icehouse, this rocky point along the north shore of Lake of Two Rivers in Algonquin Park hasn't changed at all. Perhaps some trees are taller and some have fallen in the half century that separates those laughing children and today, but the roots and rocks are so much the same that it feels, to fifty-eight-year-old bare feet, as if some genetic code of their presence, distance, height, and feel still pulses through the soles.

It certainly does through the soul.

This is the landscape Tom Thomson came to paint and was never able to finish. His fiancée, Miss Winnifred Trainor, whose sister Marie married our Uncle Roy, used to sit in a lawn chair on this rocky point and stare out over the water that runs from the Algonquin highlands down through the Madawaska Valley and all the way to the Ottawa River. The tea-coloured water ran then, and runs today, just as it did back in 1837 when the great mapmaker David Thompson—then sixty-seven years old, impoverished and all but blind—paddled by this rocky point and noted in his journal: "Current going with us, thank God."

The current went against Winnie Trainor though. She was left with a honeymoon reservation at an area lodge she could never use; left, many believe, with a child she'd have to give up; left with a dozen or more Tom Thomson originals she'd keep wrapped in newspaper and stuffed in a six-quart basket in her small second-floor apartment in Huntsville. One of those tiny sketches broke through the million-dollar mark at a recent auction in Toronto. What would she think about that? Winnie Trainor had to rent out the better part of her house just to make ends meet. She couldn't even afford to put in hot water for herself.

This is my Canada. Come sit for a moment on the warm rocks.

The wind is in the pines. The waves are licking under a rock cut at the end of the point. David Thompson paddles by on his final great journey, the last assignment the great mapmaker would ever take on.

Winnie Trainor spins her eyeglasses in her right hand as she talks, growing ever louder and more animated. While we children cover our mouths and giggle, the glasses suddenly fly out of her hand and stick high in the spruce tree standing over the handmade wooden chair she fills with her large, dark, imposing body.

Our grandfather, the old park ranger, works a hand pump down by the water, his sweat turning his faded green Lands & Forests shirt black under the arms and in a sloppy V down his back.

Our mother has the coal oil-fired washing machine running, the exhaust burping out a straight pipe like a motorcycle as she runs sheets as white as snow through the ringer sister Ann once caught her arm in up to the elbow.

Our grandmother, wearing a simple print dress, as always, is putting up wire fencing in a useless effort to stop the deer from eating her geraniums.

Our father, Saturday afternoon off from the mill on the next lake down the Madawaska River system, is far out on the waters of Lake of Two Rivers, trolling with steel line for lake trout.

All of us—Jim, Ann, Tom, and I—periodically scan the water for him and his little wooden boat, eager to be the first to shout "*HE'S UP!*"— meaning he's on his feet and reeling in what will be tonight's supper in a world where dinner is eaten at noon.

Older brother Jim and I returned to the point this past summer. I try to get there once a year; he's returned only a few times since the mid-1960s when, after the old ranger died, the family sold the place to an American and, a decade later, the new owner panicked over an impending ruling to limit park leases and had the log house dismantled, the logs numbered and carted away and reassembled like some wilderness IKEA in a very different setting far away from Algonquin Park.

Jim says there are too many ghosts and it bothers him to be there. I, on the other hand, enjoy the company of the ghosts.

When our sister Ann was dying of cancer the year she turned fifty, I asked her once, when it was beyond obvious what was going to happen, what meant most to her in a life that had included moving from the park area to a small town then to a city for university and a long career as a renowned fact-checker at *Maclean's*. (She would have caught those sorry gaffes you noted earlier.)

She never even paused: "Lake of Two Rivers, of course."

Four years later, when our mother was beginning to happily wander and was hospitalized not long before a stroke put an end to it, I happened to ask her if I could get her a drink of water. Her response astonished me. She told me where to go to get it, but nowhere in the little hospital in Huntsville. Instead, with her eyes half closed, she gave me perfectly detailed directions on where to walk along the rock cliffs and where to climb down and how to get across the beach and over the small creek to the little natural spring that bubbled with water so clear and cold it made your teeth ache if you drank it too quickly.

Lake of Two Rivers. Roots and Rocks. The place I think of first when I think of Canada.

My Pier 21—where I landed at the age of three days and have stayed ever since.

And where, one day, I may return to give my brother the willies should he happen to canoe over all by himself for a last look around.

I ONCE THOUGHT that rocky point on Lake of Two Rivers was big, then I believed Algonquin Park endless. To get to some parts of it the Lands & Forests would have to send in a floatplane to pick up the old ranger and carry him off to fight a fire or deal with poachers. Then the town we moved to from the little village seemed awfully big, but not so large as the city to the south where we would sometimes go and be overwhelmed by such simple matters as escalators and traffic lights. The province was so huge that I was grown before I ever set foot beyond it, only to discover that the country of which the province was but a portion was so big not even David Thompson's maps could hold it all.

I am grateful to journalism's *entrée* for getting me around so much of this enormous bumblebee of a country. And yet I suspect I've seen but a fraction of the fraction David Thompson saw in a lifetime of exploring. It's probably easier to cup the morning mist that rolls along the gunwales of a canoe than it is to fully grasp the width and breadth and astonishing variety of this land and its people.

I am acutely aware of how sheltered life once was here on this point. Our parents once took us to the small city of Orillia to have our eyes tested and locked us in the little motel room while they went to arrange appointments. We'd never used a flush toilet before and put so much toilet paper in that it blocked and flooded, and when the manager came pounding on the door we refused to let him in because, of course, he was a stranger. We saw so few truly different people back then that, when a black family came and set up a tent at the Lake of Two Rivers campground, word went out over the tiny crank telephones that connected the rangers and that evening we joined a virtual convoy of cars slowly making their way past the campsite. We pressed our faces to the window and stared hard at people we'd heard of but never seen—the poor family probably wondering whatever became of the promised peace of the Canadian wilderness.

Today, this great park is often filled with more visitors from outside the country than from inside. There are busloads of Japanese tourists taking pictures of the fall foliage. There are Germans on the hiking trails. There are African-Americans and African-Canadians not only in the campgrounds but in the very family that started out from this rocky point in Algonquin Park. Middle Eastern families are buying ice cream at the little Canoe Lake portage store. A Dutch tourist walking about the Smoke Lake landing tells me that the thing he'll remember most about his holiday in Canada is driving on a road and not seeing any other traffic—something he'd never before experienced.

No wonder nine out of ten of us told that *Globe and Mail* survey that the thing that spoke to them most about this thing called Canada was the vastness of the landscape. This, even with the growing fact of urban life suggesting otherwise.

Here, size matters.

On the plateau behind the rocky point there's nothing left of the log cabin today but remnants of the magnificent stone fireplace the old ranger built with his own hands. The beautiful quartz rocks he gathered from the surrounding shoreline and bush are missing, the curious having made off with them as well as with most of the lovely granite stones with the fine mica flakings. The fireplace is gone.

And yet readers will understand when I say it burns still.

On that gorgeous fall day that VIA Rail no. 638 carried Pierre Trudeau's body home to Montreal I stood at the window watching the bush and water slide by and thought about how, as a young boy, the future prime minister had been sent off to this same Algonquin Park to polish up his English. He came to attend Taylor Statten Camps on Canoe Lake, the same lake Tom Thomson painted and died on, the same lake on which Winnie Trainor kept her little cottage and where, each year, she would climb the hill behind it and clean up the grave where her Tom was first laid to rest and where some believe he still lies.

It was here, on this lake, that Trudeau gained his lifelong love for the canoe, the paddle, and the backpack filled with all the worldly goods one might require.

Years after those early canoe trips, Trudeau penned an essay he called "Exhaustion and Fulfillment: The Ascetic in the Canoe," in which he wrote, "I know a man whose school could never teach him patriotism, but who acquired that virtue when he felt in his bones the vastness of his land, and the greatness of those who founded it."

I like to think that unnamed man was Pierre Trudeau.

I like to believe that, potentially, it could be each one of us, man, woman, child—and generations of children yet to come.

Roots and Rocks ... Roots and Rocks ...

Acknowledgments

THIS BOOK came out of a happy accident. We were meeting with publishers over another project, and I happened to mention that it had been sixty years since Bruce Hutchison had written *The Unknown Country*, and, by and large, the title still holds. I have to thank Natasha Daneman and Bruce Westwood of Westwood Creative Artists for seizing on the moment and prodding me for months after to start gathering material and working on an outline—which, of course, was lost the second my fingers touched the keyboard.

I am grateful to Peter C. Newman and Andrew H. Malcolm, two wonderful writers who also poked around in the belly-button lint of this nation, for constant support and, for that matter, periodic reminders to get at it and stay at it. I tip my laptop to where they travelled before I dared set out.

Two editors deserve very special mention. Both are tough, brilliant, stubborn, smart, manipulative, persuasive, and … always right. Barbara Berson of Penguin was there from the outline that was lost, as was Edie Van Alstine of Ottawa. If Confederation can be described as a "cat's cradle," as it has been in this book, that is nothing compared to the knotted coil that thousands of pages of notes can turn into. The book, in fact, was already written—and I thought done—when these editors decided it was only half done, needed to be untangled, re-thought, and recast. For whatever this adventure amounts to, I am forever grateful to these two fine editors and friends.

My gratitude also goes to Penguin's David Davidar, who never wavered on his support and encouragement; to Jonathan Webb, who read and commented on the early version of the book; to Brian Bethune, the walking Canadian encyclopedia; to Penguin's Tracy Bordian, who kept everything together; to Penguin's art director, Mary Opper, for a wonderful cover; and to Karen Alliston, who did the fine copy editing and translated my scratches and eraser smudges and cross-outs into things that ended up looking like sentences.

I thank Brian Craik and Luci Salt for their help in Cree translations.

To Ellen, I simply say thanks, as always.

And I also must pay a debt of gratitude to a long series of editors who, over a thirty-five-year period, saw fit to send me to places and let me go to places that perhaps didn't always seem to make sense—but that in the end provided a sense of this country and the people of this wonderful country that would never have been possible to gain otherwise. Thank you, Peter Newman, Don Obe, Walter Stewart, Gary Lautens, Ray Timson, Kevin Doyle, Robert Lewis, Nelson Skuce, Scott Honeyman, Keith Spicer, Russell Mills, James Travers, Ken Whyte, and Ed Greenspon. The only expenses still outstanding are the ones I will always owe you....

Roy MacGregor
Ottawa
February 15, 2007

Selected Readings

Adams, Michael. *Fire and Ice: The United States, Canada and the Myth of Converging Values,* Toronto: Penguin, 2003.

Anderssen, Erin, Michael Valpy, et al. *The New Canada,* Toronto: McClelland & Stewart, 2004.

Archbold, Rick. *I Stand for Canada: The Story of the Maple Leaf Flag,* Toronto: Macfarlane Walter & Ross, 2002.

Atwood, Margaret. *Survival: A Thematic Guide to Canadian Literature,* Toronto: Anansi, 1972.

Barlow, Maude. *Too Close for Comfort: Canada's Future within Fortress North America,* Toronto: McClelland & Stewart, 2005.

Berton, Pierre. *The Arctic Grail: The Quest for the North West Passage and the North Pole 1818–1909,* Toronto: Anchor Canada edition, 2001.

Bielawski, Ellen. *Rogue Diamonds: Northern Riches on Dene Land,* Vancouver: Douglas & McIntyre, 2003.

Boorstin, Daniel J. *The Americans: The National Experience,* New York: Vintage, 1965.

———. *The Americans: The Democratic Experience,* New York: Vintage, 1974.

Bowering, George. *Stone Country: An Unauthorized History of Canada,* Toronto: Viking, 2003.

Bowers, Vivien. *Only in Canada,* Toronto: Maple Tree Press, 2002.

Boyens, Ingeborg. *Another Season's Promise: Hope and Despair in Canada's Farm Country,* Toronto: Viking, 2001.

Bricker, Darrell, and John Wright. *What Canadians Think: "About Almost Everything,"* Toronto: Doubleday Canada, 2005.

Brown, Craig, ed. *The Illustrated History of Canada,* Toronto: Lester & Orpen Dennys, 1987.

Cameron, Elspeth, ed. *The Other Side of Hugh MacLennan: Selected Essays Old and New,* Toronto: Macmillan, 1978.

Cohen, Andrew. *While Canada Slept: How We Lost Our Place in the World,* Toronto: McClelland & Stewart, 2003.

Colombo, John Robert. *The Penguin Treasury of Popular Canadian Poems and Songs,* Toronto: Penguin, 2002.

Coupland, Douglas. *Souvenir of Canada*, Vancouver: Douglas & McIntyre, 2002.

English, John. *Citizen of the World: The Life of Pierre Elliott Trudeau, Vol. One, 1919–1968*, Toronto: Alfred A. Knopf, 2006.

Epp, Roger, and Dave Whitson, eds. *Writing Off the Rural West: Globalization, Governments, and the Transformation of Rural Communities*, Edmonton: University of Alberta Press, 2001.

Ferguson, Will. *Beauty Tips from Moose Jaw: Travels in Search of Canada*, Toronto: Alfred A. Knopf Canada, 2004.

Francis, Daniel. *A Road for Canada: The Illustrated Story of the Trans-Canada Highway*, Vancouver: Stanton Atkins & Dosil, 2006.

Friesen, Gerald. *The West: Regional Ambitions, National Debates, Global Age*, Toronto: Penguin, 1999.

Frye, Northrop. *The Bush Garden: Essays on the Canadian Imagination*, Toronto: House of Anansi, 1995.

Fumoleau, René. *As Long As This Land Shall Last: A History of Treaty 8 and Treaty 11, 1870–1939*, Calgary: University of Calgary Press, 2004.

Gordon, Charles. *The Canada Trip*, Toronto: McClelland & Stewart, 1997.

Grady, Wayne, ed. *Treasures of the Place: Three Centuries of Nature Writing in Canada*, Vancouver: Douglas & McIntyre, 1992.

Gray, Charlotte. *The Museum Called Canada*, Toronto: Random House, 2004.

Gruending, Dennis, ed. *The Middle of Nowhere: Rediscovering Saskatchewan*, Calgary: Fifth House Publishing, 1996.

Gwyn, Richard. *Nationalism Without Walls: The Unbearable Lightness of Being Canadian*, Toronto: McClelland & Stewart, 1996.

Hurtig, Mel. *The Vanishing Country: Is It Too Late to Save Canada?* Toronto: McClelland & Stewart, 2002.

Hutchison, Bruce. *The Unknown Country: Canada and Her People*, Toronto: Longmans, Green & Company, 1943.

———. *The Far Side of the Street*, Toronto: Macmillan, 1976.

———. *A Life in the Country*, Vancouver: Douglas & McIntyre, 1988.

Ibbitson, John. *The Polite Revolution: Perfecting the Canadian Dream*, Toronto: McClelland & Stewart, 2005.

Janovicek, Nancy, and Joy Parr, eds. *Histories of Canadian Children and Youth*, Toronto: Oxford Press, 2003.

Keahey, Deborah. *Making It Home: Place in Canadian Prairie Literature*, Winnipeg: University of Manitoba Press, 1996.

Laxer, James. *The Border: Canada, the U.S. and Dispatches from the 49th Parallel*, Toronto: Doubleday Canada, 2003.

Layton, Jack. *Speaking Out Louder: Ideas That Work for Canadians*, rev. ed., Toronto: Key Porter Books, 2006.

Lynch, Gerald, ed. *Leacock on Life*, Toronto: University of Toronto Press, 2002.

MacKay, Donald. *Flight from Famine: The Coming of the Irish to Canada*, Toronto: McClelland & Stewart, 1990.

Madison, G.B., Paul Fairfield, and Ingrid Harris. *Is There a Canadian Philosophy? Reflections on the Canadian Identity,* Ottawa: University of Ottawa Press, 2000.

Malcolm, Andrew H. *The Canadians,* New York: St. Martin's Press, 1985.

Major, Kevin. *As Near to Heaven by Sea: A History of Newfoundland and Labrador,* Toronto: Penguin, 2001.

Mandel, Eli, and David Taras. *A Passion for Identity: An Introduction to Canadian Studies,* Toronto: Methuen, 1987.

Morrison, Samuel Eliot. *The Great Explorers: The European Discovery of America,* New York: Oxford University Press, 1978.

Morton, Desmond. *A Short History of Canada,* 3rd rev. ed., Toronto: McClelland & Stewart, 1997.

Morton, Desmond, and Morton Weinfeld. *Who Speaks for Canada? Words That Shape a Country,* Toronto: McClelland & Stewart, 1998.

Morton, W.L. *The Canadian Identity,* 2nd ed., Toronto: University of Toronto Press, 1972.

Nemni, Max, and Monique Nemni. *Young Trudeau: Son of Quebec, Father of Canada, 1919–1944,* Toronto: McClelland & Stewart, 2006.

Newman, Peter C. *Company of Adventurers,* Toronto: Viking, 1985.

———. *Caesars of the Wilderness,* Toronto: Viking, 1987.

———. *Merchant Princes,* Toronto: Viking, 1991.

———. *The Canadian Revolution: From Deference to Defiance,* Toronto: Viking, 1995.

———. *Here Be Dragons: Telling Tales of People, Passion and Power,* Toronto: McClelland & Stewart, 2004.

Paxman, Jeremy. *The English: A Portrait of a People,* London: Penguin, 1999.

Purdy, Al. *No Other Country,* Toronto: McClelland & Stewart, 1977.

Saul, John Ralston. *Reflections of a Siamese Twin: Canada at the End of the Twentieth Century,* Toronto: Penguin, 1997.

Spicer, Keith. *Life Sentences: Memoirs of an Incorrigible Canadian,* Toronto: McClelland & Stewart, 2004.

Stackhouse, John. *Timbit Nation: A Hitchhiker's View of Canada,* Toronto: Random House, 2003.

Staines, David, ed. *The Forty-ninth and Other Parallels: Contemporary Canadian Perspectives,* Amherst: University of Massachusetts Press, 1986.

Stewart, Walter. *But Not in Canada: Smug Canadian Myths Shattered by Harsh Reality,* Toronto: Macmillan, 1976.

———. *My Cross-Country Checkup: Across Canada by Minivan, Through Space and Time,* Toronto: Stoddart, 2000.

Studin, Irvin, ed. *What Is a Canadian? Forty-three Thought-Provoking Responses,* Toronto: McClelland & Stewart, 2006.

Vance, Jonathan. *Building Canada: People and Projects That Shaped the Nation,* Toronto: Penguin Canada, 2006.

Welsh, Jennifer. *At Home in the World: Canada's Global Vision for the 21st Century,* Toronto: Harper Perennial, 2004.

Index